HUMANITY UPROOTED

HUMANITY UPROOTED

By MAURICE HINDUS

AUTHOR OF "BROKEN EARTH"

Drawings by Arthur Hawkins, Jr.

GREENWOOD PRESS, PUBLISHERS
WESTPORT, CONNECTICUT

The Library of Congress has catalogued this publication as follows:

Library of Congress Cataloging in Publication Data

Hindus, Maurice Gerschon, 1891-1969.
   Humanity uprooted.

   1. Russia--Social conditions.--1917-
2. Russia--Civilization.--1917-   3. Communism--
Russia. 4. Russia--Foreign relations--1917-1945.
I. Title.
DK267.H5 1972   914.7'03'84   77-159716
ISBN 0-8371-6190-8

For some a prologue,
For some an epilogue.

BULGAKOV.

PREFACE

I WAS born in a Russian village, so deaf, as the Russians would say (meaning so far removed from centers of civilization), that not until I had started for America at the age of fourteen, did I see a railroad train or an electric light. After a lengthy sojourn in this country I returned to Russia in 1923 and spent a year there, wandering about the cities and villages. Since then I have visited Russia almost annually, roaming at leisure in Siberia, the Caucasus, the Volga region, the Ukraine, the Crimea and the far North. Everywhere it was the same story — humanity in a state of feverish agitation, convulsed with thought and feeling. Life in Russia is so violent an experience, so painful a trial and to him who bursts with the new faith so glorious an ecstasy, that one cannot remain simply passive. One must react somehow to the heaving turbulence, with fervour, with fury, with hope, with despair, with madness or even with death.

For good or for evil Russia has plucked up the old world by its very roots and the Party in power is glad to see these roots wilt and turn into dust. Hardly an institution — property, religion, morality, family, love — has escaped the blasts of the Revolution.

It was the learned Dr. Hu Shih in Shanghai who told me that what struck him most forcibly about the Russian Revolution was the deliberate attempt to build a

civilization based on an entirely new pattern. Of course
there is nothing new in that. Japan has done it wisely
and well. But Japan has had a model to follow. The
Western world furnished her with a complete set of diagrams. Not so with Russia. The civilization she is seeking to enthrone never was on sea or land. She has had
no ready models to guide her. She wants a society without religion, with sex freedom, with external compulsions removed from family and love, with mental and
manual workers reduced to a plane of equality, with
the individual depending for his salvation not on himself but the group. A whole generation is being vigour-
ously reared in the belief that religion is a monstrous
unreality, that the accumulation of material substance
is the grossest of wrongs and that the man in its pursuit, especially the business man, is the slimiest creature on earth. A whole generation of women is being
reared in the idea that women must be economically
independent, and must participate in the affairs of the
world — in industry, in education, in government, in
all other national pursuits, on a basis of equality with
men. Whatever we may think of feminism something
stupendous must come out of this effort to draw on the
intelligence and energies of women in the task of re-
building a civilization.

Those of us with an American or some other western
background and with a knowledge of the Russian language, who have had the opportunity to observe at
close range Russian humanity in these years of tumult
and tribulation, have had an extraordinary experience,
fraught with great sorrow, yet not void of romance.
Agony there is in Russia, more, I am sure, than in any

land in the world. Rapture also, the highest man ever has tasted.

In this book I have attempted to give a picture of the results of the revolutionary effort to uproot ancient institutions and to refashion the ways of man.

Some of the chapters, in somewhat abbreviated and altered form, have appeared in *Asia,* in the *Century* and in the *Round Table.* To the editors of these publications I wish to tender my thanks for their permission to incorporate in this book the material they have printed.

MAURICE HINDUS

NEW YORK,
May 1, 1929.

NOTE TO SECOND EDITION

Owing to the amazing spread of collective farming in the past year it has been necessary to revise the final part of the chapter on The Peasant. Otherwise with the exception of stylistic corrections and explanatory sentences the book remains unchanged.

M. H.

CONTENTS

Institutions

I.	RELIGION — COLLAPSE	3
II.	RELIGION — CAUSE OF COLLAPSE	23
III.	RELIGION — SUBSTITUTIONS	35
IV.	PROPERTY	48
V.	MAN	70
VI.	SEX — THE NEW MORALITY	84
VII.	FAMILY — TESTS AND TRIALS	101
VIII.	LOVE	119
IX.	FAMILY — THE NEW FAMILY	140

People

X.	PEASANT	149
XI.	PROLETARIAN	174
XII.	COMMUNIST	188
XIII.	YOUTH	209
XIV.	INTELLIGENTSIA	224
XV.	COSSACK	239
XVI.	JEW	259
XVII.	WOMAN	279

Quests

XVIII.	ENGLAND	307
XIX.	REVOLUTION	323
XX.	WAR	339
XXI.	AMERICA	355

INTRODUCTION

THE following passage taken from the chapter on Youth seems to me to be itself a suitable Introduction to the entire book: at least to the attentive reader it suggests the animated spirit of Mr. Hindus' extraordinary account of the extraordinary Russian scene. "Often when I would tell Russian youths that I was a writer they would immediately ask what was my political orientation. What they really meant was whether I was for or against the class struggle. They could not conceive of a writer being apolitical and indifferent to political viewpoints." The passage is intended to tell something about the attitude of Russian youth. In fact, it communicates even more about the point of view from which Mr. Hindus has surveyed the Russian situation.

To take sides, to find something to praise or to blame, and then follow the purpose of blame or praise to control all one's ideas of a social situation is almost as natural to humanity as it is to breathe. The idler on the bank of a stream can with difficulty observe two chips floating downwards near each other without thinking of them as engaged in a struggle and identifying himself with one against the other. When the conflict is actual and is human, when it includes within itself forces and interests wherein the spectator is already committed by education, prejudice and aspiration, impartiality of observation and report is well nigh beyond human power.

It is not merely Russian youth who find it hard to conceive that a writer should be interested in what is going on in their country simply as something to behold and if possible to understand. All over the world, it is assumed that a person must of necessity be interested in the scenes as one who is for the new regime or is against it. It is incredible that one should be concerned to look and to note as a spectator may assist at the unrolling of a drama in which human passions, beliefs and fortunes are engaged deeply and on the most tremendous scale. To see for the sake of seeing and to tell others so that they may vicariously share in the seeing: — that is beyond the reach of the imagination of most men in respect to Soviet Russia. To them it is not a scene to behold; it is a battle to take part in. Failure to be an open partisan is itself suspect. To my mind the striking thing about this book by Mr. Hindus is that with the most intimate sympathetic response to all the human issues involved in the revolutionary transformation, he is nevertheless content to see and to report. Nowhere does he assume the divine prerogative of blessing or condemning; nowhere is he the avenging angel of divine wrath nor yet the angel of benediction.

In consequence, readers who have not already made up their minds, who have not already formed judgments incapable of change, will find the means in this book for reaching a juster and more appreciative understanding of Bolshevist Russia than in any other book known to me. Those who have made up their minds for or against will, each of them, find plenty of material that may be isolated from its context and be used to support their pre-formed views. There is hardly a book in existence that affords more material for hearty damnation of Russia if one merely selects passages with that end in view. But there is also a dispassionate and compassionate account of all the factors that have fired the imaginative ardour of the most devout adherents of the revolution. Yet what has been said would be thoroughly misleading if it induced anyone to suppose that the book is of the " on this hand and the other hand " type. There is no weighing of good points against bad. There is a picture of a large section of humanity uprooted, torn loose from its old bearings, and striving with both fanatical madness and sublime fervour to create a new humanity rooted in a new earth. That the scene of the uprooting and the new aspirations should be mixed beyond all possibility of weighing, point by point, good against evil, is exactly what might be expected. Yet it is precisely what writers with a particular political or economic slant fail to convey.

I have asked myself what it is that has enabled Mr. Hindus to rise so completely above the trammels of partisanship and to achieve a depiction as " objective," as impartial, as it is moving and vivid. The answer which I have found for myself is that he has viewed the scene with the eye of the artist. That the most profound and extensive revolution humanity has ever known is immensely worth beholding and reporting on its own account as a human spectacle is, in the abstract, self-evident. But only, so it seems to me, an unusually large endowment of the eye and the mind of an artist will enable anyone to appreciate as a moving spectacle a revolutionary situation in which all passions and all prejudices are involved. But it is just this trait that marks off the accomplishment of Mr. Hindus. There are objective scientific studies of this and that phase of the Bolshevist revolution, political and economic; the scientific mind also attains impartiality of report. But without the vision of the artist such science stops with columns of figures and statistics. What one finds in the pages of Mr. Hindus is the revolution portrayed in terms of the human beings who experience its agonies and its exaltations.

Each reader will form his own impression of the net outcome of this overturn in the beliefs and labours of humanity — almost as much so as if he had personally accompanied Mr. Hindus in his wanderings through Russia and seen things with his own eyes. Not as a finality, then, but as the impression made upon one reader, I may say that what perhaps I carry away most of all is a sense of the thoroughly Russian character of this upheaval of institutions, traditions, and customs. I suppose a Russian communist would be obliged to deny this interpretation. To him the movement is intrinsically universal — as universal as the material of mathematics or any necessary science. Possibly, however, that conviction is but another evidence of its irretrievably Russian character. At all events, I do not see how anyone can begin to find his way into complexities and inconsistencies of the Russian scene until he has placed it on Russian soil, projected against the background of Russian history.

Without display and without pedantry, Mr. Hindus

has evidently absorbed into himself Russian history, Russian literature, the psychology of each of the classes he so brilliantly depicts. Everything is in its own human setting. Hence it is real, concrete, and it carries with it the sense of living reality. To read these pages with sympathy is to travel the road of a liberal education.

JOHN DEWEY

Part I
INSTITUTIONS

CHAPTER I

RELIGION

COLLAPSE

ONCE long past midnight I was wandering about the streets of Moscow. I sauntered up the rolling Kuznetsky, turned aimlessly into a winding side street and presently found myself, much to my own surprise, on the spacious cobbled square that fronts the imposing structure of the Foreign Office. There is a little park in the center of the square, and in the daytime scores of children with their mothers and nurses enliven it with their gaiety. Now the park was deserted, as was the square, as were the surrounding streets. I leaned against the fence, and, as I contemplated the scene about me, I had the illusion that never in my life had I been in a place more blissfully remote from human turbulence than was the city of Moscow. Bolshevism, revolution and all that the words imply and portend seemed for the moment only legend. But, as often happens in Russia when the outward placidity of life bewitches the visitor into forgetfulness of its inward turmoil, an incident quite trifling jerked me back into a full awareness of the colossal drama that Russian humanity has been enacting. " Uncle," I heard a boy's voice, " give us a ten-kopeck piece for a loaf of bread."

He was a street waif, I had not heard him approach. He seemed to have shot right out of the earth, and, even as he finished speaking, several other waifs dashed over to his side, all boys, barefoot, ragged, faces smirched with soot as if they had come out of a chimney. They explained that they had just arrived in the city on a freight-train and were fearfully hungry. I invited them to follow me, and together we walked about in search of one of those woman pedlars in Moscow who sit out until the early hours of dawn selling sandwiches, rolls and hard-boiled eggs. In the doorway of an old building we found such a woman fast asleep over her basket. I bought all her rolls and eggs; the waifs pounced on the food with delightful avidity. As their spirits mounted, they grew chummy and talkative. They had never before been in Moscow or in any other city. They were from different villages on the Volga, orphans all, and after weeks of wandering afoot, on boats and in freight-trains they had at last reached Moscow in the hope that some Soviet organization would put them into a home. They seemed not at all worried over their rags, their desolation, their aloneness in the world. They were good-humoured peasant children. Finally I asked them the question that I never failed to put to youngsters with whom I engaged in conversation, especially to peasant youngsters.

" Boys," I said, " How many of you believe in God? " " Not one of us," replied several voices in unison. " Don't any of you ever go to church? " " No." They snickered as if amused at such a query. " Are you atheists? " " Aren't you, Uncle? " countered one of them with a touch of defiance. " Why should I be? " " Because " — and there was a sense of finality in the tone of the answer as if the speaker, mere boy though he was, thought the matter beyond dispute.

" Everybody is an atheist," remarked the tallest of the group, apparently also its leader, " except of course old hags."

" I'll bet you are an atheist too," teased a red-haired lad, " only you won't let on." He giggled, and the others giggled with him.

" And why do you say that? " I demanded.

" Because there is no God, that's why," responded the leader, and once more they giggled and then guffawed with amusement.

I had previously visited a number of children's homes in various parts of the country. I had been in many schools and more than once had been accorded the privilege of putting direct questions to pupils on any subject I chose. I had been on picnics with both Pioneers and Young Communists and had talked to other youths, singly and in groups, who were under the direct influence of some revolutionary agency. Those young people were invariably atheistic, boisterously, triumphantly so. But they had been worked on by propaganda. They had heard only denunciations of religion. They had been repeatedly informed that religion, any religion, is a curse. These waifs, however, had never been in a city. They had never come under direct or indirect influence of any revolutionary body. They had never attended school. They had never hobnobbed with Pioneers or Young Communists. Whence, then, had come their atheism? They did not know and they did not care. Yet they gloried in it!

Shortly afterward, in company with a Russian student, I was making a journey, mostly afoot, in one of the most far-away and backward peasant regions. No telephone lines had yet been laid over its endless spaces. No railroad had yet cut across its vast plains. No sign of industrial civilization had yet invaded its slumbering domain. It was what the Russians call " the deaf country," aye, the deafest of the deaf. My companion and I tramped about in a leisurely way from village to village, and one day, caught in a storm, we ran for shelter into the first peasant hut we saw. A sagging log hut it was, with a thatch roof and two dusky little windows that peered into the muddy streets with the glazed dullness of the eyes of a corpse. It was obvious that this was the home of a real *bedniak,* or poor man.

A crowd of children from seven to twelve years of age had gathered there. We greeted them, but they only drew together and snickered as if abashed. I passed around lumps of sugar, a luxury of luxuries to peasant youths, and they immediately loosened up and began to talk. There were no grown folk in the house. It was summer, and all adults in the village were in the field working. There was only one girl in the group, somewhat older than the boys, barefoot and caring for a crying baby in a crib suspended by a rope from the ceiling.

" Boys," I finally braved myself to ask, " do any of you believe in God? "

Now, in the old days, when I was a boy living in a Russian village, had anyone put such a question to a group of peasant youths, they would have stared at him with terror and dismay as at one demented or possessed of an evil spirit. They would have clutched at their little crosses and possibly muttered a prayer invoking the aid of the saints to protect them against

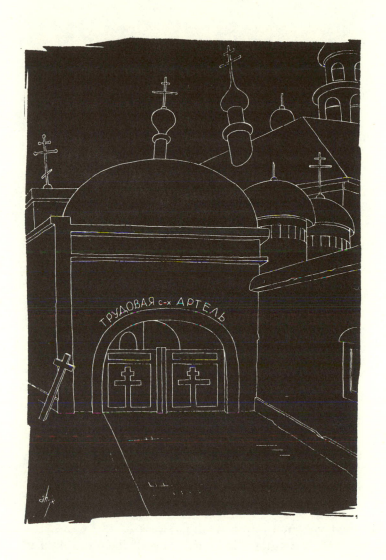

an evil power. In the old days, had a man dared ask such a question of little boys, he would have been hounded out of the village by the elder folk or perhaps turned over to the constable. In the old days the very word *bezbozhnik*, atheist, was anathema to the muzhiks, young and old. In the old days — how old? Only ten or twelve years ago! But now — what an incredible upheaval. Good-humoured mirth was the only response my question evoked.

"They don't believe in God," the girl broke in, "they are all atheists."

"And so are you," burst out a light-haired youth with glowing dark eyes.

"No, I am not," the girl protested. "I am like my mother and not like my father. I believe in God, and I go to church and light candles, too."

The boys laughed at her attempted defense, and she, as if stung by their ridicule, proceeded to expatiate on the subject.

"Well, Uncle, ask my mother if I am telling a lie. She will be here soon. She won't stay in the field when it pours like this. Look, I have got my cross on — see! " she went on, clutching at the little brass cross hung on a red string around her neck. " But you ask them to show their crosses."

"We have none," came the triumphant reply, and the boys burst into a fresh guffaw.

"Do *you* believe in God? " one of them ventured to ask me.

"No, there is no God," another shot out before I even had time to make reply.

"Nobody has seen God," added still another.

As I listened to their words, I wondered if they were really peasant children who were thus expressing themselves. It seemed so incredible — and yet here they were, unkempt, barefoot, ragged lads, as openly boastful of their atheism as if it were a mighty achievement or a wondrous adventure. I set about investigating the possible immediate cause of their riotous unbelief, and, at first, the more I searched into the social life of the community the more I was baffled. There was not even a Soviet in this village. It was governed by a Soviet fifteen miles away. There was no school, no club-house, no little theater, none of the agencies that the Revolution has brought into being to deluge the populace with the new ideas of life. What was even more surprising, there was not a single Communist in the village, nor a Young Communist, nor a Pioneer. And yet somehow, from some invisible source, the new beliefs, new audacities, new defiances, penetrated so deep into this deaf country that these peasant children, illiterate all of them, spoke of their infidelity with the same gusto as do Pioneer lads in Moscow or any other large city. The Revolution seemed to have surcharged the very air with a substance that, when inhaled, automatically burned up religious faith, especially in youth. At any rate, when I met peasant youths, especially boys, in fields, in inns, at market-places, even in church-yards, I seldom heard any of them speak with reverence of the church, of religion or even of the Deity. Only the girls seemed on the whole reluctant to make an outright break with the old faith.

My own village from which I had been away for eighteen years was a distinct shock to me. Even on the way there as I drove along with an old neighbour of ours, I observed evidences of religious apathy which, when set against boyhood memories, seemed wholly incredible. The wooden crosses which used to mark every turn of the road — tall crosses, with a wooden statuette of Jesus, crucified, nailed at the top — were now gone. I asked the driver what had become of them, and quite placidly he replied that the peasants in the neighbourhood had dug them out and cut them up for firewood. In some places, he added, muzhiks had even pulled the crosses out of tombs on the cemeteries, and burned them in their ovens. Of course it was a sin to do that, " but," he added, " our muzhiks don't believe in sin any more; that is, not many of them do," words which shocked me only a little less than those which soon followed: namely, " There are some muzhiks who no longer believe in God! "

I had not been in the village long when I discovered ample confirmation of my driver's remarks. There was the little shrine at the gateway of the village. In former times it was the most imposing little structure in the community, with a trim shingled roof, at the top of which gleamed a huge green cross, and with a neat picket fence shielding the luxurious lawn from the intrusion of stock and fowl. Any damage that ever happened to it — the loosening of a picket, a shingle, a corner-post — was always immediately repaired, and whenever a peasant passed by on foot or on horse, he bowed in reverence and mumbled a prayer.

Now the shrine was tottering to ruin. The fence was gone, the lawn was rooted up, evidently by pigs, with the big black holes gaping out of the green grass like deep gashes in the human body. The windows were smashed, and the frames hung loose like mangled arms. Inside, the picture was even more desolate. The walls were wet and grimy; the floor was overgrown with weeds; and the ikons were no longer draped in white linen, but hung there, frayed and faded, soaked in rain and dirt, mute witnesses of a dying faith. In the surrounding villages the shrines were in no happier condition, and when I asked peasants why they neglected to repair them, they shrugged their shoulders and shook their heads and offered the hackneyed explanation that they were too busy and too poor to think of matters outside of their own household! Strange language this for a once pious man!

On Sunday very few of them went to church. Instead, they gathered in groups in the street, talked, and shelled pumpkin-seeds. The parish church, which served about eight villages and a population of six thousand souls, and which in former times was jammed with worshippers every Sunday, was now fairly deserted. I counted the people there on the Sunday that I visited it, the few old men and old women and little girls. There were twenty-seven in all. I stayed to the end of the services — not another person came.

I visited the priest, whom I knew well as a boy. He had grown old and humped and feeble. His eyes were streaked with blood, and his hair, still long, had grown sparse and grey, and was matted and tousled as though untouched by a comb. He was as touching a picture as his deserted church and the tumbling shrines in the nearby villages. He lived in poverty and loneliness. His land had been taken from him by the Soviets, and he had not even a decent garden left. His once gorgeous furnishings he had to sell for bread. And now the Soviets were driving him from the property of the state, and the muzhiks did nothing for his aid. They had grown brutally indifferent to the church and to him. That was what hurt the most, he wailed. Except on solemn festivals they stopped going to church and at Christmas and Easter they came more for a bit of hilarity than for worship.

Of course there are thousands of churches in Russia that are still open, and on certain occasions, such as Easter or Christmas, they are crowded with visitors. I have been in villages where groups of older people were fanatically devoted to the church. I ran into such a village in the province of Ryazan at a time when the population in the entire district was feverishly agitated over an unusually dramatic incident. The local teacher, disgusted with the dilapidated hovel where he held school, petitioned the Soviet to turn part of the church, which was too large for its parish anyway, into a schoolroom. When the older folk heard of it, they held a secret meeting and resolved to kill the teacher. They would not desecrate their church by turning any portion of it into a schoolhouse, a Soviet school at that! To escape death the teacher fled from the village.

In the South, certain Protestant sects, like the Baptists and the Evangelicans, have, since the coming of the Revolution and the legalization of evangelistic services, won many new converts, chiefly among adults. Here and there a new sect springs into being with a new creed, a new system of conduct. Likewise healers, magicians, prophets, continue to bob up in village after village and, incidentally, to fade away shortly afterward. It is the exception rather than the rule for a peasant girl to be satisfied with a wedding outside of the church. It is estimated that not more than ten per cent of peasant brides agree to secular weddings. Indeed, one could adduce an array of facts and incidents which would seem to indicate that religion is still in a flourishing state in Russia.

But then — after all, Russia is vast, and there are millions and millions of peasants scattered over thousands of villages. What is of prime significance is not that multitudes still attend services in the churches, but that multitudes who were formerly the backbone of the village parishes have now ceased to visit the church, to pray or to believe in God. What is noteworthy in the religious crisis in Russia is that fundamental forces have been set in motion, some loosed by the Revolution, others always latent in the country but formerly held in leash by severe disciplinary measures and now given free play, which are working havoc with the old faith, with all religious faiths, for that matter. What should stir the concern of the honest believer is, not that hundreds of churches in Russia are still open and are often crowded with worshippers, but that hundreds of others have had to close and, most important of all, that a tide of atheism is engulfing the youth of the country, even the peasant youth, though chiefly boys. It is not the outward semblance of things but the basic processes at work that should command the earnest student's thoughtful reflection. These processes are everywhere breaking down, dissolving the bonds of religious fealty.

Never was I so poignantly impressed, however, with the disintegration of Russian Christianity, as when I visited Kiev, most ancient, most beautiful, most joyous of all Russian cities. Glorious Kiev! What peasant in Russia has not heard of this holy city, this Russian Canterbury? It was there that the mighty Prince Vladimir converted his savage subjects to Christianity. It was there that the first Orthodox church and school and library were founded. It was there that the first church printing press was set up. It was there that the first saint was canonized. It is there, in the caves and catacombs of the famous Pechersky monasteries, that the remains of many a holy man have been preserved.

What peasant in the old days, when misfortune crowded hard, a barren woman, a man suffering from epilepsy or demented and considered possessed of evil spirits, a child without the power of speech, anyone with a malady beyond the power of man to heal or a sorrow beyond the capacity of neighbors to assuage — what peasant, when in great travail, did not wish to make a pilgrimage to the holy city, to light candles before the miracle-working ikons, to kiss the shrouded remains of noted saints, to drink of the water in the holy well, all in the hope of obtaining surcease from affliction? From all over Russia they trudged there, men, women, youths; hundreds, thousands of them — a half-million every year — with heavy staffs in their hands and huge loads on their backs, each with a pack of woes and troubles, each full of faith, each eager for a miracle in his own behalf?

Kiev, the dream and the glory of Old Russia, the

hope of the meek, the haven of the downcast. Kiev the spirit and the soul of Orthodoxy!

Well, the city, despite the ferocious civil war that was waged within its boundaries, is as lovely to behold as it ever was. Its hills and vales, its bluffs and hollows, its parks and groves, are as ever drowned in sunshine and fragrance. Its Kreshchatnik, to me the most wondrous street in Russia, more so even than the famous Nevsky in Leningrad, is as gay as it ever was; evenings after dark the city turns out on it, as in the old days, for a promenade — a glamorous procession of all manner of folk, the best dressed in Russia and the best looking, especially the women, also outwardly the happiest and certainly the most genial. Kiev is one of those cities so full of intrinsic vigour and beauty that no hand of man or whim of nature ever can mar or degrade its majestic comeliness.

I hied me to the Pechersky Lavra, that ancient sanctuary, where are spread the most famous monasteries in Russia. First I walked all around the place, and then I entered the gateway, and no sooner had I stepped inside the yard than I felt the desolation that had come over everything there. Fowls and goats were strutting about the grounds, nibbling zealously of the weeds and grass that had shot out of the crannies in the broken sidewalks and in between the cobbles of the pavement. The rows and rows of halls and dormitories that formerly housed monks and pilgrims were now occupied by proletarians, and out of their interiors issued not the sounds of sacred chants and invocations but the strains of profane revolutionary anthems. Somewhere an accordian was playing a sprightly tune to the accompaniment of the shouts of men's voices — proletarians evidently having a jolly time in the very heart of the Pechersky Lavra! Few were the visitors around, and these not pilgrims nor beggars but stray excursionists out sightseeing. Not a peasant in view, and strangest of all but few monks about.

I passed a group of them leaning in stolid contemplation against a tottering board fence. They were bearded men, stately enough in their flowing robes and their shiny crosses, yet with an air of forlornness pathetic to behold.

Lonely men they must be in these days of Revolution, with youth and officialdom gnawing fast and hard at the very core of things religious. I introduced myself to them. They responded warmly, glad evidently that a stranger from a far-away land could speak to them in their own language. Other monks came out of their cells to join in the conversation. They bombarded me with questions — and what questions! Had they lived in caves shut off from all physical contact with outside humanity, they could not have been more dismally misinformed of life beyond their own immediate little world. How far was America from Russia? Was it really safe to travel on the ocean? Was there a Soviet government in America? Did Americans have ikons in their churches? Was the government supporting the brethren in the American monasteries? Questions without end.

They invited me to join them in their afternoon repast — tea, black bread and apple jam, which they themselves had made. They apologized profusely for the scantiness of their fare. They were poor now, poorer even than muzhiks. They could afford no meats, eggs, cakes. Fast-foods were all they had to live on. The lands and shops and hostelries that once yielded them rich revenues were no longer under their control; nor were tributes from thousands of pilgrims pouring into their treasuries. Though their robes, shirts, shoes, were worn threadbare, they could afford no new ones. They could afford nothing new, not even a teakettle, a sock or a handkerchief. What was actually keeping them alive was the sale of candles, pictures and other relics, not to pilgrims, not to pious muzhiks — no, alas! — but to excursionists, infidels most of them, who were daily coming in search of fresh weapons of attack on God and Christ. That was what Russia had come to — this sacred place a mere playground for unbelievers. But then — the Lord would not desert them. Maybe He had permitted these privations just to test their faith. They would not forsake Him, even if all Russia, aye, the entire world, were to deny Him. It was comforting to hear at least this note of heroism in their otherwise despairing speech.

Two of the brethren volunteered to take me through the famous *peshchery,* or caves, that wind in a network deep underground. With lighted wax candles in our hands to illumine the way, we descended into the ancient tunnels, where so much dramatic history was made. And not only by churchmen — knights, princes, warriors, during feuds with neighbouring rulers, fled there to find shelter and to hatch grandiose conspiracies. Holy men, sick of the world with its pain and allurements, retired there for penance and meditation. Not a few of them interred themselves in the ground and remained there, living corpses, until they breathed their last. As we wound our way around these caves, we came now and then on open coffins containing the remains of some of these saints, draped in red cloth. " In old days," mourned one of my guides, " thousands of pilgrims would come here daily to kneel beside these *moshtshui,* to kiss the cloth enveloping them, and to spend hours, aye, days, in prayer and meditation in these underground chapels. But now — " he did not have to finish the sentence. The utter stillness of the place told the story of its abandonment more eloquently than could any words of his.

" How do you account for this sudden apathy of the Russian muzhik? " I asked.

" Ah, this muzhik," replied one of the monks, a small man with a bristly red beard and sparkling little eyes that gleamed with despair as much as with rancour. " He is a beast, that's what he is, this muzhik of ours. He is the ruination of our great country, he more than all the infidels and Bolshevists and other Reds. He knows nothing. He never had God in his heart. That's the truth, my friend — the real truth. The muzhik never took Christ to his heart, because he never understood Him. Oh, this damned muzhik, this human beast."

" Yes, this brother is right," remarked the other monk, a tall man with a flowing black beard, more reserved than his companion, " the muzhik is at heart a *bezbozhnik.* Otherwise — well, atheists would not be ruling our country. Do you understand what I mean? I can say no more."

Several hours later I left them, and, as I was walking back to town and catching a last glimpse of the towering cupolas growing dim with dusk, it seemed to me that night was settling not only over this ancient lavra but over the old faith that it symbolized, aye, perhaps, over all religion in Russia!

Afterward, as I wandered about Russian villages in other sections of the country, observing everywhere the pronounced religious indifference of the peasant, especially of the rising generation, I asked myself and others what had happened to the muzhik, this ancient and stalwart pillar of Russian Christianity or Orthodoxy? What has happened to the man of whose piety and godliness so many rhapsodic books have been written, who was always pointed to as the symbol of Holy Russia, the great sufferer and the great mystic, in brief the man with the soul of a saint? How has it come about that this valiant protagonist of Christianity has yielded or is yielding so readily to the blandishments of infidelity?

I know the answer some people will make. I have heard it so often from the lips of believers, Russians and others. It is a simple enough answer — Bolshevist propaganda! But such an answer invests Bolshevist propaganda with a power too terrific to contemplate, as if it were an omnipotent force. Of course there has been Bolshevist propaganda, wide-spread and eloquent, but why has it seemingly been so successful? Why has it been overcoming the propaganda of which Russian Christianity, or Russian Orthodoxy, has held an undisputed monopoly for about a thousand years?

That the Bolshevists are hostile to religion, that they hope ultimately to stamp out all churches and all faiths, they frankly and proudly admit. No believing person is accepted to membership in the Communist Party, and should a member exhibit a leaning toward religion, if only out of deference for his wife or mother, he would be immediately expelled.

In their treatment of Orthodox clergymen they have been openly and sometimes brutally severe. But that was inevitable in view of the past record of the Orthodox church. It had been an integral part of the old government and naturally enough the Bolsheviks suspected every functionary of the church as an actual and potential counter-revolutionary. The conduct of the heads of the church defying to the last the Soviet government and calling on the laity to disobey its mandates did not of course weaken this suspicion.

Roman Catholic clergymen likewise have from time to time been sternly treated. But here again the political motive is pre-eminent. In Russia the Roman Catholics are mainly Poles, and the feud between Russia and Poland has been too intense not to react with some vehemence on as patriotically minded a body of Poles as are the Polish clergymen on Soviet territory and especially along the Polish frontier.

Aside, however, from these considerations which made the Bolsheviks from time to time lay a heavy hand on Orthodox and Roman Catholic clergymen, they have never shown a disposition to favour organized religion. In a subsequent chapter I shall explain at length the reason for their hostility to religion. Here I only wish to emphasize that they regard it in every way as inimical to the purpose of the Revolution and will allow it no more liberties than necessary to fulfill the principle of freedom of conscience which they have proclaimed, and which, of course, they interpret in their own way. No church is allowed to engage in cultural or social pursuits. Libraries, clubs, hospitals, dispensaries, nurseries, co-operative stores — no church may embark on any such welfare enterprises. This limits the function of church and religion purely to the pursuit of worship. Whether or not the Bolsheviks can enforce this policy, time alone will tell. If they can, the Protestant sects will be the chief sufferers. They had so skillfully woven the revolutionary methods of social service into their church life that during the early years of the Revolution they had made hosts of converts especially among the older generation. A further damaging ordinance, in force since the very rise of the Soviet government, prohibits religious instruction to youths under eighteen years of age outside of the home. This, while not interfering with the church attendance of youth at any age, automatically bans Sunday and parochial schools for children.

Such regulations alone, however, can hardly account for the religious apathy which, save among Protestant sects, has spread among the Russian masses including the peasantry. The Bolsheviks have disinterred and placed on exhibition the remains of certain saints, but they have not prohibited pilgrimages to Pereyeslavl, to Kiev, to Poltava and to other places that formerly drew annually hundreds of thousands of worshippers. Why then are there practically no more pilgrims in Russia? Even the beggars that trudge the bazaars with accordions or other musical instruments are beginning to sing revolutionary limericks instead of their ancient religious chants. The Bolsheviks do not fine or tax

people for attending religious services, yet even in villages the Orthodox churches are hardly half as well
attended as in the old days. Hundreds of them have
actually had to close because of lack of support. Witness especially the desolation that has come over Kiev
— not enough pilgrims now coming to provide sustenance for a mere handful of monks, whereas in the
old days several thousand of them could thrive on the
fees and contributions of visiting worshippers.

Yet even if religion were subject to persecution in
Russia, that would not explain its collapse. History
bristles with examples of contrary effects of persecution. Witness the early Christian Fathers. Consider the
case of the Jews in Spain or in any land where forcible
attempts were made to break them from the faith of
their ancestors. Inquisition, torture only strengthened
them in this faith.

For the real cause of the religious disintegration in
Russia we must search in the condition of the people,
especially the peasantry, and in the faith which they
professed.

CHAPTER II

RELIGION

CAUSE OF COLLAPSE

I ONCE attended a lecture in Moscow by Archbishop Vvedensky, perhaps the most eloquent clergyman in Russia and one of the most scholarly. He was discussing the shortcomings of the Orthodox church — the official church in Russia in the old days — and among other things he said:

" The extraordinary Byzantine glitter of our Orthodox services has been our greatest curse. Our church has striven after external gorgeousness at the expense of inner virtue, after showy splendour at the cost of spiritual perfection. It acquired pomp, power, riches, but lost its soul. Only now are we beginning to realize what a feeble spiritual infant our Orthodoxy has been. That is why it is disintegrating."

History corroborates the learned clergyman's diagnosis. Too exclusively had the Orthodox church given itself to the pursuit of ceremonial and externalism. Coming to Russia at the end of the tenth century by way of Byzantium, it brought with it both physical magnificence and a new morality, for those days radical enough to have subdued even as lustful a ruler as Prince Vladimir of Kiev. But it soon stagnated, having acquired tremendous wealth and become a plaything in the hands of rulers. It did not seek to fit into the varying mould of an expanding civilization with its power to stir new ideas, new questions in the human mind. It hardly heeded the challenge of science, the humanities and the rising social movements. It hardly took cognizance of their existence. It seldom engaged in combat with its intellectual and spiritual adversaries as did the Roman Catholic church. It did not have to. It was always shielded from outside encroachments and questionings by the strong arm of the government. It never, therefore, acquired the intellectual and spiritual endurance of the Roman church. It really remained aloof from earthly life, from the problems and burdens and conflicts that harassed and lacerated Russian mankind.

Nor had it suffered the strengthening agony of an inner purgation. Self-doubt, self-criticism it vigilantly suppressed. Once a year it would pronounce an anathema on those outside of its fold. It considered itself the beginning and the end of all spiritual wisdom and justice for all times and all mankind. Now and then a waft of Western questioning would blow into the mind of some monk or layman, and a voice of dissent would rise from some monastery or village. But it was stifled soon enough. True, the Orthodox church in Russia went through a rather dramatic split with the so-called Old Believers, but characteristically enough mainly over matters of form, over the corrected spelling of the church books instituted by Patriarch Nikon, over the proper way to make the sign of the cross, with two fingers or with the entire hand. The spiritual forces at work in the world outside its own confines it chose to ignore. Hence it never grew in spiritual stature. It had only its mechanistic mysticism to lean upon. With its conversion into a state institution in the days of

Peter the Great, it lost all semblance of independence, and became merely a weapon in the hands of the czars, with its doors even more tightly shut to the invigourating influences of the outside world. No wonder that Tolstoy felt constrained to say:

" I cannot but be hostile to this harmful sect . . . which is seeking to corrupt the dark masses and the young generation by instilling in them false notions of God and His law." Or as the noted Dr. E. J. Dillon once put it — " The Russian church is a museum of liturgic antiquities."

The ministration of the Orthodox church had a sterilizing effect on the spiritual life of the peasant. It depended for its appeal not on living sentiment, on understanding of the real purpose of faith and the meaning of service, but on miracle, magic, ceremonial. It had always emphasized the form rather than the substance, the technique rather than the spirit of worship.

I was present once at the Donskoy Monastery when the late Patriarch Tikhon was canonizing a Siberian bishop. The services were aglow with colour and action, stirring to the eye and the ear — spectacle, pageantry, drama. Beautiful music, jewelled ikons and symbols, glittering vestments, always marked the Orthodox form of worship. But the peasant, who was the chief bulwark of the church, never made any mental connection between this gorgeous ritual, this extraordinary ceremonial, and his humdrum personal affairs.

The Orthodox church never even sought to wean him from his pagan superstitions. It was tolerant of the witches, sorcerers, magicians, incantation — charmers that infested the villages and preyed on the muzhik.

It saw him wallowing in alcoholism, in thievery, in cruelty, in other vices and hardly made an effort to regenerate him.

Christianity never had become part of the peasant's inner self, rarely had been the source of a great inspiration. The Bible he scarcely knew. In most instances he could not read it; he was illiterate. I once asked a group of peasants on a boat on the Volga how they liked the Sermon on the Mount? I might as well have asked them what they thought of Einstein's theory of relativity. They had never heard of it. With rare exceptions the muzhik acquired his knowledge of God and religion not from the Bible, personal study or contemplation, but from the Orthodox church which, as already pointed out, stressed the symbol instead of the spirit of faith, the method rather than the meaning of worship. Consequently, the peasant had come to associate religion, not with an inner mood, but with an external act. He felt it was something vital and indispensable, but aloof and detached, residing not within, but without himself, a ceremony, a ritual, to perform and observe, not an ideal, a revelation, to meditate upon, to absorb, to transmute into that joyous identity and communion with the invisible spirit of the Deity, which constitutes at once the essence and the florescence of true religion. With rare exceptions, that " individual psychological experience " which Fosdick speaks of as the fountain-head of religion was alien to him.

In its concrete manifestations the peasant's faith showed itself literally enough. It resolved itself into a calculated formalism, piously executed. He went to church, observed his numerous fasts, lighted candles before his favourite ikons, visited monks and saints who for a consideration could perform miracles — invoke a cure of a malignant ailment, bless the applicant with the arrival of a much wanted child, grant other petitions. He always stressed the performance of the external act as the price and the means of attaining the desired end. He went on long pilgrimages to distant monasteries, to the Holy Land, not so much in search of spiritual solace as in quest of a definite reward. The question of morality and righteousness did not always enter into his considerations. Peasants have been known to invoke the aid of God for success in robbery, arson, murder.

Such a mechanistic conception of religion could not survive the shattering effects of the Revolution, with its fierce onslaught upon non-rationalistic faith and practice. His atrophied spirituality could not lift the peasant above the inconsistencies and contradictions which the Revolution had been hurling at him. Orthodoxy, for example, was in his mind an impregnable and inviolate institution. To rise against it was a sin fraught with cruel retribution. The dignitaries of the church, bishops, archbishops, he always held as above possibility of harm by mere man. But Patriarch Tikhon, the most holy one, was arrested and jailed, and the men who effected the arrest did not turn into stone. Gold and jewels were gathered from holy ikons, and the hands that did the gathering did not wither. Graves of saints were dug up, and the men who wielded the picks and shovels did not drop dead. The saints themselves proved to be only huddles of bones, with no living energy spurting out of them. Bishops, archbishops, holy monks, miracle-workers, were driven from their homes, jailed, exiled, executed, like common criminals, and their enemies and tormentors remained unharmed. The very people to whom the peasant went for guidance, in whose power to invoke the intercession of a supernatural force he implicitly trusted, could not even extricate themselves from the fierce clutch of adversity.

There was no miracle. The saints seemed helpless. All incantations, ceremonials, anathemas, were like so much wasted breath. The wicked revolutionaries had triumphed over the church, over magic, over miracle, over saints and bishops, over the very God that the peasant knew!

Literal-minded man that he is, with no inner spiritual reserve to sustain him in time of a crisis, these and other similar events and incidents had a devastating effect on his faith, broke the spell of Orthodoxy over him.

The consequences of its mechanistic mysticism were doubly calamitous to the Orthodox church. It failed to develop a reserve of vitality that would enable it to withstand with safety and effectiveness an outside onslaught such as the Revolution had launched on it, and it failed no less dismally to make the peasant, its chief pillar of support throughout the ages, loyal enough so that in a crisis he would rally to its rescue. It overawed him with its temporal power. It bewitched him with its grandiose magic. But it did not stir in him the fealty that comes from close fellowship, from a kinship of spirit, from a reciprocity of sentiment.

In time the peasant began to follow the line of least resistance. He stayed away from church, and nothing happened. His appetite was as good. He slept as well. He could work as hard. He experienced no feeling of regret or remorse. Life flowed along as evenly as it had when he worshipped regularly. And there was the boon of material gain. He was no longer under the obligation to make contributions of sacks of rye, loaves of bread, bundles of flax, or rolls of linen to the church and its officials. So the motive of material advantage, predominant in all of a peasant's calculations, was an added incentive to infidelity.

The reader will naturally wonder what has become of Holy Russia of which so much was written in the pre-revolutionary days. He will ask where has disappeared the saintly all-suffering muzhik of the Stephen Grahams, with his out-going warmth and pity for all fallen mankind, his sublime faith in God and Christ and his eternal search for spiritual verities?

Again and again I would ask myself this question as I wandered about the villages in the far-flung Soviet empire, and I must confess that I never found him, this Christ-like muzhik, and for a very simple reason — he never existed outside of the exuberant imagination of irresponsible romancers. Holy Russia is a mawkish myth! A Christ-like peasant is a preposterous fable! Even Tolstoy with all his revolt against modern civilization, his deification of primitivism, his exaltation of the simple life of the peasant, never deigned to picture the muzhik as a saintly person with a faith that moveth mountains. Neither Turgeniev, nor Chekhov, nor Gleb Uspensky, nor Chirikov, nor Bunin, nor Gorky, nor Andreyev had ever encountered this all-suffering, all-forgiving muzhik. Humility the peasant has, patient and all-enduring he is — at times — not through choice, but compulsion; submissive he has been not by virtue of the power of an inner spiritual grandeur, but because of sheer physical impotence. Yet what a savage he could be when he felt the shackles of repression removed from his hands! What orgies of slaughter he could perpetrate when he felt power on his side, or when he reached out for its possession! Let the reader consider the sanguinary uprisings in which he has participated — under Stenka Razin in 1669, under Yemelyan Pugatchev in the reign of Katherine the Second, the continuous outbursts of rebellion in the nineteenth century, the Revolutions of 1905 and 1917, when peasants all over the land, gun or axe in hand, swooped on landlords to settle ancient grudges!

All the romantic palaver of a peasant in search of spiritual perfection through pain and self-denial is a mere legend. The very words " spiritual perfection " are not part of his vocabulary, are beyond his comprehension. Warm-hearted he is — at times. So are other peasant peoples, so are all primitive peoples. The Tatar or the Kirghiz peasant is as meek, as all-suffering, as is the muzhik, and is even more kindly. Visit him in his tent on the steppes where he tends his stock, and he will joyously slaughter the fattest sheep in your honour and will overwhelm you to agony with his hospitality. And he is no Christian at all. He hates Orthodoxy. He is a staunch Mohammedan.

Despite his outward show of piety and religiosity, at heart the peasant has remained a pagan with no real comprehension of the meaning and spirit of the faith which he professed. The rise of numerous religious sects among the peasantry, which both government and church had sought to suppress, was in rebellion against the externalism which the reigning church so exclusively emphasized. Peasants wanted something more warm, more vital, more responsive to their spiritual yearnings than the old church had offered them. Incidentally it is these sects, Protestant in nature, that show the greatest resistance to the spread of infidelity.

Even as I write my mind teems with incidents, typical enough, that reveal an absence in the peasant of that spirit of reverence and devotion which we expect of a true follower of Christ. Once at a mass-meeting in a village at which several thousand peasants had gathered — I asked if any among those present had Bibles in their homes. Not a hand went up. I then asked if any of them had possessed Bibles in the old days. About half a dozen hands shot upward.

" What," I continued my question, " have you done with them — sold them? "

" No, indeed," came the reply from someone in the crowd, " during the civil war we could not get anything from the city, not even cigarette paper, so we smoked up our Bibles." On investigation I learned that that was precisely what peasants had done in numerous villages — had used up their Bibles for cigarette paper!

At another time, while passing through a village, I was attracted by a gigantic brick structure that was as if in process of demolition. The tin roof was gone, windows and doors had been taken out and several layers of brick had been removed from the top. It was dusk and a militiaman in uniform, rifle in hand, was standing on guard. I asked him why he had been stationed there, and he replied that, if he had not been, the peasants in the village would have taken apart and carried off bit by bit the entire structure, which, he emphasized, was not the home of a former landlord, on whom muzhiks might wish to wreak vengeance, but a newly-built church, finished just before the Revolution, and which had had to close because of lack of attendance. I visited other villages where churches had had to close and where the local peasants had begun taking them apart, stripping the tin off the roof, removing iron, glass, lumber and other materials that might be of use to them. Only after local Soviets had stationed guards armed with rifles around these places, did the plundering cease. And how many monasteries in Russia did the peasants loot in the days of the civil war, when monks were beginning to flee and the Soviets had not yet organized strongly enough to protect public property! When I asked peasants why they were inconsiderate of a former house of worship, which they might some day need, if not for a church, then for some other communal purpose, they had no real explanation to offer. It was a *kazenny*, or government, building, they would say, and, as long as it was not in use, they might as well help themselves to anything in or about it that might be of service to them.

Once again while I was driving to a distant village, my coachman stopped at a crossroad to water his horse. I noticed that the watering trough was resting on a huge and fine marble slab. On investigation I discovered that this was a tombstone, evidently out of the grave of some landlord. The peasants seemed to have had no qualms about lugging it to this place and putting it to ordinary use. On another occasion, as an elderly peasant was showing me around his barnyard, I saw a mud-hole plugged up with two large marble tombstones. I asked him where he had secured them, and he said that his boys had brought them home from the private chapel-grounds of a nearby estate after the landlord had fled to foreign parts. But, I remonstrated, was it not a sin to put tombstones to such use? In reply he shrugged his shoulders — perhaps it was a sin, he remarked, but his boys had done it, and youths in Russia no longer believed in sin!

Certainly these incidents and many others which space does not permit me to cite, do not speak of a stirring reverence in the peasant, of an outgoing devotion to the Christian faith or to the Orthodox church. If the peasant were the holy man depicted by impassioned Slavophiles, would he have dared or been willing to " smoke up " his Bible? If he were the Christlike soul that the Stephen Grahams had once pictured him, would he have pulled tombstones out of graves to use as stands for watering troughs or to plug up holes in a barnyard? Would he have had the courage or the heart to strip a closed church of materials that he could utilize for household purposes? Would he have prayed as peasants have sometimes done for success in robbery, in arson, in murder? Would he ever have tolerated with such indifference the stripping of the holy ikons all over the country of gold and jewels? The religious world must face the fact that at heart the peasant has always been a pagan, except, I must emphasize, when he came under the influence of certain sects. The sectarian peasant, because of his knowledge of the Bible, his understanding in his own way, of course, of the purpose and the mission of Christianity, is the only peasant in Russia who in spite of the Revolution has remained staunch in his faith. His problem is to pass on his faith to his children so that they will possess sufficient inner strength to resist the many-sided and dynamic onslaught of atheism.

CHAPTER III

RELIGION

SUBSTITUTIONS

THE feature in the religious disintegration of Russia that is especially provocative of reflection is the defiant atheism of the youth. Everywhere so-called advanced youth is openly and hilariously atheistic, and this youth is sucking into its fold the other youth of the land, save possibly that of the Protestants. I say possibly, because, while the Protestant youth has hitherto held to its faith more firmly than the other youth of the land, it is still a question whether in the end it will not break away from the religion of its fathers.

There are religious leaders who smilingly dismiss the notion that atheism can remain a permanent condition in Russia. They argue that religion, Christianity especially, has survived all attacks in the past, and it will as surely survive the opposition of the Bolshevists. In reply I must emphasize the consideration that never in its history has any religion, and Christianity in particular, faced a foe as formidable as it is now encountering in Russia — a foe so determined, so energetic, so intelligent as the Bolshevists are. There is no use deriding or dismissing their fighting strength. They are not following in the footsteps of other anti-religious crusades — not quite. Violence and brute repression, for example, form no part of their attack. They know that violent procedure would court certain defeat.

Why are they so implacably hostile to religion? It is not enough to say that they are relieving themselves of rancour against the Orthodox church for its docile submission to the old government, for its ancient enmity of social progress, for its tireless persecution of revolutionaries. That may account for their contempt of the Orthodox church, but does not explain their hostility to all religions.

One must reckon with antecedents. The spiritual atmosphere in which they grew up has kept them from cultivating a feeling of sympathy for any religion. Consider the old revolutionary movement in Russia out of which they have sprung. Here men and women were banded together for the purpose of liberating the dark masses from an age-old tyranny. They studied, suffered, planned and plotted — always for the sake of others. They lived for something outside of themselves. They cared not for their own welfare. Money, glory, career — these were of no consequence. Today they were in their home — tomorrow they might be in hiding in some cave. Today they were walking along the Nevsky Prospect — tomorrow they might be on their way to Siberia. Today they were in the embrace of their wives or loved ones — tomorrow they might be piloted across the boisterous Neva to the living tombs of the Petropavlovsky fortress. These men and women had passion, faith, love, an out-going spirit of self-sacrifice. One cannot read the biographies of men and women like Kalyayev, Gershuni, Zheliabow, Breshkovskaya, Figner, Zassulitch and others without feeling that here were not merely heroes and heroines, but the very flower of human goodness, the very soul of nobil-

ity, the very fulfillment of the word and the deed of
Christianity.

And yet it was neither Christianity nor any other
religion that had roused in them their revolutionary
fervor. They had come to their beliefs and deeds entirely through non-Christian and non-religious sources.
Church had not offered them aid or encouragement,
no church. Seldom do you find in the utterances of these
men and women any recognition of indebtedness to any
religion for their espousal of the revolutionary faith.
Seldom has there been any effort made by a revolutionary leader to make the Revolution a vehicle of
religious precepts, an expression of religious ideals.
Men like Kalyayev composed some stirring poems
about Christ. Also there were churchmen, though
not many, in the movement, but the movement itself
derived its inspiration from sources remote from church
or religion. The revolutionaries were not in the service
of God. They did not regard themselves as fulfilling the
will or the word of Christ. They were in the service of
the Revolution and the " dark masses " which they
had set out to liberate. The passion they cherished
for their faith, their spirit of self-abnegation, their
readiness to give all they had, including their life, for
their cause, were free from any religious influence. Indeed, intellectually and spiritually the Russian revolutionary movement derived its inspiration from the
fathers of the French Revolution and from German
materialism, and both were hostile to religion. The
Russian Bolshevists reared emotionally and intellectually in the old revolutionary movement, were naturally enough imbued with a hostility toward religion,

any religion. Marx was their spiritual godfather, and it was Marx who had first declared that " religion is the opium of the people."

Now that the Bolshevists are in power they make no secret of their hostility to religion. Unlike socialists in other lands, men like Ramsay MacDonald, for example, they disclaim any identity in aim and purpose between socialism and religion, especially Christianity. As Mr. Krasikov, an associate of the Commissary of Justice in Moscow, once said to me, " It is preposterous to think that Christianity and socialism have anything in common, and what is worrying us is not that Christianity in Russia is dying, but that it is still surviving."

The Bolshevik indictment of religion and especially of Christianity, since it is the leading religion in industrial lands, is many-sided. Being materialists or calling themselves such, the Bolshevists repudiate emphatically all types of mysticism or idealism. Belief in God, they contend, is not rooted in matter, therefore, it is a mere invention, a myth. " The transition," says Bukharin, " from the society which makes an end of capitalism to the society which is completely free from all traces of class-division and class-struggle, will bring about the natural death of all religion and all superstition."

As for Christianity in particular they regard many of its teachings anti-social and highly perversive. It teaches, they charge, acquiescence and therefore dulls man's urge to fight for a better life. It promises a paradise in the life to come, and thereby lulls man into a tolerance of injustices on this earth. It seeks to make man righteous by persuasion, but has failed to stop the strong man from exploiting his weaker brother. It has only ideas but no social methods. It preaches the brotherhood of man but in reality it has served as a weapon for social cleavages and racial feuds. The golden rule they find utterly subversive, and against it they set the class-struggle. However modernized the conception of religion, any religion, they will have none of it. " Sacredness," " worship," recognition of duties as " Divine commands," which Kant spoke of as religion; " reverence and love for ideal conduct," which John Stuart Mill and Huxley recognized as religion; " a saving experience of inner spiritual devotion and daily spiritual power," which Fosdick enunciates as the very soul of religion; the belief " in an everlasting God, a Divine mind and will ruling the Universe and holding moral relations with mankind," which Dr. Martineau lays down as the essence of religion; " the championship of personality," which Fosdick proclaims as the mainstay of Christianity — the Bolsheviks emphatically and scornfully reject any and all of these approaches to religion. They do not even capitalize the word God in their writings. Religion to them *is* " an opiate of the people."

In their method of attack they proceed on the theory that religion is not the result of an inborn force or impulse, but of training, of something that is superimposed from without. If children, they declare, are reared without religious guidance, they will grow up to be non-religious, and then religion will dry up at the source and will die of its own accord.

Intrinsically the religious crisis in Russia has resolved itself into a struggle between the Church and the home on one hand, the Communist Party and all the agencies at its command on the other, for the control and allegiance of youth. It is a stupendous conflict, the outcome of which will not be without its effects on the outside world. The active agencies of the Communist Party are formidable. They embrace the Red army, the schools, the children's homes, the playgrounds, the lecture platform, the moving pictures, the press and all the other institutions under direct and indirect Communist control, including such organizations as Octobrists, Pioneers, Young Communists — the youth movements of Russia — with a joint membership of some five millions. Rich, or comparatively so, in material resources, in energy, in daring, these agencies seek to make the Revolution and therefore atheism, which is an integral part of the Revolution, a force in their everyday life. Let us note here also, that not a policy or an idea the Russian Communists urge youth to support, but they seek to inject into it the thrill of an adventure; and so the espousal of atheism they have likewise galvanized into a gallant adventure.

They do not confine themselves to destructive attacks on religion. Therein alone they are quite unlike other atheist movements in history. They know that to blast out of life an institution which for centuries has constituted an integral part of civilization is more than likely to create a void which sooner or later might be filled by a return to the banished institution in its original or in a modified form. They realize that there are features in religion which appeal to man's sense of beauty, to his self-importance, his sense of superiority,

his gregariousness, his search for a key to the mystery
of life and the universe. So they purpose to minister to
these cravings with ideas, practices, institutions of their
own. They seek to deprive religion of the least justification for its existence, of the slightest element of utility
to man, materially, spiritually, psychologically. They
are confident that they can permanently rid Russia of
religion through the spread and application of science,
art, morality, sociability, social service and a new faith.
These, roughly speaking, are their chief methods of
combat upon religion.

Science is the rapier with which they hope to cut
through the intellectual fabric of religion, to demolish
the acceptance of the biblical version of creation, of
God, of Christ, of worship — of any religion. Science,
they insist, is the key to the mystery of life, its origin,
scope, purpose. Science, which is the handmaid of communism, shall be the force in which man shall repose
his faith. And they are spreading science with the zeal
of missionaries distributing Bibles in heathen lands.
Their presses are churning out mountains of scientific
tracts, written in simple and vigorous style, which are
given wide circulation. At every possible occasion these
are read, explained and discussed with groups of youths
and older people, but especially with youths. Indeed,
the word *nauka* — science — is almost a holy word in
present-day Russia, synonymous with, and therefore, a
symbol of a new redemption, a new adventure.

In their advocacy of morality they are no less ardent.
Of course, the word has a somewhat different meaning
to them than it has in the Western World, both prag-
matically and theoretically. To them all morality de-

rives chiefly from one source — absence of exploitation of one man by another. That is why making a profit in business is to them highly immoral, for profit, according to them, is a result of exploitation. Therefore the possession of private property which can be utilized for profit-making purposes in also immoral, and so is the accumulation of wealth through investments. In matters of sex they reject many of the tenets of morality that prevail in the outside world, as I shall point out in a subsequent chapter, yet laxity in sex life they unflinchingly condemn. They have banned the houses of prostitution which in the old days infested every town and every city in Russia. While they do not regard it as immoral to smoke, drink liquor, gamble, they have been conducting a vigorous propaganda against all such indulgences. There is a group within the Party that is hostile to dancing. A personal experience will prove enlightening, no less than amusing. In the company of an English journalist I once attended a ball of a laundry-workers' union in the Hotel Europe in Leningrad. Several of the girls with whom we had become acquainted proposed that the orchestra play a fox-trot in honour of the foreign visitors, but the chairman of the ball, a handsome youth of not more than twenty, with the taciturnity of a man continually preoccupied with weighty thoughts, apologized for having to rule against the request on the ground that an American fox-trot was improper as a dance for a class-conscious proletarian! During the years when the Charleston was the rage all over the world including China, Russia was the only land that banned it.

The art appeal of church and religion the Bolshevists

are equally determined to nullify. The peasant hangs ikons in the house, not only because of their religious significance, but because they are a contrast to the dulness of the bare walls. In church the frescoes, the paintings, the draperies, the vestments, the gilded crosses, stir and gratify the sense of colour and beauty. The lighted candles add to the scene of splendor. The singing wakens the emotions. But the substitutes they propose to introduce will, they insist, stir the art sense in man more abundantly than did the church. The peasant will decorate his lowly hut not with ikons, but with pictures of the leaders of the Revolution; pictures vividly depicting the evils of drinking vodka, of ignorance, of superstition, of cruelty; pictures inculcating love of children, of birds, of animals, of nature; pictures reproducing ancient forms of life and the appearance of our planet in geologic times; pictures depicting scenes from the every-day experience of the common man in the city and in the village; pictures of the Red Army in its various daily pursuits — pictures always rich in meaning no less than in color and realism. In village after village I saw the living rooms of muzhiks plastered with such pictures, and Soviet offices and club-houses in the provinces, despite untidiness, have all the appearance and atmosphere of finely decorated studios.

And if the ceremonies of the church have a distinctive art value, so will the non-religious ceremonies of the Soviets. The church has well-trained choirs? The Soviets will build such choirs; only, instead of religious hymns, they will sing of toil and sacrifice for the Revolution and of the trials and triumphs of the proletarian and peasant in their struggle to overpower the bourgeoisie. The church dramatizes births, weddings, funerals? So will the Soviet through a ceremonial of its own, fitting and appealing and with a rich anti-religious flavour. A Soviet wedding, they say, for those who want it, can be made to give man a finer sense of exultation and self-importance than a church wedding ever did. A Soviet christening may be made an occasion of more ample festivities and joviality than a church christening. A Soviet funeral may solemnize man's passage into nothingness more impressively than a church funeral — with flowers, red bunting, red flags, a red canopy over the hearse, a band, a choir, and speeches by members of the Party and friends of the deceased. Soviet funeral ceremonies, executed with the dramatic feeling which is innate in the Russian, are touching enough to move the most stolid person.

And the village and town club-house will provide a more ample outlet for man's social yearnings than the church ever did. Every community, every factory, will have at least one club-house, which will always be richly and appropriately decorated with pictures, flowers, flags, bunting and which will have a stage for concerts and for dramatic performances. Peasants and workers will gather there to see friends, to gossip, to listen to lectures, to engage in discussion, to play games, to learn to read and write, to hear concerts, to see motion pictures and theatrical performances. There are few villages and factories in Russia now without such a club-house or away from convenient reach of one. In communities far removed from railroads I attended dramatic performances which, despite crudeness of staging, would delight the heart of the most exacting critic. I know of no country where amateur theatricals are so widespread and where sociability is so diligently fostered as in Russia, or so glowingly appreciated by the mass. Anti-dullness is, indeed, one of the cardinal features of the Bolshevist attack on religion, as well as one of the methods to gain and to hold a following, especially of the youth of the country.

Social service under the banner of the Revolution, insist the Bolshevists, will likewise bring to man new interests and new raptures. Everybody in Russia is to be an *obshtchestvennik* — a social worker. A physician, a teacher, an engineer, an agricultural expert, a locksmith, a kitchen maid — all must understand the purport and value of social work. Social service is to be the great method and the great goal, the great motive and the great fact — the big reality and the big inspiration in the everyday tasks of man. It will open new channels of self-expression, and will be a prolific source of gratification. Instead of prayers, fasting, lighting of candles or retirement to a monastery, all of which, argue the Russians, aside from being of no practical value, draw man into himself, his own well-being, his own inner glorification, he will give himself to building things for the new society — new factories, new cities, new homes, new schools, new enjoyments, new aspirations. These tasks will take him out of himself and link him inextricably with his fellow man and the new society. It is into such activities, they plead, that man is to pour his time, energies, talents. It is such enterprises, they never cease to emphasize, that will give man a fuller sense of dignity, of personal worth, than any form of worship, for they will inculcate in him a sense of mastery instead of submission, or triumph instead of fear. Social service is, indeed, to be one of the chief means of nullifying a variety of appeals that religion has made to man.

Then there is to be the new faith — in a new day, a new civilization, a new happiness, a new conquest, a new man — on this earth now, and for all mortal souls. It matters not, of course, that judged by western standards this revolutionary faith is utopian or subversive. The passion is there and so is the outgoing earnestness and readiness to bring all in its sacrifice. One only has to watch a parade of Russian revolutionaries or to attend a celebration of a revolutionary holiday, to become aware of the depth of passion that the Russian revolutionaries have for their new faith. This faith may in time become a mere matter of routine, a dogma without a breath of warmth. All faiths finally do burn themselves low if not out. For the present, however, to those who have been inoculated with it, it is a reality and a power that transcend anything else in their life, anything else humanity has to offer to them.

I submit that this is a novel crusade against religion, a well calculated effort to strip it of all meaning and all appeal to man, utilitarian, mystical, social, artistic. It is, I think, a challenge which religion has never before faced in any land; not, at any rate, in such basic and intensively diversified forms, with the forces of science, morality, art, sociability, faith and social service in a multitude of appealing ways, marshalled against it.

The Orthodox church is unprepared to meet the challenge. The Protestants are worried. They shrug their shoulders when asked about their future in Russia. The Roman Catholics are in despair. There are about a million and a half of them in Russia. The confiscation of their properties, as well as the law prohibiting religious instruction to youths under eighteen outside of the home, has been of especial damage to them.

Meanwhile the forces of infidelity bore deeper and deeper into the life of the people.

CHAPTER IV

PROPERTY

A BEZPRISORNY, a Russian street waif, had been befriended by a locksmith. He learned the trade of his benefactor — learned it well. He was earning good wages, as wages are in Russia, and he was not spending his money recklessly. He had bought a new suit of clothes and a wrist watch. He had moved into a comfortable room. He had purchased a radio-set and an accordion and loved to while away his leisure listening to the one or playing the other. He had begun to save money. Clearly he was a youth of perseverance, diligence, ambition, qualities that are exalted in Western lands and perhaps nowhere so much as in America.

Yet one of the journals of the revolutionary youth of Russia threw its columns open to a debate as to whether this youth was the type of man needed by the new society. An avalanche of letters poured in on the editor and loud were the voices in condemnation of the former street waif. Not because he was diligent or ambitious, but because he was wrapping his life around himself, his own pleasures and advancement, all of which, so ran the verdict, were cultivating in him a love if not a lust for personal possession, for private property.

Flitting incidents like this dramatize the true measure of the Russian Revolution more trenchantly than volumes of edicts or tomes of theoretic dissertation. With implacable clarity they unfold the human values involved. The very person who in the outside world would be envied, lauded, set up as a model for other youths to follow, is to the Russian revolutionaries a nuisance, a curse. They would subdue him with all the power at their command, and only because he is or might become a devotee of private property!

For it is on this institution that the Bolsheviks have centered their fiercest attack. " The theory of the Communist," says the Communist Manifesto, " may be summed up in one sentence: the abolition of private property." This is the burning kernel of the Bolshevik idea, the blazing essence of the Russian audacity. It is the institution of private property that they seek to uproot, to wipe out of the very consciousness of man.

By private property they mean primarily " the means of production." " Communism," says the above Communist Manifesto, " deprives no man of the power to appropriate the products of society," meaning that certain forms of private property man may legitimately acquire. Clothes, for example, a home, a garden, a little farm, but only for personal use. Man may store food in his cellar for winter months — but solely for his own consumption, not for trade, not for profit. It is really *functional* property, which can be exploited for gain, for the accumulation of more property, that they wish to outlaw. " The middle class owner of property," continues the Communist Manifesto, " must indeed be swept out of the way." This goes beyond the means of production. It embraces the means of distribution no less — salesmanship, retail and wholesale trade, and any and all their adjuncts. The ideal condition will come when " individual property can no longer be transformed into bourgeois property, into capital." It is in this sense that the Bolsheviks employ the term private property, and it is in this sense that it is used in this book.

Such property the Russian revolutionaries pronounce the chief scourge of mankind. Is it wars, poverty, prostitution, crime, charity, that they discuss? Is it greed, malice, hate and their power for mischief that they consider? Is it racial feuds, international conflicts that they interpret? To them all these spring largely or wholly from the same poisonous fount — private property!

It matters not to them that there are schools of economics, philosophy, which not only approve but exalt the institution. It is of no concern to them that certain religious bodies have officially sanctified it. They care not that an overwhelming mass of humanity has come to believe that the urge and search for its possession is a maker of character, a builder of individuality, a promoter of progress. They will not admit that in this day of scientific advance private property has redeeming features. To them it is the supreme villain in the world, sowing everywhere only havoc and desolation, debauching, perverting, wrecking mankind. Unlike reformers, political philosophers, religious prophets, they would not bother to humour this villain, to discipline him. They would not compromise with him. They would slay him, pronounce a curse on him and make his very memory a reproach. They would do this without struggle and without sacrifice of life if possible, but if necessary, at any price and any sacrifice of life and substance.

Attacks on private property are not new. Since ancient times there have been thinkers, rulers, prophets, who viewed its possibilities for evil with dismay and horror. In our leading religions the urge to accumulate property and the search for riches have been under scorching condemnation. Gotham Buddha and his order of mendicants in their protest against the " craving for prosperity " wandered forth in rags with only a begging bowl, razor, needle and water-strainer as their possessions. Moses laid down rigid laws on property. " The land shall not be sold forever, for the land is mine; for ye are strangers and sojourners with me." And again, " At the end of seven years thou shalt make a release and this is the manner of the release. Every creditor that lendeth aught unto his neighbour shall release it, he shall not exact it of his neighbour or of his brother because it is called the hoards' release."

No more excoriating assaults on the search for private property which makes man " sell the righteous for silver and the poor for a pair of shoes " have ever been voiced, than by the old Hebrew prophets. The utterances of Christ bristle with pronouncements that stigmatize and anathematize accumulation of riches, which again is private property.

In the writings of early Christian churchmen we find sentiments which but for the difference in rhetoric might have been uttered by Lenine or Marx. " Property," said Ambrose, " hath no rights. The earth is the Lord's, and we are His offspring. The pagans hold earth as property. They do blaspheme God." St. Jerome was even more mordantly outspoken on the subject. " Opulence," said he, " is always the result of theft, if not committed by actual possessor then by his predecessor." St. Augustine had almost hit on the Marxian theory of surplus value when he said, " Those who possess superfluities possess the goods of others."

Under the inspiration of Buddhist, Jewish and Christian religions, societies sprang up whose members withdrew from the pursuit of private property and entered into a life of some form of communism. Such were the Buddhist monks, the Essenes, the monastic Christian orders, numerous Christian sects, some of whom, like the Russian Doukhobors in Western Canada, are still struggling desperately to steer clear of private property as though it were a malignant scourge.

But there is a gulf as wide as the sky between the attacks on private property by the Bolsheviks and by all those who have preceded them since earliest times, including the numerous reform movements of the nineteenth century. The religious prophets, for example, Buddha and Moses, did not seek its outright abolition. At any rate they are not explicit enough on the subject, nor was Christ. That is why it is possible for the Russian Doukhobors to repudiate private property as unchristian and for the Roman Catholic Papacy to uphold it as properly Christian. The attempts to live without it, that is to practice communism, as exemplified in the early communistic movements, were purely voluntary and local in nature. To please a supernatural power and to renounce the flesh were the guiding motives. Material progress in and of itself, whether for the individual or the commune, was held in the background and even frowned upon. This communism was an individual ideal rather than a social goal, a utopia rather than a reality.

Not so with the Russian revolutionaries. They do not mince their words. They have sworn death to private property and they mean to carry out the sentence, not merely in a local way but universally. Hence the conception of world revolution. " The whole of society," said Lenine, " will become one office and one factory." The Russians do not propose to leave the matter to the discretion of the individual. They give him no choice. He submits or he is cast out. If he rises in opposition he is destroyed, with no more compunction than an annoying insect. The will of a supernatural power enters not into their motivations. God has no place in their world. A renunciation of the flesh for purposes of spiritual perfection is to them the very height of absurdity. They see in the flesh not a flitting and putrid illusion but a lasting and pulsating reality, which they would always glorify. They seek not a curtailment but an expansion of material progress. Their motto is not a renunciation but an equalization of the joys of the flesh. In aim, scope, method the Bolshevik attack on private property is without precedent in the history of mankind. That is why it is at once so audacious, so unsettling, and so stupendous a performance.

Karl Marx of course had warned his followers that no one nation, least of all like Russia with a primitive economic culture, with a mass of illiterate peasants, could alone build a society without private property, that is of communism. But Lenine after recovery from disappointment at failure of the proletarian world to respond to seductive promises and impassioned appeals for world revolution, gave, so at least Stalin and his followers insist, a new twist to Marxism. He laid down the proposition that one nation even as backward as Russia can launch even if it cannot perfect the Communist society.

The Leninist idea has triumphed and the Russians are proceeding on the assumption that Russia alone can build the new society, not at once, but slowly and with infinite pains. Meanwhile as a means of facilitating the passage into this society the Bolsheviks have created the *nep* — the new economic policy — which is a concession to private property, retrieving it to the right to be, but without any of the social attributes and the political power it formerly enjoyed. It is a temporary concession, or so the Bolsheviks would have it, the period of whose duration they themselves do not know, and implies neither an abandonment nor an abatement of the crusade against private property. Let there be no misjudgment on this point. The Bolsheviks have not had a change of heart. The achievement of their final aim according to their own words is predicated on the destruction of private property as inevitably as is the position of the earth in space on its revolution around the sun.

This aim, while originally unfolded by Marx and Engels in the Communist Manifesto, has been restated with fiery vehemence in the program passed by the Third International during its sixth congress in Moscow in the summer of 1928. The chapter entitled " World Communism," flashes before the reader a bold picture of the Communist society. Anarchy in production, we are assured, is eliminated. Exploitation of one man by another is ended. Economic life is integrated and planned in accordance with actual needs. Crises due to over-production and their aftermath of human distress are banished. Hunts for foreign markets, spheres of influence, fields of investments, are no longer necessary. Hence the chief cause of war is demolished. Labor ceases to be a means to an end and becomes a primary need. Gone is poverty. Gone is economic inequality. Gone are slums. Gone are the differences between manual and mental effort. Gone are the inequalities of the sexes. The state itself, an organ of class control, melts away. Compulsions disappear. Man becomes fully emancipated. Gone is the monopoly of education. Culture becomes a common heritage and a common right, of all men, and their innate gifts flower forth in a fresh burst of glory. Gone are national boundaries. Gone are state frontiers. Mysticism dies. Religion disappears. Prejudices and superstitions vanish. A new era, a new age, a new man are enthroned!

This is the ultimate aim the Russian revolutionaries hope to achieve, and it can, they insist, be brought to fruition only when private property is no more. Hence, though compelled at present to tolerate its existence, they are yet determined to keep it from adding flesh to its bones, blood to its veins. They have hedged it about with economic, social, political, curbs that keep it shut within tight quarters, where it can be watched, tamed, half-starved and if necessary asphyxiated without much ado and effort.

The economic strictures they have imposed on pri-

vate property are in themselves sufficient to hold it at
their mercy. Consider the case of taxes. Certain of
these, like the license and turn-over taxes, the collective
enterprises that are pitted against the private businessman pay in amounts no less than he. But they enjoy
favours which lighten their burdens. Their income tax,
local and national, comes to about ten per cent. Super-
taxes they do pay, but on rental of premises they
occasionally enjoy discounts. They obtain credits from
state banks. They are the first to receive raw materials
or goods from state distributing agencies. Had the
private businessman been accorded such treatment he
would have regarded himself a child of fortune.

But his income tax alone devours a large share of
his earnings — often leaves him gasping with horror.
I do not wish to clutter these pages with an explanation of the involutions of the Soviet income tax as
applied to private enterprise. How damaging it is the
reader can glean from a bare statement of its results.
On the first one thousand roubles it is light enough,
only three per cent of the income, but on subsequent
sums it mounts in rapid progression until, when the
income is ten thousand roubles, the tax is one fourth
of the amount, when the income is twenty-four thousand roubles, the tax is one third; and when it exceeds
twenty-four thousand roubles, the tax is fifty-four per
cent of the income. This is the national tax. The local
tax carves off another rich slice of the income equal
to about one fourth of the national tax.

Nor does this exhaust the tax burdens of the private
businessman. He has to reckon with a drastic super-
profit tax, which is likewise based on an involved

formula and which it is not necessary to unfold here.
Let the reader note that profits in Russia are regulated
by laws and vary in their amounts with different communities and with the enterprise operated. In Ivano-
Voznesensk, for example, the legitimate profits on
groceries are eleven per cent, hotels twenty-five per
cent, restaurants twenty-two per cent, dry-goods sixteen per cent. Other types of enterprise run to similar
percentages. All amounts earned over and above these
percentages come under the heading of super-profits.
If these reach the sum of only one thousand roubles and
constitute ten per cent of all profits, the super-tax is
only six per cent, but if these one thousand roubles make
up twenty per cent of all profits, the super-tax bounds
to ten per cent. It keeps on bounding swiftly with the
rise of the sum of the super-profits and with the percent-
age that these constitute of all profits. When the entire
sum of the super-profits rolls up to ten thousand roubles
and makes up one fourth of all profits, the super-tax is
forty per cent, and if the super-profits are one half of
all the profits or over, the super-tax is fifty per cent.
But super-profits are regulated. In no case must they
leap beyond fifty per cent of all profits. Woe to the
entrepreneur if they do! He is liable to the charge of
speculation — a dastardly offence in Russian jurispru-
dence. Many a man has had his possessions seized by
the state, entire or in part, and himself banished to
some remote part of the world for edging profits into
the forbidden frontiers of speculation.

Because of this inequality in taxes alone the private
entrepreneur faces a grinding enough task in his struggle to hold his ground against the collective business

bodies. But he has other economic hurdles to clear before he squares his accounts with the government. There is his rent — especially for his residence. The amount differs with the community in which he lives. Let us see how this works out in a city like Moscow. The normal living space allowed an individual is approximately sixteen square yards. A businessman pays from twenty to forty roubles a yard. If the space he occupies exceeds eighteen yards he pays for each additional yard three times the initial amount, that is, from sixty to one hundred and twenty roubles a yard. Workers and officials likewise pay three times for each unit of extra space, but the initial payment they make is paltry compared to the sum exacted from a businessman.

For his children, when they are admitted to school, the businessman must pay high tuition fees — the higher his income the higher these fees. If he has a son of military age he must pay a military tax for him in lieu of service in the army, from which children of businessmen are barred. When it comes to credits the state banks ban him from eligibility, and nearly all banks in Russia are state banks. About eighty-five per cent of the wholesale trade is in the hands of the state, and unless he is an exceptionally shrewd manipulator and risks heavy consequences, he cannot always obtain goods as readily as the state or cooperative concerns. If he makes any infractions on existing laws he suffers mete punishment — quite mete, depending on the locality and on the temper of the prevailing administration. I have been in places where for keeping the shop open five minutes later than the law allowed, the private entrepreneur was made to pay a heavy fine. Once I wandered around hungry for several hours in a small town in the province of Kazan because no merchant would dare sell me even a loaf of bread. It was after five o'clock in the afternoon, the local closing hour, and since a few days previous a local shopkeeper had been fined twenty-five roubles for selling a supply of eggs to an out-of-town visitor after the legal closing hour, none of them would run the risk again of infringing on existing law. On another occasion I saw a policeman draw up a complaint against a *nepwoman* in a village for not having swept up the shells of sunflower seeds that peasant customers had scattered about the floor of her little shop. The charge was that she had not kept her premises as clean as the law demanded. Yet later in the day, when I visited the cooperative store in that village, peasants, a good-sized group of them, were zealously pursuing the popular Russian pastime of shelling sunflower seeds and strewing the floor with the shells, and neither the chairman of the Soviet, who was with me, nor the visiting cooperative inspector who happened to be there bothered to say a word of reproof to the manager of the shop or to the offending peasants. There are numerous ways in which the businessman is made to feel the pinch of existing laws more crucially than his collective trading competitors.

With such taxes, rentals, profit regulations, penalties for delinquencies, tuition fees for children, military exemption payments, the private businessman has a thorny enough path to traverse in his quest of riches or of an accumulation. Only the most shrewd and most energetic man can manage to squeeze through with some sort of an estate. But he can hold it in his hands only during his lifetime. With his passing the state comes in with its inheritance tax and cleaves it to pieces. Wearing apparel that he may leave, furniture, and other personal effects which are not luxuries, are exempted from the inheritance laws, as are one watch, one piano, one dozen pieces of utensils made from precious metals such as silver, platinum, gold, as are art works not exceeding one hundred roubles in value, except when they are the creation of the deceased and are not offered for sale. All other properties, save to the value of the first one thousand roubles, are subjected to a severe toll. The higher the value of these properties the higher the share of this toll. On two thousand roubles it is only two per cent and it mounts rapidly until it is fifty per cent on one hundred thousand roubles, and ninety per cent on sums above this figure.

Whichever way the private businessman turns in life and in death the state keeps watch over him, ever ready to strip him of the economic substance he may have gathered. It must keep him economically lean, else he might prove dangerous. Did not Rykov, Premier of Russia, say once that the government will shear the fresh coat of wool off the Russian businessman as soon as he has grown it? And was it not Bukharin who once likened the private businessman to a milch cow that must be assiduously milked and with no more compunction than necessary to preserve the beast's milk-giving capacity?

Melancholy also and devastating is the political

assault on holders of private property. A businessman forfeits his citizenship rights and that in Russia is a stark calamity. Not because it automatically bars a man from a voice, however indirect, in the affairs of the government. It degrades him almost to the position of an outlaw. His children are admitted to a school only if there is a vacancy open and then on payment of a high tuition fee. " Why don't you send your daughter to school? " I asked once a hotel proprietor in a small town. " Because," he replied, " they demand two hundred roubles for tuition and how can I afford it? " " And if you don't send me to school next year," remonstrated the girl who was only fourteen years of age, " I'll run away from home and disown you forever and ever." The father said nothing in reply. He stared at his daughter, tears came to his eyes, and when she left he leaned close and whispered: " She will do it, too."

Once I stopped in a tea-house in a small town run by an old man and his eighteen-year-old son. The son was an omnivorous reader of books and I asked him why he was not seeking admission to a university. He assured me that he had tried desperately enough, but his father had once been rich and now, though he was poor, he was the owner of the tea-house and therefore without citizenship rights, so there never seemed to be a vacancy for him in the university. He could, of course, disown his father, change his name, declare himself independent, and doors to institutions of learning would open up. Some of his friends had done so. But he could not follow in their footsteps. His father was old, a widower, and he would not abandon him, even if he had to remain an outcast to the end of his days.

" My son," said an authoress to me once, " has just entered high school. He is a bright lad, very ambitious. He is already talking of the university and his plans for the future. He does not know that I, because of no special friendliness for the Revolution, have no citizenship rights and on that account the doors of the university are likely to be closed to him. I have not the heart to tell him. When he learns of his predicament he will have to make a momentous decision. He will either have to abandon me, not only to live apart, but to disown me legally and depart from me perhaps forever, or else bid good-bye to the university and to a career."

In defence of these harsh discriminations against children of the despised bourgeoisie the revolutionaries urge the consideration that at present when every skilled worker, whether teacher or engineer, is worth to them his weight in gold, they must fill the seats of learning with men and women on whose devotion they can count rather than with those of whose loyalty to the new society they are in doubt. A practical enough defence, but it does not lift the load of torment from father and mother, nor the pall of frustration from their children.

Most harrowing is the social contumely with which the Russians have saddled the businessman. Not even Christianity in the Middle Ages had invested the occupation of trading with such a scorching sense of sordidness as have the Russian revolutionaries the pursuit of private enterprise, save of course in the case of peasants and artisans who do not come under the heading of *nepmen* and *kulacks*. They no longer use the word *koopetz* — trader — or the word *promyshlenik* — industrialist — to designate a person engaged in such pursuit. They have coined a new word — *nepman* — and no person who has not visited Russia can appreciate how mean a word it has become in that country. *Nepman* — symbol of degradation, object of scorn and contumely! Pariah, social swine! Villain on the stage, villain in the motion pictures, villain in everyday life! *Nepman* — label, curse, anathema! "I'd rather that my children became bandits than *nepmen*," exclaimed once the daughter of a former millionaire; "they'd be stood up against the wall and shot, and that would be more merciful than the eternal damnation they would suffer as *nepmen*."

Small wonder that men of prominence in the business world of Russia in the old days, have fled from private enterprise. They eschew it as they would a deathly trap. They have entered the service of the state. They live modestly and inconspicuously in small apartments and on limited salaries. But they enjoy the privilege of sending their children to schools, whichever ones they choose, and best of all they can preserve their self-respect. They are never haunted by the dread of certain transactions being construed by the state as speculation or as an infringement on some legal regulation. Their minds are free from worry and their hearts from tribulation over goods, credits, reports, inspectors, and all the other nerve-shattering by-products incident to private enterprise in Russia. They would rather live humbly and keep their dignity than reap harvests of gold and suffer the fate of a door-mat.

Outside of the village, private property is continually losing ground. It cannot under existing conditions withstand the onslaught of governmental repression and of the collectivist machine. Like an insatiable monster this machine is devouring everything in its path. In time it may so overglut itself as to burst from sheer inability to digest all it swallows. Its enemies prophesy for it just such a doom. For the present it stalks along safely enough. No less than eighty-five per cent of industry, a like proportion of wholesale and a somewhat smaller amount of retail trade, are already under collectivist control. Foreign concessionaries, though guaranteed against social stigmatization, must yet subscribe to the principle that whether or not they enter into a partnership with the Russian government or exploit a concession on a basis of royalty payments to the Soviets, the concession, after the lapse of a certain stipulated period, becomes automatically the possession of the Russian state. Of course, the Russians propose conditions which, they hold, will enable the outside investor to gain back not only his original capital but a sumptuous profit. Most manifestly they will grant no concession in perpetuity or for very lengthy periods, unless some mighty catastrophe compels a change of policy.

I am not proposing to make comparison between the operation of collectivist and private control of property. That is a subject for a book in itself. Indeed, not one but hundreds of such books will be written for hundreds of years to come. At present the Russians themselves admit that on the economic side their collectivism can boast of no successes which private enterprise is achieving, neither in the province of production nor distribution. Here, however, I am merely seeking to set down the motive, the method, the scope of their attack on private property and also certain international implications. These must be of special interest to America if only because it is in America that private enterprise has scored its richest triumphs.

To succeed, Russian collectivism must surpass not only European, but also American individualism in economic achievement. The Russians themselves grant that much. " We are acquainted," says Trotzky — and on this point there is no difference of opinion between him and the other revolutionaries, " with the fundamental laws of history; victory belongs to that system which provides society with the higher economic plane. The historic dispute will be decided — and of course not at once — by the comparative coefficients of labour productivity." Precisely so, and these coefficients, Trotzky further argues, " must include quality; otherwise they become merely a source or instrument of self-delusion." In other words Russian collectivism in the field of productivity alone must outdo individualism — must show a higher output of goods per unit of energy and per unit cost of this energy, and the goods must be cheaper in price and superior in quality. It must do this or else find itself outdistanced and eventually beaten by individualist endeavour.

Indeed, beneath all the bluster and frenzy and rancour over Bolshevism or communism this contest between individual and collective control of property resolves itself into a conflict over a matter of fact proposition, over a purely business problem. It is a historic contest, the outcome of which, one way or the other, must change the face of the world. I say contest, but in reality it is a war, the most stupendous, though the least obvious, that the world has fought since possibly the rise of Christianity. Subjective graces, sympathies, wishes, patriotism, though everpresent, play hardly a helpful part in it. It is a war between forces almost as objective as the weather, and is being fought out in office, laboratory, factory, through brawn and brain, through mechanical ingenuity and organizing talent, through coal, iron, oil — like any other war almost, except that the sides involved, to attain real and lasting victory, must outdo each other not in destruction but in construction. Propaganda is only an incident and not an important one though the outside world is wont to cry to heaven that it is the only issue that matters. Not at all. It is like the buzzing of a drone. It frightens, irritates, but has no sting with poison in it and can have none, until results have armed it with one.

On the surface this war seems almost ridiculous. What has Russia to match such giants of economic power and efficiency as the Krupp industries of Germany, the Ford Motor Company, General Motors, United States Steel Corporation, International Harvester, General Electric and the host of other privately operated industrial units which in productive output are performing miracles that would stagger the fancy of a Jules Verne? What has Russia to offset such marvels of organized distribution as Sears-Roebuck Company, Montgomery-Ward Company, the five and ten cent stores? What has Russia to equal not to say surpass the promptness, the reliability, the dispatch, the courtesy, of American business service? Nothing concrete as yet, nothing but a vast land of mammoth resources, barely sprinkled with smoke-stacks, its idyllic calm hardly riven by the whine and whir of engines. Its chief asset is an audacious engineering idea, tried out in a number of lands in a limited manner and in a feverish mood during the past war and having the theoretical indorsement of no small galley of re-nowned bourgeois engineers and economists. The sub-stance of this idea is not that the collectivist method of property control will breed superior engineers, executives, workers (though the Russians insist it will do this, too) but that the integrated planning and operation upon which such control is based, will elimi-nate wastes incident to a system of unintegrated in-dividual control of property. Wastes in production, in distribution, in consumption. The contest centers chiefly in the problem of waste or of savings. We know well enough that as Wesley Mitchell says, " in detail the economic activity (of private enterprise) is planned and directed with skill, but in the large there is neither plan nor developed direction." Individual economic units such as a Ford Motor Company do operate under a system of most heroic elimination of wastes, but the economic life of the country as a whole, because of the absence of coordination in economic activity, involves colossal wastage of energy, of raw material, of natural resources. In his " Tragedy of Waste," Stuart Chase computes that the waste incident to the absence of an integrated scheme of economic effort in this country entails a loss equivalent in value to about fifty per cent of America's man-power. David Friday in speaking on the same subject says:

" We have increased (during the war) our output of products twenty-five and thirty per cent over the pre-war period through the complete utilization of national resources, our plants and our machinery and our labour. If production is allowed to return to pre-war level output will slump by twenty per cent. This would mean a corresponding waste of productive resources and decreases of fourteen billion dollars per annum in our national income as measured by the present level of prices." Hoover himself, than whom there is no more prophetic defender of private property, is constrained to admit that during the war with the economic efforts of the country planfully integrated by the government and with " twenty per cent of man-power withdrawn into the army, we yet produced twenty per cent more commodities than we are now doing." The question is whether the Russian brand of collectivism banishing the stimulations which private property kindles, and upsetting established habits of life and work, holds within it the power to achieve the expected results? The Russians themselves cherish no more doubt of eventual victory than the ploughman of the ultimate fruition of the seed he plants. They read triumph in the pages of history, in the very elements of nature. They bank for it on the superiority of their engineering idea.

If they do succeed, collectivism in one form or another will sweep the world and private property as a source of income will vanish. Superior engineering ideas do win in the end, whatever the obstacles in the way and whatever the sacrifices entailed. This is as immutable a law of history as any law of nature we know of. But if they fail, then private property, however modified in form, will continue to function and perhaps to flourish even in Russia.

CHAPTER V

MAN

WHAT does man live by?

Is material incentive essential to man's best effort? If so why do men seek military careers? Why do they yearn to become captains, colonels, generals in an army? Why a Foch, a Hindenburg, a Grant, a Wellington? Why do men enter the civil service? Why do they choose teaching as a life-pursuit? Why do they become clergymen? The material rewards in these occupations do not permit of expansive living nor of substantial accumulation of wealth.

Why do men enter politics? Often enough political office is a vehicle for personal enrichment, but the method is illicit and more and more in non-feudal lands, it is vehemently condemned. Witness the tradition of honest public service, especially in Germany and England. Consider Asquith, Grey, MacDonald and an endless line of heroic figures in English history who served their country with brilliance and with no thought of material aggrandizement. Consider Roosevelt, Wilson, Hoover, Hughes, who, whatever one may think of their policies and principles, have given the best of themselves to America without any thought of material reward.

Does genius need the lure of affluence as a spur to achievement? Why an Einstein? Why a Lincoln? Why a Burbank? Why a Steinmetz? Why a Pasteur, this great-grandson of a serf? Why a Spinoza, grinding lenses for a living? Why a Luther, a Galileo and the host of other luminaries who stretch along the vistas of the past like stars on a darkened night, and who pursued their quest for truth and beauty in spite of poverty, the pillory and threat of death?

Why do men sally forth to explore the polar regions? Why do they die in the attempt to scale Mount Everest? Why do they enlist in an army and go to war knowing that they may get killed in battle?

Only when we turn to the business world do we find material reward almost as inseparable from achievement as the roar from falling waters. Material reward has been a driving force in business pursuits. Perhaps America would have attained her grandiose material development in the absence of opportunities for personal aggrandizement. But perhaps not. The undeniable fact is that under the spur of such opportunities she has soared to heights of economic success unheard of in the history of mankind.

To the businessman wealth has furnished inspiration. It has been a symbol of power, progress, achievement, distinction. It has meant creation, something almost like the painting to the artist, the printed word to the writer. Stirred by the lure of material reward man dared, risked, gambled and pushed on for the biggest stakes in the world, built machines, factories, railroads, cities, towns — and nowhere so magnificently as in America. No wonder that when an American businessman visits Russia and discovers that the men at the helm of Soviet trusts, railroads, industries, receive a salary which a chauffeur at home would scorn to consider, he shrugs his shoulders and prophesies imminent collapse of the whole collectivist venture. " Every time an American visits me," remarked the chairman of the Soviet textile industry, " whether he is an officer of a large bank or a journalist, one of the first questions he asks is why we work as we do, what is there in it for us anyway? "

What, indeed?

Certainly not wealth, not a glimmer of a chance to amass it. No man excepting a foreigner, whose sojourn in Russia is always temporary, need ever think of material accumulation if he wishes to have peace of mind. Hardly any of the attributes and rewards which wealth bestows on a man in a western land, and chiefly in America, are attainable in Russia. Is it power? No man can have less than the person with capital or in the pursuit of capital. Politically he is a nonentity. Socially he is a pariah. His word means nothing. His influence is nil. He cannot even make himself articulate without inviting an avalanche of scorn. Is it distinction? No criminal ever has had to disguise himself from the outside world more completely than has the man of wealth in Russia. Is it achievement? That is not impossible, but it is beset with so many hazards that chance of success is negligible. Is it self-importance? What self-importance or even self-esteem can man cherish when at every step he is reminded that he is only a putrid scavenger? Is it conspicuous consumption, which Thorstein Veblein assures us is both a stimulus to and a symbol of success in a bourgeois society? Nothing is more dangerous in Russia for a Russian than display of opulence in public. Is it security? Hardly even that, for the man of means never knows when and what deed of his will through some new law or a fresh interpretation of an old law be deemed contrary to the best interests of the proletarian society and cause a court to lay its hands on all or a sumptuous part of his accumulation. Confiscation of property is one of the commonest sentences Russian courts impose on holders of private property.

Neither power then, nor self-importance, nor achievement, nor even security does wealth make possible in Russia, and the person who starts out with the aim of building up a personal fortune, unless he is a foreign citizen, must sooner or later come to grief.

What then do men live by in Russia?

Material self-interest, of course, has not been banished. It has only been limited. " To everyone according to his needs," the slogan of the communist for his final communist society is still a matter of the faraway and impenetrable future. The present motto is, " to everyone according to his ability," as ability is measured in Russia. That is why sixty per cent of all work in Russian industry is done on a piece basis. Gradations in wages and in salaries are as wide-spread as in any capitalist society, save that they never reach the same amounts. The unskilled labourer receives less than the skilled, and more in one locality than in another. The skilled worker obtains less than the expert and again less in one locality than in another. The system of promotions, carrying with it increases in earnings, is in full blast in every enterprise. Special rewards for meritorious service or for economic use of materials is in wide vogue. Engineers of locomotives who cover their mileage at a saving of fuel receive a premium. So do chauffeurs of state automobiles. Sometimes the premium is a sum of money, sometimes it is a trip to an interesting part of Russia, or to a foreign land. One fourth of one per cent of all the profits in Russian industry is at present used for such premiums.

Managers, directors, executives, inventors, men in positions of command, unless they are members of the Party, receive salaries much higher than ordinary proletarians, however skilled they may be. Material incentive, therefore, has not been eliminated. It has only been restricted to a point where accumulation is practically impossible, at least in substantial amounts. In the textile industry, for example, the highest salary any executive received in 1928 was seven hundred roubles a month, or about half that many dollars. There are hardly any industries in which the highest officials receive more. Only foreign experts when invited for special consultation are paid fees which measure up to the best they command in their own lands.

The Russian revolutionaries not only condemn accumulation but regard it as unnecessary in a collectivist society. Originally, they contend, accumulation was prompted by the desire to provide against possible mishaps. It was a source of security, a means to an end, which in time man has transmuted into an end itself. But in a collectivist society the individual needs have no concern for his personal security. The society will provide him with a job, an opportunity for advancement, protection against unemployment, sickness, old age, accident. It will offer children the chance they need to develop themselves physically and mentally, and fit them for an adequate place in the world. It will lift from the individual the burden and the torment of security for himself and those dependent on him. He will be as sure of shelter, food, clothes, social diversion as of air to breathe and water to drink.

At present there is no adequate security in Russia, hardly even for a proletarian, save in instances of disability when a member of a trade union receives, to the end of his life, the same salary that he earned while in unimpaired physical condition. These short-comings in security the Russians hope to overcome with the growth of the prosperity of the new society. Let us here assume for the sake of this discussion that the collectivist society which the Russians are building will in time provide adequately for all man's needs under all emergencies. If it does not it is as doomed as a straw stack set afire.

But what, the reader will ask, of man's instinct of acquisitiveness, which certain psychologists inform us is as innate in man as his desire to eat or to mate? Stoutly the Russians deny that it is an obstacle to collectivism. In the text-book on psychology which is in wide use in Russian schools and colleges acquisitiveness is spoken of as being " much more of a habit than an inborn tendency . . . for it is either not present or present only in very different forms in certain primitive peoples." Being merely a tendency, the manner in which it expresses itself need not necessarily assume the form prevalent in a bourgeois society. It can, say the Russians, be transferred from the individual to the group, from personal to social acquisitiveness if the individual knows it will be used for his benefit. It can further be sublimated into non-material values, into the purely mental and emotional gratifications which material values make possible — such as an opportunity to read books, to attend lectures, theatrical performances, motion pictures, concerts, to participate in sports and to partake of whichever new enjoyments the new society affords. Flagrantly the Russians deny that a hankering after personal acquisition of material things is the sole manner of gratifying man's acquisitiveness or is as irrepressible as the instinct of hunger and sex.

The psychic incentives the Russians have brought into play are in some instances a new departure in modern life. There is, of course, promotion with all its accompanying gratifications — prestige, responsibility, power. There is competition with one enterprise pitted against another and there is the excitement that follows in the wake of strife for special distinction or recognition. There is the plan of achievement mapped out for the year by the State Planning Commission, and constantly held up as the goal to be reached and, if possible, to be surpassed. There are the celebrations of outstanding attainments — parades with banners, songs, mass-meetings at the opening of a new factory, a new bridge, a new artesian well. There is the appreciation of merit through bestowal of the title of " hero of labour " and the banner of the " red labour flag," both, and especially the latter, conferring on the recipient honour, glory and a host of special privileges. His name is mentioned in the press and in official publications. He is always pointed out to visitors. I have never been in a Russian factory but the " heroes of labour " were introduced to me and spoken of with special pride, almost with rev-

erence. They are the elite in the land. They get the best
in living quarters, education of children, vacations —
anything and everything. In an egoistic sense these
titles are the highest rewards possible in Russia.

And how strenuously the Russians are striving to
inculcate in the individual and especially in the worker
the sense of proprietorship! "What stimulates me
most," once remarked a youthful manager of a packing
house, "is the advance we are making. Every time
we start a new engine, not only here in this plant but
anywhere in the union, or we lay a foundation of a
new factory, or dig a new canal, I feel thrilled, because
I know it is done not for any one individual or group
of individuals, but for the mass and for me as much as
for anybody." This is precisely how the revolutionaries want every worker and official in industry to feel.
They are to speak in terms of proprietorship, such
as, "our factory," "our shop," "our cooperative,"
"our club," — our everything. They are ever to
remember that the more successful the enterprise the
more lavish will be the rewards, material and others,
which it will make possible for them.

New entirely in economic life is the idea of social
service which the Russians are seeking to convert into
an incentive. I say new because it has a different conno-
tation in Russia than it has in other lands. It is stripped
of altruism. It is drained of the spirit of sacrifice.
"The building of socialism," writes a youthful revolutionary, "requires sacrifice, but not the psychology
of sacrifice . . . sacrifice shall have an objective and
not a subjective quality. . . ." "To accept the workers' Revolution," wrote Trotzky in the day when he

still was the hero of the mass and its most brilliant spokesman, " in the name of high ideals is not only to reject but to slander it . . . the Socialist Revolution tears the cover off ' illusions and elevating ' . . . can it be that the Revolution which is before us, the first since the earth began, needs seasoning of romantic outbursts as a cat ragout needs hare sauce? " . . . Hard language, acid in its bite and brutally decisive, yet characteristic of the Russian revolutionary. He will inject no sentimentality into his conception of social service. He does not view it as a diversion but as a duty, not as an escape but as a fulfillment, not as a means to an end but as an end in itself. There is none of that spirit of pity for the lowly that pursues so unendingly Tolstoy's Nekhludov in the novel " Resurrection," and that harassed Tolstoy himself no less poignantly. Rather would he invest it with a spirit of pugnacity if not heroism, akin to that an athlete feels when preparing for a contest. All this of course, is, as the Russians love to express themselves, " a matter of principle." But this principle is to become a basic motive, a part of the very nature of man.

Not appreciable is the respect of the Russian revolutionaries for the purely egoistic instincts of leadership, hunting, ostentation, vanity, which according to Veblein have come so powerfully to the fore with the rise of an industrial civilization. They recognize the egoistic urge in man, and accord it some recognition, as already indicated, but they will not pamper it. Therefore individual leadership in Russia is at best a precarious affair. No enterprise, for example, whether a factory, a shop, a publishing house, is ever identified

with the name of anyone associated with it. If it is
named after some person it is usually after some outstanding revolutionary hero. Nothing like a Ford Motor Company, a Woolworth store, a Marshall and Field
shop, to perpetuate the name of founder or owner is
possible. Curtailed also is the power of the individual
manager, however high he be. He is always working
under orders of someone, of a group, of a collective
body. He is always under the control of a committee,
a board, and also of the mass of workers under him
who now and then at meetings lay their criticisms and
grievances before him or some board he is associated
with. He is always checked up, ratified, corrected, ve-
toed. He is really submerged.

How does such a scheme of incentives, material and
psychic, effect Russian humanity? Those who were
reared in the pre-revolutionary days respond but feebly
to them, if at all. The old intelligentsia — engineers,
managers, architects — are not visibly stimulated by
them. The limitation of their earning power with a view
of eventually eliminating all distinctions in incomes
between mental and manual workers, the impossibility
of making profitable investments, the subservience to
a group, the curtailment of individual power — all
these are displeasing to them. They have absorbed
none, or very little, of the sense of proprietorship which
every worker in the new society is supposed to cherish,
and not much more of the spirit of social service. They
take pride in the purely nationalistic aspects of the new
society — after all it is Russia they are helping
to develop — the Russia they have always loved.
The opportunity to comprehend and build projects

on a large scale which the unified control of all economic life makes not only possible but inevitable, likewise brings its mite of satisfaction. Otherwise they are uncomfortable. They draft plans and help carry them into practice. They are creative men and the instinct of workmanship functions powerfully in them. But — "we have no future, — do you understand?" complained a noted architect to me once. He meant a personal future, and of course there is none and there can be none to an old-time unreformed intellectual who at best is an outsider looking in.

Even the proletarians reared in the old days do not respond with exceptional fervour to the new incentives. Otherwise there would not have been such nation-wide complaint of drunkenness of proletarians, of absences from work, of carelessness with raw material and machinery and even of petty larceny. The proletarian talks loudly enough of his factories, his industries, his cooperatives, but often he behaves as though these belonged to the old Russian landlords or to the old bourgeoisie. In the textile industry, search of workers is periodic, and only for the purpose of preventing stealing. The same is true of other industries. I ate once in a cafeteria in Ivano-Voznesensk, opened for proletarian convenience. When a customer there receives his utensils he deposits a brass check which he is handed on entering. If he returns the utensils he recovers the brass check and on giving it back to the attendant at the door, he is allowed to go out. Otherwise he is held up and investigated to make sure that he has not tucked a knife or spoon or fork into his boots or into his bosom.

. . . Old habits do persist in spite of new incentives and new ambitions. . . .

It is not, however, with the men, whether intellectuals or proletarians, reared in the old habits and old ambitions that these new incentives must win. It is with the young generation who know of the old life mostly by hearsay, that they must register a triumph. This young generation is being impregnated with the idea that private business enterprise and personal accumulation are the grossest of vices. I have never met a university student in Russia who would admit that on the completion of his course of study he would seek to establish himself in a business of his own. Russian student youth, with but rare exceptions, looks forward to a life of service for the new society. It does not disregard material reward. It is not unresponsive to the urge for comfort and distinction. It thinks of advancement, of rising to positions of managers, directors, superintendents, but not of palatial homes, exclusive country clubs, yachts of their own, and of other material acquisitions possible for men of success in a modern bourgeois society. It thinks in terms of salaries and not of profits. Wealth is a measure not of success but of failure, the most heinous possible to man. Never did the words " what profiteth a man if he gain the whole world but lose his own soul," apply with such cogency to any people as to the seekers of affluence in Russia. Wealth is not only a contagion but a disease, a curse — the most loathsome that can afflict man.

For the first time in history is this extraordinary thing happening — a whole generation deliberately being schooled and habituated away from personal acquisitiveness, from personal wealth. Still, impressive as such a spectacle may seem, stirring as it may be to the imagination and the emotions, the question after all is if man in the long run will be the gainer from such an approach to life? The world must have inventiveness and creation if it is to march on to a destiny of greater grace of body, mind and soul. Will this new youth of Russia, when it comes of age, measure up in creative effort and capacity to the men holding positions of responsibility in a capitalist society? In such pursuits as literature, art, music, science — endeavours which cannot be collectivized, and which always require special aptitude and personal application — the sheer instinct of workmanship will stir man into high attainments in spite of lack of adequate material returns. Genius seldom has been deterred from achievement by an absence of material compensation or social recognition.

But in the world of material development, material stimulus has been a fire which has kindled man's mind and heart and has spurred him into heights of achievement which are the envy of the most implacable revolutionary in Russia. What land in the world adores Ford more earnestly than Russia — not Ford the man, but Ford the builder, the creator, the achiever of miracles? Under present Russian conditions a Ford is as impossible as a Czar. The rise of a magnate in industry, in finance, is unthinkable in a society where the individual in his economic pursuits is always subject to a group, which limits reward and also power.

Can Russia make man as inventive, as creative, as constructive as a capitalist regime which lays at the

feet of a Ford, a Rosenwald, a Woolworth, a Rocke-
feller, all the rewards that this earth can afford? This
is the crux of the Communist challenge to capitalism.
It is easy for the Communist to dismiss the question
as stupid, as easy for the capitalist to dismiss the
Communist venture as idiotic. Raillery alone will prove
nothing. The problem has now been lifted out of the
realm of speculation. The tests it suggests have been
carried beyond exhortation, mystical or rational. The
age-old question as to what man does or should live by,
which has perplexed and tormented philosopher and
prophet since the beginning of time, is being answered
anew in Russia, at cost of great agony to a whole
generation of people, but with a compactness and a
possibility for veracity which have hitherto been un-
attainable. The answer is still wrapped in nebulous-
ness. It may be several generations, if not centuries,
before it comes to view as unmistakably as patches of
black in bright daylight. When it does shine out of its
impenetrable shroud we shall perhaps understand more
about the nature of man than the world has yet been
able to discover.

CHAPTER VI

SEX

THE NEW MORALITY

TOUCH Russian life below the surface and you discover an absence of inhibitions, restraints, suspicions, in the customs regulating the relations of the sexes, that astonishes and often even embarrasses. You go to lectures on sex and no matter how delicate the subject discussed, the audience is always made up of men and women. Now and then, as a means of dramatizing the evils of venereal disease, some organization will stage a mock trial of a man who had supposedly infected his wife with a venereal ailment. Witnesses, physicians, nurses, will go into minute explanations, in language audaciously frank, of the function, physiology, hygiene, technique of sex, and again the audience invariably is mixed. You buy a ticket in a compartment in a wagon-lit — sleeping car — and you never know whether your neighbour will be a man or a woman. On my first trip to Russia when I was paired up once in a compartment in the wagon-lit with a woman, I concluded that it must have been an error and proceeded to enlist the aid of the conductor to have it rectified. But the conductor stared blandly at me, and with a feeling almost of pity, declared that insomuch as the woman had a ticket for a berth in that compartment she would have to stay there. Later in the evening as he passed me in the vestibule he paused long enough to ask what countryman I was, and when I informed him I was from America, he chortled good-naturedly and remarked, " Are American men afraid of strange women? "

In Russia it is considered most proper for men and women, young and old, married and unmarried, to visit each other at all times of day or night in their private rooms whether in apartments or hotels. Russian girls go to men's rooms in hotels with no more reserve or abashment than to a class-room, a library, a theatre or any other public place. They never think of it as improper, as liable to invite suspicion or reproach from anyone, anywhere. In the universities men and women live in the same dormitories, though in separate rooms, but they constantly visit each other back and forth to regale themselves with tea, black bread and sausage, to study together or just to sit and discuss problems of life and of the Revolution. I have gone to numerous parties of Russian youths, in club-houses, universities, and have never seen chaperons in attendance. The Russians of the present generation do not even know the existence of the institution. And of course, since Will Rogers' visit to Russia we all know that Russian bathers when swimming have as much use for a bathing suit as American bathers have for a fur coat. Men and women in Russia mingle with each other most freely on all occasions, at all times and without the faintest show of embarrassment or reserve.

Yet it is well to remember that this display of sex unconcern, while more pronounced now than in the old days, is no new phenomenon in Russia. The Russians had never surrounded women with the heavy barriers which so many western lands have deemed indispensable for the safeguarding of woman's virtue. True, at one time the women of the nobility were held in a *terem* — a garret — under locked doors. But Peter the Great, who did so many astonishing things for Russia, smashed the doors of the *terem* and dragged women out into the open, and they have since stayed in the open. Of course, Russia has had her *domostroy,* a book of rules for the behaviour of man in his household. This book lays down some of the most savage rules to which women have ever been subjected in any land. It invests man with complete authority and power over his household, especially over women, and admonishes him to use the rod freely to achieve submission.

Yet even the *domostroy,* while it made man master of the household, failed to effect a pronounced social cleavage between the sexes, especially among the big mass of the people — the peasantry.

Perhaps the chief reason for this condition is the fact that neither chivalry nor puritanism had secured the clutch on Russia that they had on other lands. Chivalry swept by Russia without convulsing her. Its tenets and usages dribbled into the land second-hand through foreigners visiting Russia, or Russians going to foreign parts, and perhaps even more through foreign, and especially French literature, injected a new spiciness and also a new stiffness into the relations of the sexes. But such influence as chivalry had made possible was confined chiefly to the upper crust of Russian society, and even there chivalry never had become a cult. Hence the absence in Russia, among all classes of society, of that sense of aloofness and mystery with which chivalry had invested women.

Puritanism, likewise, save among certain religious sects or groups of churchmen who revelled in asceticism, was never part of the Russian Church and only faint echoes of it reached Russia through visiting German missionaries. Hence the puritanic attitude toward sex, the sense of terror and sin attached to it, has hardly made its way into the Russian mind or become a part of Russian folkways. Men, therefore, had not the stimulus and did not feel the necessity of erecting social barriers between themselves and women. They did not separate women either intellectually or physically from themselves to the extent that this was done in western lands. This is especially true of the Russian intelligentsia. The relations of the sexes in their midst remained always close, simple, unaffected.

Even more is it true of the peasantry, who had never been touched by either chivalry or puritanism. Since ancient times large peasant families have been living together in one-room huts, men and women sleeping beside each other on the brick oven, on the *polati* — the platform — or on the hay in the barn. Even now there are parts of Russia where young people in summer take their horses to pasture, and while there sleep on the grass in groups right near each other, with lovers invariably in each other's embrace. When I visited the Cossack settlements in the Kuban in the summer of 1928, I learned that to this day many youths there follow the old custom of wooing a girl by sleeping with her, usually in the barn, at frequent intervals and for a lengthy period. Of course, the girl preserves her virginity. Such customs, however, and many others which might seem utterly indecent to a Westerner, but which have been part of the folkways of the peasant since days immemorial, show emphatically that the mass of the Russian people, the peasantry, has ever regarded sex with undisguised frankness, without that sense of curiosity, mystery, horror and sin with which chivalry and puritanism have endowed it.

When we remember the conditions of sex-life in old Russia the revolution in sex morals which the new regime has launched does not seem inordinately drastic. Only when we compare this revolution with conceptions and standards that obtain in Anglo-Saxon lands are we apt to be bewildered by the audacity of the innovations proclaimed.

The gist of the new sex morality is freedom of personal judgment and action. This at one stroke wipes out the old tenets of morality. The Russians will have none of the old strictures and old precepts. They do not regard morality as something inviolate, eternal, irrevocable. " We do not believe in eternal morality," said Lenine. " Morality serves the purpose of helping human society to rise higher, to get rid of exploitation of labour." That is why the Russians have thrust all responsibility for sex conduct on the individual, on woman as much as on man. Sex-life is nowhere regulated by law, save in cases of seduction or other forms of violent approach. There is no adultery in the Russian legal code and also no such provision as a Mann Act. Likewise metaphysics has no place in it. Nor has sex morality been exalted into a fetish. It is not viewed as something to be followed and worshipped, in and of itself, as though it were almost a conscious force detached from, but vital to human life and with power in some devious manner to visit punishment for misdeeds or even mistakes.

Religion with its multifold taboos and ascetic flavourings has likewise been cast aside. " To us," said Lenine, " morality derived from a power outside of human society does not exist — is merely a deception." The Russians will have no God commanding or terrorizing them into a prescribed mode of behaviour. The Paulist stricture on sex, expressed in the well-known words, " For I would that all men were even as I myself," that is, celibate and continent, meets in Russia with fierce contempt. Against this maxim of Paul, the Russians set the words of Lenine, " Communism must bring the joy of life and vigour which comes from completeness of love-life."

The Russians see no good purpose in an escape from an all-pervading and powerful an urge as sex. Nor do they cherish appreciable sympathy for the notion that sex is merely a means to an end — the end being the propagation of the human race. Some Communists, older men with stern views on sex, would indeed impose such a conception on the mass. But the mass will have none of it. Propagation of the human race, say its young, and some of its older leaders, may have been nature's sole intent in the creation of sex. But does man follow nature in all his pursuits? Does he eat, drink, dress, love as nature intended him to? In nature there is no imagination, no exaltation. In nature, that is, in the animal kingdom, there is no sex-love; there is only purely physiological gratification. But to man sex-love is a mighty passion, and it is of no use, say they, to shut one's eyes to its overpowering stimulations. As Lenine expressed himself once, "In sex-life you have biology plus culture," and the one should be as important as the other.

Sex to men, the Russians hold, is more than a mere physiological satisfaction, more than a sheer instrument of race propagation, though it is and should be that too. Sex is a high and never an inglorious part of man's self. There is nothing, say they, in sex itself to be ashamed of, to fear, to hide, to hate, no more than there is in eating, drinking tea, reading books, listening to music, attending the art theatre. They are, in other words, seeking to emancipate sex from legal, metaphysical, religious and certain social prejudgments, for women, as much as for men.

There is nothing they strive so strenuously to bring into life as the conception that in sex as in other human relations no greater liberties or advantages shall be permitted to men than to women. All the argumentation that this might lead to social debasement, conveys no meaning to them. If women, say they, will abuse their sex liberties as men have been doing, well and good. They shall have the right to do so. To allow one sex to enjoy pleasures denied to the other is, they hold, no less preposterous than to allow one class privileges withheld from the other. In both instances there is exploitation, in the one of labour, in the other of sex, and exploitation, they insist, is the grossest of sins, always flagrantly out of tune with the new morality. "We have to carry on a heartless civil war in

ourselves," says Dusha in the recent Russian novel
" Cement," when her husband seeks to exercise his
prerogative as a male in violation of her will. " There
is nothing more powerful, more alive than our habits,"
she lectures to her dismayed mate, who, though a
Communist, had not thought of a new attitude in
women toward men. " Jealousy," she continues to remind him, " rebels inside of you, and that is worse
than despotism," especially, the revolutionaries would
add, if mingled with the sense of masculine domination
over women.

Now when women enjoy the same sex liberties as
men, the ancient doctrine of virginity topples down like
a heap of snow struck by a rock. There is nothing to
hold it together. Chastity, as a principle and a practice,
as a canon and a custom, in and of itself, ceases to have
any meaning, any virtue, any glory. It is certainly ceasing to have these in Russia. The Russians avow that
once for all they are done with enforced chastity for
women. Just because women are women is no reason at
all, they declare, why they should be subjected to trials
and tests that men do not necessarily have to uphold
or endure. They are willing to leave sex behaviour to the
judgment and to the conscience of women themselves.
Once, while on a train, a German scientist with whom
I had been travelling, expressed the opinion to a group
of youths, who had gathered around us, that the Russian disregard of chastity in women, is a pernicious
doctrine and might debase Russian society. Women, he
protested with energy, are the mothers of the race and
that alone imposes a heavier responsibility on them
than on men. The youths howled with protest. The

male members of the group were especially vociferous in their denunciations. To them the German scientist's view seemed as ancient and barbarous as landlordism, czarism or witchcraft.

The Russians realize, of course, that biology exacts its own dole, and that in the nature of things in matters of sex, women are at a disadvantage. They know that with their own powers they cannot remove this disadvantage, but whatever ameliorations science makes possible, they will not withhold from women. They have made both birth-control and abortions legal, though they encourage neither the one nor the other. They are war-panicky. They imagine themselves surrounded by enemies who are awaiting an opportunity to pounce on them. They do not wish their birthrate interfered with at present. Hence an absence of intensive propaganda of birth-control. But the information may be obtained freely by anyone seeking it, and in the cities, in spite of the misgivings of Party leaders, it is spreading with amazing rapidity. Abortions, they regard at best as a necessary evil. They are constantly pointing out the dangers to health even of a most successful abortion. They are however warning women not to go to *babkas* — midwives — for an abortion but to a hospital where competent physicians can perform it with the least risk to their physical welfare.

Set against the morality prevalent in the outside world the new departures of the Russians are, for good or for evil, a landmark in history. No half measures; no step by step experimentation; no piece-meal reforms; no mere birth-control panaceas such as Mrs. Sanger is championing; no mere half-covert freedom such as Mrs. Bertrand Russell is seeking; no mere dawdling efforts to lift companionate marriage to a plane of respectability. Complete liberty to men and women with all the benefits of science at the disposal of both, but not at the expense of personal welfare, aesthetic appreciation and responsibility for possible social consequences.

The Russians make it clear to the individual that his own welfare and that of society demand judicious self-control. There is the question of personal health which must suffer through undisciplined indulgence. Poor health not only lessens a person's enjoyment of life — this life on this earth, for to them there is no other life — but impairs his capacity to render his best services to society. Besides, it might lead to over-absorption in self, a waning interest in the social group and a de-basement of the social consciousness. " The proleta-rian," says Lenine, " is not in need of the intoxication that excites and stupefies. He needs neither the intoxi-cation of sex nor of alcohol." Both are depraving, so-cially and physically.

Nor must the individual ignore the aesthetic aspect of sex. More and more do the Russian revolutionaries emphasize aesthetic values. The more refined, they de-clare, man's approach to sex the higher he rises above the beast and the more abundant is his enjoyment of life. " Does a normal man," queries Lenine, " under normal conditions drink from a glass from which dozens of others have drunk? " The implication is clear. Lenine was not especially given to aesthetic evaluations or en-joyments. But he sensed and in his own matter-of-fact way glorified the need of beauty and delicacy in sex-

life. Promiscuity, he insisted, cheapened and vulgarized
sex and reduced it to an act no more refined or elevating
than " drinking out of a mud-puddle."

Above all, the Russians emphasize to the individual his personal responsibility for social consequences.
" Get together, children," says Semashko, the commissary of health, " and separate at your will, but do not
forget your little children, and if you do — well, by the
ear we shall drag you into the sun of the people's
court." And they do drag them into this court, not by
one but by both ears, and even by the nose. The law is
merciless in enforcing responsibility for offspring. But
this law is only a makeshift. It is temporary in intent,
necessitated by the impecuniousness of the state and
the new society. When Russia at some future date
grows prosperous, homes will be provided for all children whose parents would care to place them there.
Then economic responsibility for children will be lifted
from the individual. Yet even now offspring need not
come, for, as already emphasized, both birth-control
and abortions are legal.

In the final analysis, however, despite considerations of personal hygiene, the individual's obligation
to society, his responsibility for children and aesthetic
values, the individual is his own arbiter. He is a free
agent unless his acts become anti-social and then society must discipline him. If a man and woman wish to
go off on a trip on the Volga or to the Caucasus for a
love-life of their own for a week, a month, a year, any
period, it is their affair, and only theirs. The law will
not interfere with them; nor will public opinion; nor
anybody or anything else. It is as respectable a pro-

cedure or indulgence as a honeymoon with one's own spouse.

So violent a plunge into a new sex morality with historical restraints brushed aside; with metaphysics, religion, law, fetishism, and the customs and standards grown out of these scrapped; with man and woman placed on a level of equality in use as well as abuse; with birth-control and abortions legalized; with a new self-discipline based on rational, earthly motivations launched so suddenly, it was natural that a maelstrom of maladjustments should break upon the scene. In the early years of the Revolution this new freedom had pushed wide open the floodgates of sensuality, especially as it had come on the heels of a chain of catastrophes — the World War, the Civil War, the famine, which, in and of themselves, are always upsetting to existing habits and standards.

Groups of youths plunged into an orgy of excesses. They did not care. They had no God to frighten them. They had no parents to control them. They had no teachers to restrain them. They had no public opinion to bother about. They had only their own immediate impulses to consider. They did not stop to weigh consequences, personal and social. They did not have time. They were too excited, too distressed. Today they lived, tomorrow they were dead. Today they had food, tomorrow they were starving. Today they had a home, tomorrow they might be vagabonding. In those terrific days nothing personal was of serious consequences. People lived with the rush of the joy or the passion of the moment.

Besides, the spirit of rebellion was at white-heat —

it had become to youth not only a task but an adventure. Youth pounded away with uncontrolled fury at anything and everything the old world had sponsored, including self-control in sex. There were instances when girls who protested against reckless liberties or refused to acquiesce in the " revolutionary " demands of men were rudely castigated, placed beyond the pale of good-fellowship. Sex was to be as free and simple as drinking a glass of water. The older revolutionaries were outraged. But they were on the battlefields busy fighting their enemies. Lenine himself was frantic with indignation. " The theory of a glass of water (in sex-life)," said he, " has made our youth mad . . . and this is anti-Marxian and anti-social."

With the coming of political stability and a modicum of economic security, the wave of riotous indulgence has been subsiding. Youth has grown more contemplative. New voices have been roaring of dangers ahead. Personal hygiene, aesthetic approach, social responsibility as measures of self-discipline have been pressed with increasing assiduity through all available channels of publicity, especially the drama and the cinema. Yet old standards and conceptions have remained in discard. The basic philosophy of the new sex morality has remained unshaken. Personal liberty is still its cornerstone.

When seeking to make an appraisal of the possible outcome of such an approach to sex behaviour, it is always emphatically necessary to keep in perspective certain conditions and traits peculiarly Russian which are, for the present at least, inextricably interwoven with the issue. The Russians are an unrepressed and an uninhibited people. They are not overburdened with sex consciousness. Under normal conditions, when not overwhelmed by some physical disaster or spiritual strain such as failure or success of a revolution, sex is to them a vital but not an all-absorbing object in life. They do not play with sex — not much, at any rate. They have not made sex a conspicuous part of their mental life, a form of intellectual diversion or intellectual self-expression.

This sex-unconsciousness the revolutionaries are seeking to perpetuate. They are death on commercial exploitation of sex. They have closed the old houses of prostitution, which in days of czardom were as distinctive a feature of every Russian community outside of the village as vodka shops or bazaars, and they have been waging a relentless war on underground harlotry. From studies made of university students and proletarians, two of the chief patrons of prostitution in the old days, it has been ascertained that there is a marked drop in resort to it as a means of sex relief.

The injection of sex lure in any form into commercial life they have likewise banned. There is nowhere a hint of sex in the displays in shop windows or in the amusement places. There is scarcely a trace of sex suggestiveness in Russian motion pictures. If a Russian producer were to make sex intrigue the central point of interest in a picture he would be mercilessly howled down. The Russian public would not be stirred. The Russian newspapers and magazines are singularly free from sex scandals or sex tales. The new plays and operettas do not build their plots around sex entanglements. I saw once in a summer theatre in Moscow a presentation of " Rose Marie." The production was as unlike the American version of it, as a peasant girl is unlike a Ziegfeld Follies beauty. There was scarcely a trace of pulchritude in the performance. In the new literature no subject outside of the Revolution itself commands as stirring attention as does sex. Yet despite the amazing frankness with which it is approached, it is not made intriguing or seductive. There are two night clubs in Moscow, both meagerly attended; both are maintained more as a concession to foreign visitors than in fulfillment of a need of the Russian public. But sculptural posturings of semi-nude girls are never part of their cabaret performances. Nowhere in restaurants or theatres are there displays of pictures of voluptuous maidens in a variety of semi-nude poses, such as greet the eyes of the visitor at every step on certain streets in Berlin. The revolutionaries regard the exploitation of a woman's body for commercial gain as a vicious insult to womanhood. Nowhere in Russia are pornographic pictures peddled around openly or secretly — they are not to be had. The Russian public does not crave and does not demand vicarious forms of sex excitement.

We must also reckon with the sex attitude of the Russian woman. She never has regarded sex with disdain. She talks of sex with no more reserve than of music, the theatre, the weather. Conventions never did have a special meaning to her. Yet she has always been astonishingly unfrivolous in her love-life. In its early days the Revolution had unbalanced her, as it had others, but she is rapidly regaining mental and emotional equilibrium. She does not enter into liaisons with men light-heartedly. There are exceptions of course, but it is not of these I am speaking. Foreigners who have come to Russia imagining that because of the new freedom in sex they would find the country steeped in a perpetual sex orgy, with women everywhere ready for sex association, have learned soon enough that the contrary is the case — that the Russian woman, despite all her frankness and all her freedom, is not easily won to sex association. When stirred by a great passion for a man or a cause she yields readily to sex approaches. Were there not girls in the revolutionary movement in the Czarist days who played the part of sweetheart and mistress to noted reactionaries and gendarmes, only to spy out their moves against revolutionaries?

Yet despite the emotional earnestness of the Russian woman, the sex unconsciousness of the Russian people, the measures of self-discipline that are a part of the new education of Russian humanity, one cannot help wondering if the Russians are in danger of sinking into a morass of animality. Personal liberty and personal judgment are the new watchwords, the new guide, if not the new god in sex behaviour. May it not be that the Russian woman in her new condition of rising economic independence and equality with men, with the findings of science at her ample command to avert child-bearing, with the spread of state nurseries for children — may it not be that she will become as lax in her sex-life as man is reputed to be? The Russians feel assured that through their education and their social action and interaction between the group or the individual, the woman will acquire too stirring a sense of social responsibility to abandon herself to a reckless search of sex pleasures. But this is only a supposition.

It may also be, as Havelock Ellis suggested when I discussed the possible outcome of the Russian experiment with him, that there will be a reaction in the opposite direction, that instead of women becoming more, men will become less lax. He seemed not at all sure that man's reputed polygamous proclivities are an innate part of him — they may be only a result of repressive conventions. The world, he emphasized, needs experiments like the Russian one to determine a host of puzzles in the sex behaviour of men and women.

Of course if in the end it should prove that under the Russian condition of liberty, libertinism will diminish and men will become less given to promiscuity and women will remain as disinclined toward promiscuity, or more so than tradition holds them to be, we shall have a new form of monogamy in the love-life of human beings, the highest yet attained, if only because it will flow out of inner desire and be free from outward compulsion. This would be a new power in the world, and would revolutionize sex morals everywhere.

Supposing, however, that this experiment instead of dissipating only emphasizes polygamous proclivities in both sexes? Then no doubt the Russians will curb personal liberty in matters of sex. They will intensify the emphasis of the disciplinary measures mentioned. They will bring into play the weapon of social censure, so effective in their battle on drunkenness. They will expand the fields of social diversion above all social work with a view of sublimating sex into fresh channels of self-expression. They may resort to external compulsion to curb libertinism, for they regard it as a product and a symbol of bourgeois decadence.

CHAPTER VII

FAMILY

TESTS AND TRIALS

THE new sex morality which Russia is forging would seem, to an outsider at any rate, to strike hard at the family, at least at marriage. By offering the individual complete freedom of action the Russian revolutionaries would appear to encroach on one of the most exalted purposes of marriage — sex-life. But modern civilization everywhere has injected a corrosive force into this aspect of marriage. Yet that alone does not imply family disintegration. It is the vast array of other conditions the Russians have sown into life that is subjecting the institution of the family to the most arduous tests it ever has faced in all its history. Never before have the forces which have for ages bound it together been so rudely shaken as now in Russia.

Not that a conscious effort is being made by the body in power to annihilate it as in the case of religion and private property. There are revolutionaries, men and women, who would deliberately dissolve the family and wipe it out of existence. But they are without power. They are held in the background, they and their views on sex and the family. The real rulers of Russia find the family at this stage of readjustment and national impecuniousness indispensable to the maintenance of social stability. They are not unaware of the menace the family holds to their ultimate aims. Its em-

phasis of individualistic proclivities hinders the unfolding of the collectivist spirit, which must be the foundation of the new society. At present, however, it still
performs a host of useful functions. Substitutes, many
of them varied and appealing, are only in process of
development. Besides, the high priests of communism
have spoken approvingly of the family. So the Russian
revolutionaries do not wish to speed its collapse, yet
will not resort to measures *compelling* its survival.

It is this last condition that lifts the problem of
the family in Russia to a condition unknown and un-
dreamed of in any other land. In America the family
has been a subject of endless solicitude. Witness the
incessant discussions in the periodical press and in
books. But in America the problem is still in a stage
of discussion. Doubt and uncertainty still harass both
public and leaders. Besides, the conscious social forces
of the land — the state, press, pulpit, school and even
the motion pictures are jointly and separately bent on
halting the process of disintegration. They view home
and family as a spiritual basis of civilization, as a great
sanctity and a great compensation.

Not so in Soviet Russia. There, while discussion is
still heated, the period of doubt as to immediate procedure has long since passed. The Russians have embarked on a definite program of action. They have
made the family a matter of voluntary union. They believe that even in this period of transition and national
poverty the family must justify its own existence, must
hold together by virtue of its own inner power and
vitality or else fall into disuse. " If, like a man of infirm
body," argued a revolutionary with me, " the family

must always lean on an outward clutch for support, then it is better that it go down into dust."

For the present, while in some cities, and notably in Moscow, divorce has reached immense proportions, during certain months equalling and once in March 1928 actually exceeding the number of marriages, the family, while rapidly changing its form, has not lost its staying powers. In the village, while somewhat shaken, it still has its roots in the soil, and, after all, Russia is essentially a village nation. The forces that have made for such stability are visible enough. There is the power of sheer inertia dragging people, though with ever increasing feebleness, into established tracks of behaviour. There is the family tradition of the race, so deep-rooted, especially with the peasantry, that life to them outside of the family circle is futile, almost criminal. There is the bond of economic pressure, again especially strong in the village, though collective farming is shattering this bond and weakening the family tradition of the race.

Above all there is the innate nature of the Russian. Violent as has been the jolt it has received at the hands of the Revolution, it has left the Russian the elemental human being that he was, possibly the most elemental of all white peoples. He still lives with his nose, as it were, in the earth. His emotions and instincts have not been warped by the artificial stimulations incident to a highly organized urban civilization. He is a man of simple habits of body and mind. Outside of the few large cities he is hardly aware of the existence, not to say practice, of sex perversion. He is a rugged animal, vital in his physical urges and natural in his mode of gratifying them. Incompatibilities resulting from erotic abnormalities, so much a cause of social restlessness and of family disunion in western nations, are hardly known to him.

He is also a highly emotional and gregarious fellow. He is not the self-contained, self-sufficient man that the American, or still more the Britisher is. No man in the world is so unaccustomed to aloneness as he, or dreads it more. The Russian loves people. He must lean on friends. That is why he is always so sociable, so informal, so bountifully hospitable. That is also why the family has been to him a source of social and spiritual gratification.

Above all he is a lover of children. I say this in spite of the much deserved reputation of the muzhik for cruelty to offspring and of the daily occurrences of infanticide in city and country. Peasant speech drips with sentiments of child love. I was once in a village with a Russian physician and as we were sitting in a peasant home eating breakfast, a middle-aged neighbour and his wife dashed into the house, unloaded from their bosoms apples, pears, eggs — gifts to the physician, and with tears in their eyes — the woman actually breaking into a paroxysm of cries — begged him to rush to their home and save their sick two-year-old daughter, the only child of five that had survived. " Little son mine," wailed the woman, " saviour mine, little angel mine, don't let her die. Oh, what will I do if she goes? " The man, illiterate as he was, gave utterance to an expression of child love as poignant and poetic as I ever have heard, an expression which unfortunately loses in translation much of the beauty and profundity of its pathos.

"Without a child, my dearest, without even one child, you blunder about like a lost soul." This was no exceptional burst of sentimentality. It was expressive of the innate feelings of the race. Communists, despite all their worldliness and supposed hardness, are no exception to the rule. I have known more than one stiff-souled Party man with a theoretic disdain for the family to leap with glee at the approach of his own tot, seize it, lift it high in the air, hug it tenderly and deluge it with kisses.

The question is can these forces of family unification, inertia, tradition, the biologic naturalness of the Russian, his inviolate gregariousness, his love of children, can these withstand the onslaught of the multitudinous forces of disintegration? Their extent and violence are not losing but gaining momentum.

Private property, for example, has always served as a cementing bond in the family. One does not have to be a pious Marxian socialist and agree with Engels that the monogamous family " arose through the concentration of considerable wealth in one hand — a man's hand — and from the endeavor to bequeath this wealth to the children of this man to the exclusion of all others," to appreciate the real cohesive power of private property in family life. Until about a century ago everywhere the family was the unit of economic production. It still is the unit of economic accumulation. Father, mother, brother, sister, all have a vested interest in the family fortune — the family home, automobile, investments, bank-account. Consider the feverish rush of the average American father to amass material possessions so as to provide comfort, luxury and not infrequently ostentation to wife and children, and to woo, through his wealth, prominence and distinction for his family. Private property has been the material rock on which the family has been securely resting for centuries, not merely the monogamous but the polygamous and clan family, as in China, to this very day. But in Russia private property is in a state of eclipse, especially in the city. The most feverish efforts of the new society are directed toward its demolition. This cannot but shatter one of the basic pillars of the Russian family.

The decay of religion is surely another blow at the family. Whether or not the Marxian socialists are right in attributing the emergence of the modern family to the rise of private property is of slight consequence. There is no gainsaying the fact that religion, and especially Judaism and Christianity, has sanctified and exalted it; have woven a sentimental halo about it; have pronounced it the expression of the will of God and of the florescence of man's spiritual genius. Not even the state has been so jealous a guardian of the family as the church, with one of the largest churches in the world, the Roman Catholic, practically banning to this day dissolution of family ties.

But in Russia religion and church are in a cloud of disrepute, in process of decay. Scriptural injunctions, church ordinances regulating human life, including family relations, have ceased to hold sway over a vast portion of the population and especially of the youth. " Honour thy father and thy mother? " Yes, says the revolutionary, if they have faith in the new gospel and are willing to give themselves to making it a reality. If

not, run from them as from a plague. " Whom God hath
joined together let no man put asunder? " Ridiculous,
flames the revolutionary, neither a God nor man has or
can have anything to do with the joining and the sundering of men and women from one another. " Until
death do us part? " Rubbish, shouts the revolutionary, life is too precious to wait for death to offer redemption from a union that may be blighting your
every hour of existence. He is depriving the church
and clergy of power to decide or influence the fate of
the family, and simultaneously he is stripping marriage of all sense of mystic sanctity and separation of
all sense of human wrongness. Thus, while with his attack on private property the Russian revolutionary is
shattering the material basis of the family, with his denial of religion he is blowing to pieces one of its oldest
spiritual props.

Certainly the new position of women is not without
serious import to family stability. The Russian women
are now living a freer life than they ever had in the old
days and in some respects the freest of any women in
the world. I shall return to the subject in a subsequent
chapter. Here I must emphasize that all the man-made
disabilities which they had for ages.been enduring have
been wiped out, legally at least. Chastity is no longer
a badge of honour or glory. Its loss is no longer a disgrace or a source of torment, save only to the extent
that the old tradition is still a part of the individual's
consciousness. Women are under no compulsion to endure maltreatment just for the sake of saving their
reputation or their honour or even their meal ticket.
They are encouraged to become economically independ-

ent. In Russia there is never any discussion as to whether the career interferes with the family but the reverse, as to whether the family interferes with a career. For women to attain economic independence and to make a contribution to the productive powers of society is held to be the height of social realization and personal glorification. Women are achieving economic independence on an ever-mounting scale. All of this, of course, makes them more self-assertive, more demanding, less liable to endure discomfort or abuse merely for the sake of preserving the family.

Consider further the new attitude toward the family that the youth is acquiring. How strangely out of tune it is with what we have in America! Despite the vast numbers of celibate folk here, the ideal of the family is constantly held forth to the youth of the land as the ultimate realization of their social selves. Youth sees everywhere men and women studying, planning, scheming, achieving, investing, suffering, sacrificing with the purpose, somewhere in the foreground of their minds, of eventually having families of their own on which to lavish their acquisitions and with which to share their triumphs. Even if fate intervenes and frustrates the realization of this purpose, the recognition of its supreme desirability continues to hold sway over them. Even though industrial development and city life, with its small apartments, its numerous delicatessen stores, its moving picture palaces and its multitudinous diversions and excitements, have made stern encroachments on the family and family life, it still remains the one ideal that somehow continues to lure and overpower both mind and heart.

But not so in Russia — not any longer. When I once told a group of Siberian students that in America the average individual, in his youth at any rate, looks to the family as the ultimate fruition of his chief life purpose, they looked at me with dismay. The idea seemed to them almost absurd — narrowing and devitalizing to human personality. How could it be otherwise? From its earliest days Russian youth, and especially outside of the villages, comes under revolutionary influences. Its mentality is moulded largely by agencies outside of the home, away from the family circle. In the kindergartens, schools, in the Octobrist, Pioneer, Komsomol (Young Communist) organizations, it is everlastingly made to feel that the supreme aim in life is the promotion of the purposes of the new society. Not that the family and home are held up to ridicule. Russian youth is not taught to deny the family or to regard it in the same light as private property and religion, as a symbol of a brutal age fit for the garbage pile of history. It is merely being habituated to the belief that the big tasks, the big adventures, the big glories, lie outside of its portals, are to be found only at the doorstep of what they regard as the largest all-embracing and noblest of all families — the collectivist society. Russian youth is brought up in fact to depend not only economically but socially and spiritually on the club, the factory circle, the sporting organizations, the trade union and the multitude of other groups outside of the home which are both the carriers and the builders of the ideals and achievements of the new society. Nowhere is the family set up as an ultimate ideal, as a final objective. Youth, therefore, grows up without a sense of reverence for the family and with a feeble sense of family responsibility.

In the background of the new social purpose there lurks another menace to the present-day family, the socialization of the physical and many other functions of the home. To the revolutionaries the home is an economic and even a social monstrosity. Would it not be cheaper, say they, to have community kitchens where specially trained cooks would be preparing food instead of obliging the individual housewife to stew and scorch over an individual stove? Would it not be more saving to have a community laundry where modern machinery with the aid of a well-trained corps of workers would do the washing instead of obliging the individual housewife to stew and sweat over the individual wash kettle and ironing board? Would it not be more politic to have a community nursery where children would be tended by expert nurses instead of having each mother often, in Russia especially, preposterously ignorant of child care, look after her own baby and be a slave to it by day and by night? The socialization, they argue, of these functions of the home would lift the load of drudgery from women and enable them to cultivate their minds and personalities and to engage in pursuits of some use to the new society. " No nation can be free," said Lenine, " when half the population is enslaved in the kitchen."

This idea in itself is not new or revolutionary. In the newest apartment houses in America not a few of the features which the Russians advocate have already been installed. The movement of childrens' nurseries — places where children can be left for the day and some-

times for the night in the care of competent attendants
— is likewise gaining in appeal in this country, though
for the present it is confined mainly to the well-to-do
who can afford the price of a nursery, and to the very
poor who are provided with nurseries by and in settlement houses. But in Russia it is a goal for the mass. It
has reached the magnitude of a national ambition.

Now to a Westerner and to an American the mere
mention of state nurseries for children in Russia rouses
a feeling akin to horror. In part this is due to reports
that appear occasionally in the press or that greet us
from the lecture platform to the effect that the Russian
revolutionaries are aiming at compulsory and perma-
nant separation of children from parents. That, of
course, is absurd. The revolutionaries never speak of
compulsion save in instances where by reason of parental neglect or abuse such a step is deemed advisable
to offer the child the protection it needs. The idea of
state nurseries is predicated on the supposition that not
only the mother but the child will benefit immensely
from the arrangement. The project, the Russians insist, must have not only the consent but the active co-
operation of the parents, especially of the mother. The
nursery is to be located within her convenient reach,
perhaps on the same street on which she lives. In the
new homes that are to be built the nursery may be in a
separate part of the building or in a house of its own
in the yard. The mother and father can and will be
encouraged to maintain ample contacts with the child
— play with it, fondle it, take it home at frequent intervals and assist in its physical and spiritual development. In the nursery, the Russians protest, the child

will get not less but more and better protection than any but the very rich homes could possibly offer. It will be fed, bathed, clothed in accord with the latest discoveries of science. In time of illness it will receive the immediate attention of a child specialist. It will not be pampered. It will not be abused. It will not be suppressed. Above all it will be kept from contact with vices, especially alcoholism, which now so brutally debauch the masses, the proletarian even more than the peasant. . . . It is significant that of all the schemes the Soviets and the Communists have proposed for the new society, this one of nurseries for children has, to my knowledge, roused the least concern. The only exception is the Protestant sects who see a possible clash with the government over the question of religion. But they are beginning to build their own nurseries as a means of combatting atheism.

The building of nation-wide nurseries must be a slow process, depending on the amount of prosperity the state enjoys. This is true of the entire scheme of socialization of the home, at least of its chief domestic functions. In places, however, such socialization has already been carried to an astonishing degree of effectiveness. An instance of it I saw in the city of Kiev. I was visiting a shoe factory for the unemployed, that is started by and for unemployed men and women, with state aid of course. I was shown through the workrooms, the offices, the club-quarters, the dining place, and I discovered soon enough that this was more than a mere factory. It was a little world in itself, a community almost complete in the ministrations it offered to its members. It had its own mural newspaper, the largest and most flamboyant I had seen anywhere in the city, carrying the chief news of the place and liberally scattered with cryptic remarks and criticisms of things and officials in the factory. It operated a library and schools, not only for workers but for members of their families, with classes in hygiene, in domestic science, in literature, in politics, in international affairs. It maintained its own summer home and a recreation center in a park in the city. It held excursions, athletic contests. It was projecting the erection of a little theatre for movies and for dramatic performances by and for its own crowd. It was a complete society in itself, assuming and fulfilling with notable and rather un-Russian expertness a multitude of the offices of the old-fashioned home.

Not everywhere in Russia have factories already achieved as high a degree of socialization of the private life of the worker as has this shoe factory. The significant thing is that a complete scheme of such socialization is in the very foreground of factory management. In such towns, as Ivano-Voznesensk, Russia's chief textile center, Shakhta, one of the largest coal towns in Russia, the building of community restaurants, laundries, clubs, parks, nurseries, theatres and other institutions with a view to drawing the worker away from the home into the larger society is proceeding with amazing speed. When you see the mammoth community kitchens in Ivano-Voznesensk and the fleet of trucks dashing about the city at meal time, distributing in thermos-containers food to individual households, you become dramatically aware of the earnestness with which real socialization is being pushed.

It is significant that in the new homes which are

being built in Russia the apartments are small — between two and three rooms, rarely four and never more. Large apartments for a single family will never again be built in Russia while the present regime remains in power. Home never again can be a physical nor any other kind of castle. There is no need, say the Russians, for large homes, because so much of the life of the family has already been transferred to outside places.

Like the new sex morality the new marriage laws in Russia hardly have an element of external compulsion, save in the matter of alimony, especially for children, which is intended as a temporary measure. For this reason we have in Russia if not a condition certainly a spirit of free love, and the Russians not only fail to resent but welcome with an abundance of joy such a characterization of their marital life. Couples may live together without going through the ceremony of a civil wedding, without even " inscribing themselves " in the registry office. The government does not bother them and friends do not ostracize them. It seems that most of the couples I have met in Moscow, Communist and non-Communist, live in a state of free union. Do they hide the fact or speak of it with a sense of shamefaced guilt? Not at all. They regard such unions not only as highly proper but as expressive of the truest spirit of affection and respect of man and woman for each other. Whenever I would express doubt as to the advantages of such unions, particularly to women, good-humoured laughter rather than serious argument would be the reply I would evoke. Once when I ventured to criticize the popularity of such a manner of mating to a charming mother of two children, who was herself living in a free union with an engineer, her only comment was, " Truly, you talk almost like an uncivilized man." She meant no offence, for she was a woman of marked culture. To her it was simply incomprehensible how any other kind of union could be reasonable. It is when one hears words like hers that one realizes with a sense of overwhelming amazement how far from the rest of mankind the Russians have migrated in their whole social philosophy.

Divorce, of course, is as easy and as simple as marriage. If the union is not entered in the registry books, men and women part without formalities. If they have " inscribed themselves " all they have to do is " write themselves out," that is, record their separation in the books. Either husband or wife can obtain a divorce with or without the consent of the other. A young lady I met in Moscow told me once how she had " written herself out " of wedlock. She had married a man she never really loved. He had been a persistent suitor and had once threatened to do something desperate — kill himself or her or both of them, if she should continue to refuse his hand. So she gave her consent and they got registered. He was supremely happy, but she was not, and when a few days after this marriage he left for a trip to the Caucasus, she went to the registration office and obtained her divorce, and he, she explained, " would be notified by mail that I am no longer his wife."

All divorces in Russia are as simple. No legal representation is necessary. No briefs of complaint are required. The clerk in attendance of this registration may be only a grammar-school graduate. He does not ask many questions. He does not always demand grounds for separation. He does not make attempts at reconciliation. If he tried he would throw himself open to rebukes. He is merely a clerk, an office worker. He enters names and dates and places on the divorce sheets with no more concern than other clerks record the cost of herring or kerosene. It is all so informal, so matter of fact. People stand in line for their divorce with the same display of patience and good nature that they show when they wait their turn to buy a loaf of bread in a bakery or a yard of calico in a department store. I have been in registry offices in several cities. Nowhere is there a suggestion of drama, of conflict, nowhere a hint of the epochal meaning of this most simple procedure, which is in itself one of the greatest revolutions of the ages.

The law, of course, steps in when there are children, and then not to hold the family together — that always is regarded as an attempt to outrage the freedom of the individual — but to make provision for the children all of whom, I must emphasize, are legitimate, whether born in or out of wedlock. The parents must care for them. As a rule the mother receives the custody of the child and the father pays alimony, one third of his salary until the child has attained the eighteenth birthday, and more than that but never over one half of his earnings, if there is more than one child.

There are instances, of course, when the process is reversed, when the father receives the custody of the child and the mother pays alimony. I personally know of such a case in Moscow. The mother is a physician, the father an engineer. Both sued for the custody of the child, a boy of nine. Since the father was a Communist the court ruled that he was the more competent parent to give the child the proper upbringing, but since the mother was earning more than he, she was made to pay him alimony — one third of her income — until the son should reach his eighteenth birthday.

In the event that there are no children in the family and both husband and wife are in good health, no alimony is paid to either party. But if the wife happens to be incapacitated for work she receives for her support one third of her husband's income, but never for more than a year. If the husband happens to be the incapacitated person, the wife pays him alimony, if she works, likewise one third of her income, and again for no more than a year.

What then is likely to be the fate of the family in Russia? Is it doomed? To an outsider it would seem that the odds are stacked against it. The forces of dissolution both objective and subjective would appear to be too multitudinous and too persistent. With private property in disrepute and on the decline, with religion in a state of collapse, with old sex standards and family sanctities in discard, with birth-control and abortions legalized, though discouraged, with women sweeping into economic independence, with children growing up with but a feeble sense of family responsibility, with the socialization of the functions of the home already launched, with all these new and mighty social effects constantly gaining momentum, that is with legal, economic, metaphysical, religious, conventional and even some domestic and social bonds of family life in process of dissolution, one wonders what counteracting or stabilizing influences are left or will remain to keep home and family together? Of course there is the bond of love — of man and woman for each other and for children. Russian women in the cities avow that father love is on the rise. If so it must be chiefly among the old intelligentsia and bourgeoisie who, deprived of former outlets for their emotional energy, find themselves lavishing more of it on their children.

Yet it is still a question if children can, under prevailing conditions, ever again be as powerful a binding force in the family as they formerly were. Will not the fact that they lean on the new society, much more than on parents, for their education, their recreation, their material welfare, their preparation for the future, tend to weaken their filial devotion and simultaneously the devotion of their parents toward them? Nowhere in the world does the life of the child pass so extensively outside of the home as in Russia. The parental instinct in man will of course continue to function and assert itself, and children will ever rouse warmth and tenderness and to that extent they will constitute a cohesive force in the family, but it is not likely to be as compelling as it formerly was. Love of men and women for each other must remain the basic unifying force in the Russian family. How is it then with such love in Russia?

CHAPTER VIII

LOVE

THE intelligentsia the world over, and perhaps nowhere so much as in America, has of late been visibly perturbed over the fate of romantic love in our age. Certainly nowhere else are they according the subject such conspicuous attention. Fictionists and publicists alike, on the pages of the leading literary journals are busy intoning laments over the passing of the "great and glorifying illusion of love." They see only gloom ahead, unredeemed by the faintest flash of radiance. "Many young people," wails Andrés Maurois, "are quite willing to see romantic love die a natural and speedy death."

An American writer, Joseph Wood Krutch, goes him one better by declaring that "with vertiginous rapidity it (love) is being reduced to no more than a physiological act; with no more than a physiological act's importance and value." Of course to a historically-minded person the logic of this plaint must seem strained. Love, we know, has come into being somewhere between savagery and civilization, a period marked by man's rapid ascent higher and higher over the beast. Love, like art, is a product of this ascent. To assume that we are reducing love to the position it held in savagery, is equivalent to assuming that we are stripping ourselves of the cultural heritages we have acquired since the advent of civilization, and in which love has had its birth and growth.

A coterie of young writers — Ernest Hemingway, D. H. Lawrence and Aldous Huxley, toy around with love as though it were only a putrid appendix to man's psychology, fit to be slashed out and cast into the garbage pail.

Even Bertrand Russell feels constrained to join in the chorus of disenchantment. " Religion, tragedy and love," says he, " have all decayed through . . . the diminution in our estimate of the stature of human beings."

Havelock Ellis alone has remained unswerved in his abiding faith in love. " Love," he said in a personal interview with the writer, " is too deep-seated in the human breast ever to die out."

No modernist, however, has been so distressed over the fate of love in our age as Keyserling. His words drip with despair and rancour. He sees love " lying on its death bed . . . in Europe to-day love has become openly unmodern . . . from now on love is to exist no more." Why? Because " the most modern women in the world treat with men as equals . . . in most countries women are becoming amazons," which word he defines in its literal sense as meaning breastless. " The boyish bob, the changed figure, the wearing of glasses, the destruction of all that is provocative of love by exposure to wind and weather, the sport-fury — all these are the external signs in the change of feminine structure . . . independent young women have caught the spirit of the age . . . and this brings with it the progressive atrophy of all the characteristics which define the woman as a love being. . . ."

Stern judgment, and one would infer from it that the way to preserve love or retrieve it to its former glory is to push back the flood of liberties that has come to women. How to achieve this miracle and blot out of women their newly won self-respect and courage which stir them more and more into a search of their own salvation in their own way — on this question Keyserling remains tactfully mute. Characteristically enough he informs us that France " is perhaps the last refuge place of love," and characteristically enough he omits informing us that France is also one of the last refuge places of woman's subjection to man. One cannot help wondering what will happen to the unspoiled and over-hallowed love of the French women when they, like the Russian and American women, begin in earnest to hurl down the loads of medieval disabilities which their men stubbornly persist in pressing on them.

Those who sigh for the day " when love was best " need to remind themselves that we no longer live in an age of leisure, diletantism, inbound individualism when folk of the propertied and intellectual classes were absorbed in their emotions, mainly because they had no other interests to occupy their attention. In those pacific times women especially, lived chiefly and almost solely for the fulfillment of their love. They talked, thought, dreamed of it perpetually, because they had so little else to talk, dream and become excited about.

But that precious day is dead. Science, democracy, popular education, have scorched all life-blood out of it. Women have discovered new diversions, excitements, obligations, ambitions. They have pushed open the portals of hitherto untried forms of self-expression, and have found these intriguing. They have begun to have faith in their own intelligence and have not hesitated to put it to use for their own advancement and advantage, and not without success. This together with the new knowledge we have been acquiring of the psychology and physiology of sex have necessitated a reappraisal of the value of love and a loosening of the conventions that have clustered about it.

However, the sheer attempt at such a reappraisal, as inevitable with the advance of our knowledge of ourselves as the refashioning of technology with the discovery of new laws of nature, has made some men quiver with fear and pain. Modernists and radicals, proud at least to be known as such and professing a readiness to welcome and champion new departures in thought and usage, they yet turn away with grief and horror from a transvaluation of love, or even the conventions that have surrounded it. A tender divinity love is to them — too tender to be closely approached or touched without suffering defilement and demise. Like the fundamentalist in religion they perceive only one possible outcome from challenge — demolition of the value itself.

Incidentally, is it only an accident that in this cry of despair at the collapse of love it is the voice of the male that rises the loudest? May it not be that this protest of the male is only a rebellion, conscious and subconscious, at his dethronement from a position of command in a sphere of life in which he had held himself supreme?

But whatever the opinions and misgivings we may be cherishing on the subject, the tests and conditions to which Russia is subjecting romantic love must waken ever-growing attention the world over, if only because the very forces which to a Keyserling and a Maurois spell the death of love, convey an opposite meaning to the Russian revolutionaries, inspire in them faith in its eventual revitalization. If love, argue they, is to fulfill its rightful function in human existence, it can do so most freely in the environment which they have created for it, the very environment which to Keyserling means the asphyxiation of love.

Clear-cut and irreconcilable is the clash between the two *Weltanschauungen.*

When you first dip into modern Russian life and literature you come upon an outburst of scorn against romantic love beside which Aldous Huxley's cynical blasts fade into a paltry jest. Panteleimon Romanov, for example, has written a short story, " Without Flowers," which as a social document, rather than a work of art, will take its place beside Turgenev's " Fathers and Sons " and Artzybashev's " Sanine." The heroine of the story, a university student, in writing to a girl chum, discourses gloomily, " There is no longer any love among us. There is only sex relationship. Girls easily unite with our comrades for a week, for a month or casually for one night. . . . Those who seek in love something more than physiology are viewed with ridicule like mere half-wits." Echoing these sentiments only more robustly the student revolutionary, Khorokhorin, in another audacious work of fiction exclaims boastfully, " Love is only a bourgeois caper which hampers the advancement of the cause. It is a diversion for the glutted."

Lest the reader think that such expressions of negation are an invention of over-confident or over-cynical fictionists, I shall quote from actual pronouncements of Russian youths, university students, who have been canvassed for an opinion on the subject of romantic love. "Love," says one student, "our fellows deny. They regard it as stupid and puerile." Twenty-eight per cent of the students questioned admit that in sex a feeling of romance may be desirable, but is not indispensable. Thirty-six per cent deny that it is even desirable. As one of them phrased his reply, "The majority of my acquaintances believe that in sex all that matters is that the woman be clean and in good health." Another is even more outspoken. "In general," he writes, "I pay little heed to romance, if only the woman be well and is agreeable to my demands. I need just one thing and what place has romance in it?" A revolutionary lecturer on the subject of sex, in reply to questions by his auditors as to whether there is such a thing as love, and if so must they allow a place for it in their lives, candidly answers, "Love as a separate emotion, as some distinctive and wondrous experience, does not exist at all, or only in the imagination of old maids and naïve coeds. . . . Communists are possessed only of a physical urge — not a feeling, but a plain indispensable physical need."

Plain speech this is, racy enough and boisterously decisive! Yet it would be easy to read a false meaning into it, to accept it as the crystallized opinion or aim of the mass, or as an integral part of the social program of the new regime. It is neither. Clamourous as it is, it has been mainly an affair of the male, of that portion of it which, in Russia, has always been over-exuberant in its intellectual vagaries — namely, the university students. The Russian woman has hardly been a part of this crusade. She has held aloof, or largely so, perplexed, amazed and not at all happy. The very writers of fiction who have given us the most unabashed portrayals of youth's revolt against love, have been cautious enough to confine it almost exclusively to men. Their women have remained not unshaken, but neither emptied of a capacity to idealize love nor of a wish to enjoy its rewards.

The very girl of Romanov's above-mentioned story who wails at the collapse of romantic love is herself the very epitome of romance. She thrills to sunsets and shadows, to music and flowers, to poetry and above all to her love. She seems as if lifted in body and spirit from the pages of Turgenev, whose women are the very soul of romance. In " The Moon on the Right," another devastating work of fiction, the heroine, Tanya, who within a brief space of time skids through twenty-two marriages and in despair attempts suicide, finally finds redemption in the devotion of a sturdy and unspoiled peasant youth. . . . In still another novel, the most sensational of all, " A Dog's Square," the author ushers on the scene a whole coterie of girls and all of them at the end, if not in the beginning, come to acknowledge the beneficence of real love. Even Vera Volkhova, the medical student, who has thrust scruples to the wind and has the reputation among her classmates of accepting male callers with as little discrimination as a harlot, is constrained to exclaim once, " Yes, I'll submit, but only for the sake of passion, for the sake of love. . . ." Her friend Anna, who prances into her revolutionary career with a boisterous disregard of all restraints, and is quick to mock as bourgeois the least suggestion that there is value in reserve or glory in idealization, comes in the end to visualize the tragic folly and the horrible hollowness of her behaviour. Varya, the factory girl, who knows so little of life and love and sex, is swept into a transport of feeling by the attention that the eloquent and mighty Khorokhorin bestows on her. She has not the heart to resist his masculine approaches, and when she yields to his wishes her dream is that some day she will have a son as big, brave, learned and important as her lover. . . . Indeed hardly a writer in the new fiction or the new drama of Russia but weaves a halo of romance around his women characters.

Nor does the present rebellion gain in potency or significance when viewed in historical perspective. It is not without precedent. Because of the temperament of her people and the peculiar social storms that have burst on her, Russia, to paraphrase Hoover, has been subject to cycles of emotional booms and slumps, under the spur of which idealization of sex has been flittingly doubted, mocked, tabooed. In the days of so-called nihilism, with its denial of aesthetic values and its worship of utility, romantic love was cast into discard. " You care for a woman," discourses Turgenev's master nihilist, Bazarov, " try and come to an understanding with her, and if you fail — no matter — the earth will not crack under you." Years later Sanine appeared on the scene and proceeded even more brashly than Bazarov to make merry sport of romantic love. Yet neither nihilism nor Saninism had banished it from the Russian heart.

The present outburst is by far the most tempestuous Russia has ever experienced, which is natural enough. It has come in the wake of a Revolution, that has heaved up a swell of emotion more mighty than any other movement in Russian history, not an emotion of despair, but of exaltation which always inflames defiance. It has lashed Russian youth into a frenzy of hate against the old world and all its values, so much so that youth had at one time come to regard it as an act of heroism and virtue to smash brutally into everything this old world had cherished — collar and tie, curtains over windows, hats for women, clean shirts, and of course, romantic love. But as the destructive phase of the Revolution recedes into the background, so mere negation of the old bourgeois world is giving place to a reappraisal of its old values. The proletarian himself is taking to collar and tie, to curtains over windows, to clean shirts — in short to a display of increased care and improved taste in personal appearance. Aesthetics, in other words, is lifting its head again in Russia and with it has come, or is coming, a change of attitude toward romantic love.

However uproarious and brazen the voice of revolt, however busy the new literature parading before the public the fiery rebel with vials of hot scorn for " bourgeois perversions and sentimentalities " in his hands, the more contemplative revolutionary has nevertheless gone beyond mere negation. He has been turning to his high priests for guidance and he has discovered, now to his dismay, now to his joy, that they are at dramatic variance with the notions of the rebel. Lenine spoke of sex as a product of biology plus culture. Engels has written with eloquence of the power and beauty of sex love. So has August Bebel. So in a more sober vein has Marx himself. Even Madame Kolontay, enunciator of the work-bee theory — that is of man born to flit from love to love, like a work-bee from flower to flower — recognizes that " from a purely biologic phenomenon love has acquired a psycho-social significance."

So the Russian revolutionary is beginning to take romantic love to his heart again, but on entirely new terms. He will not make it an end in itself, the final justification of life. He has only vitriolic disdain for the so-called " religion of love," but he acknowledges that love has power to vitalize and enrich man's life and make him more fit a warrior for whatever cause he is pursuing. That is why he would strip love of all extraneous interferences of whatever nature or origin, whether religious, social or even poetic. He would let it soar off on a wave of its own, propelled only by its own powers and in full sweep with advanced feminist wishes and radical pronouncements of biology and psychology. He is convinced that only through such a violent break with past curbs and encumbrances can love be saved from decay or " bondage," as one writer expresses himself — can it win a new body and a new spirit, and attain the fulfillment of its highest function in human life. He is pouring his Revolution into sex love with as much audacity as into sex morality, the family, religion, private property and international relations.

To begin with he holds that his attack on private property is in itself a boon to love. In this he is not without warrant or authority. " In days far away,"

Andrés Maurois reminds us, " it was on the man at her (woman's) side who could best assure her security that her wiles were employed. In days nearer to our own she has sought to appropriate the rich man — the man who can best assure her economic security." Under a system of private property the lure of riches does hang like a dread shadow over the free play of love. How often do we read of a woman sacrificing love for the sake of the distinction and comfort that wealth may confer, or of a man pocketing his love, or pushing his emotional life into the background for the sake of winning a wife with a rich inheritance? Nor are parents insensitive to economic values. How often do they resort, in Europe especially, and principally with daughters, to modes of persuasion that border on coercion? Novels, short stories, plays, motion pictures teem with stories of love frustrated by money considerations. But when accumulation of wealth, says the Russian revolutionary, is rendered difficult or impossible, utilitarian motivations cease, and men and women mate through the bonds of affection they cherish for one another.

Love makes a further gain, argues the revolutionary, through the possibility of early unions. Russia is indeed a land of such unions. She always was that in the village, where boys and girls united in wedlock under the age of twenty. Now all classes mate young. They have no special reason to wait. Accumulation of an estate against possible mishaps does not bother them. It would do them little good if it did, for as already explained in a preceding chapter, under Russian conditions accumulation of wealth is scarcely possible, and at best is fraught with too many harrowing risks. With

the gulf between the biologic and economic age of mating wiped out, men and women in Russia unite at an
early age, when love makes its initial approach, when
sex impulses are at an especially acute tension, and
that, the Russian revolutionary regards as an especially
salutary gain for love.

Love scores another triumph, argues he, through
the economic independence that the Russian woman is
rapidly achieving. A woman, he protests, will not endure
a union grown void of romance or replete with disgust
and pain just because she must depend on the man for
material sustenance. When she can provide for her own
needs she will not hesitate to break this union and
sally forth into freedom and into a new life in quest
perhaps of a more agreeable liaison. Nor will a man
be kept from separation by qualms over the fate the
woman may suffer if left to shift for herself. Man and
wife will be held together solely by the affection they
may have for each other and not by the economic
dependence of one on the other, especially if, as in
Russia, neither custom nor law maintain barriers to
separation.

The very removal of these barriers, discourses further the Russian revolutionary, brings another victory
to love. It leaves the doors open to escape from disappointment resulting from temperamental, physical or
other incompatibilities. In this again he is not without
warrant or authority. What are movements for trial
marriage, companionate marriage, but attempts to rem-
edy love frustration? What are the theories of Mrs.
Bertrand Russell, Ellen Key, Judge Lindsey and a host
of others, but an effort to help the individual taste his

share of love after venture into it has resulted in misfortune? Under the Russian system with birth-control
and free divorce, all marriages are trial marriages, all
matings are companionate matings. There is and there
can be no other kind of union under Russian conditions.
Of course this scraps the notion of the sacredness of
marriage. But the Russian revolutionary would not
tolerate this or any other theological interference with
the love-life of the individual. " Marriage," once exclaimed a revolutionary in the course of a hot debate on
the question, " is for man and not man for marriage."
In no other way, argue the Russians, and through no
other measure or method can equality of sexes be maintained and the *right* to love preserved.

Closely linked with this phase of love there is another of which the revolutionary seldom speaks but
which has roused the widespread interest of Russian
and other scientists. I am referring to what Havelock
Ellis calls " the erotic rights of women." We have of
late had a deluge of literature by men of science and by
outspoken feminists assuring us that women, because
of conditions they have been helpless to influence, have
not always achieved the full enjoyment of their erotic
rights. Much of the unhappiness and emotional frustration in modern civilization they lay directly to this
cause. Havelock Ellis phrases the difficulty succinctly
in the following passage:

" The practice and the ideals of this established
morality were both due to man, and both were so
thoroughly fashioned that they subjugated alike the
actions and the feelings of women. There is no sphere
which we regard as so peculiarly women's sphere as

that of love. Yet there is no sphere which in civilization women have so far had so small a part in regulating. Their deepest feelings, their modesty, their mater-
nity, their devotion, their emotional receptivity — were
used with no conscious and deliberate Machiavellism,
against themselves, to mould a moral world for their
habitation which they would not themselves have
moulded. . . . In the erotic spheres woman asks nothing better of a man than to be lifted above the coldness
to the higher plane where there is reciprocal interest
and mutual joy in the act of love. . . . Therein her
silent demand is one of nature's. . . . The erotic claims
of women are not publicly voiced and women themselves would be the last to assert them. . . ." But under a system of equality of the sexes, which Russia
makes possible, women may make their demands manifest without perhaps a need of voicing them in the
open. They may acquire silent but none the less effective ways of forcing a reconsideration of their wishes
and a readaptation to their needs. In fact women the
world over are beginning to do so, even in America,
and perhaps in America more than in other lands. Under a condition of freedom of choice and separation
which Russia makes possible, men will be compelled to
take fresh stock of themselves, to learn new methods
of adaptation or else go down in defeat. This is the
theory I have frequently heard expounded by Russian
medical savants. " Women," a noted woman psychia-
trist in Moscow once said to me, " will not suffer further mutilation of their love-life just for the sake of
pleasing men. Under our conditions, despite all our
difficulties and agonies, love in its physical aspects will

no longer remain primarily an erotic right and enjoyment of the male."

If the revolutionary glides over with unconcern the purely erotic aspect of love leaving it to the scientist to discuss its possibilities in his new society, he most emphatically does not pass over lightly the question of sex education. He is stripping sex of mysteriousness. He is spreading enlightenment on the subject with a lavish hand through lectures, motion pictures, posters, plays, books, pamphlets sold everywhere even at the kiosks in railroad stations and bazaars. He is bringing sex education to the schools. Through this campaign of enlightenment he hopes to mitigate and eventually to eliminate the doubts, distresses, errors and bewilderments that youth so often has to countenance. This again, he holds, is a decided gain for sex-love, purifies it of false notions and of the morbid exoticism which ignorance of sex often invites.

There is nothing, however, which the Russian revolutionary deems of such salutary value to the love-life of men and women as an all-pervading spirit of comradeship between the sexes. With feverish energy he has hewed down the barriers between them. From their earliest days, in and out of school, boys and girls in Russia are constantly thrown together, far more so than in any land in the world. They study together, play together in parks, club-houses, theatres. They swim together, exercise together, frolic together. They are fed on the same thoughts and sentiments. They are being impregnated with the same ideas of devotion to the social purpose of the Revolution. When they grow up they work side by side in shop, factory, office.

The Russian revolutionary is convinced that under the spur of this new relationship and in the absence of special privileges for either party, the sex conflict between man and woman will abate, will yield to a more rational understanding of one another, to a more comradely approach, which will strengthen the bonds of their love. However intense, says he, the ardour arising from a purely sex attraction, unless it is interwoven with a spirit of actual comradeship, with a hearty devotion to some social purpose, with an outgoing wish to help one another always, not only in personal struggles but in the big issues of life; unless, in other words, it is interlaid with a host of mutual interests and devotions, it may soon spend itself, create an emotional void and degenerate into antipathy. The greater the comradeship between men and women, says he, the more robust will be their bonds of love. In the new literature, motion pictures and theatrical productions this comradeship is always glowingly emphasized. It is as if the revolutionary were expecting it to usher in a new age of reconciliation between the sexes and a fresh burst of romance.

Now the bringing together into life with a gush of enthusiasm all these new forces — the abolition of private property, the economic independence of women, sex freedom, sex education, free divorce and the promotion of closest social contacts between men and women, has, as already suggested, caused no little dismay to a coterie of men of note to whom love is the supreme joy and glory in life. These men lay much of the disillusionment with love, which they note in all western lands, to the spread of the very ideas and prac-

tices which Russia has loosened with such a bold
hand.

Of course, these men hold largely to notions of love
which were nurtured in chivalry. The essence of chivalric love in the words of Andrés Maurois was " the
deification of womanhood," made possible through
the constant separation of men and women from each
other, by " the functions and manner of life of the two
sexes." But chivalry flourished in a civilization of which
hardly a vestige has remained, and it is surely pertinent
to question, as the whole world is doing and especially
America, whether the old garment of love fits the new
body and soul of man? Is the deification of womanhood so essential to the existence of romantic love, and
is such love so utterly contingent on the separation of
the sexes? At one time opponents of coeducation in
America prophesied that if men and women would sit
together in the same classrooms, listen to the same lectures, look at each other at all hours of the day, they
would cease to be enamored of one another and love
would perish. When the movement of woman suffrage
had gained momentum in America, again the plaint was
loud that women, by getting messed up in politics — a
man's affair — would cease to lure or be allured. In
fact whenever woman ventured to invade any sphere
of life in the control of men protests were thundered at
her from everywhere that she was, with her own hands,
slaughtering love!

This man-made conception of love reduced to simplest
terms means nothing less than this — that man could
indulge in all the laxity and grossness, open and secret,
that his pocket-book or his good luck would allow, and

yet retain unimpaired his power to love and to be loved. But woman, when she ventured beyond the limits of physical and emotional activity prescribed for her by tradition and convention, was supposed to ruin her capacity to experience, and her power to awaken " exalted feeling." The differentiation between the nature of man and woman, which such a theory presupposes, must seem even to a Keyserling both monstrous and absurd.

For the most striking proof of the falsity of the chivalric creed " that a continuous life in common is the ruin of exalted feeling," we must turn to Russia, her history and her literature. As already explained in a preceding chapter, Russia had never been swept by chivalry, had gotten a taste of it only second hand, and then in a thinly diluted form. Amidst the Russian intelligentsia, for example, women never were shelved off into a little world of their own, in which they were supposed to devote themselves to but one purpose — making themselves alluring to men and dreaming of their love or loves, as in the days of chivalry. In the Russian revolutionary movement men and women always associated intimately — worked together, planned and plotted together, saw each other continually, on their bright days, on their off days, in all their strength, all their weaknesses, all their moods, all their failings. Yet some of the most fervid loves recorded in Russian history have flowered within the ranks of the revolutionaries. Is there romance in Russian literature? Is there exalted feeling in Pushkin's " Yevgeny Onyegin "? Is there love in Turgenev's novels? Yet consider how intimately the men and women in these novels have always associated.

Consider further the Russian peasant, or still better the Russian Cossack, this age-old and implacable warrior. He had never heard of chivalry. He had never sallied forth to battle for the honour and glory of some lady love in the manner of medieval knights. His women have always been among the most proud, the most self-assertive in Russia, and he had never erected substantial social gulfs between himself and them. Yet he has created some of the most exquisite love-lyrics in the Russian language — replete with exalted feeling.

The plain fact is, that given sex instinct and imagination — and what forces are there to deprive man of either? — there will be exaltation, sublimation, response, there will be romance and love. In love as in anything else human nature is inordinately plastic. Because the Keyserlings and the Maurois' had habituated their emotional responses to a woman of certain standards and quality, it does not at all follow that a new generation of men reared in a new set of standards and values, cannot habituate their emotional responses to the new type of woman. And vice versa of course. New conditions evoke new reactions. New tastes beget new inspirations. At one time in Russia it was the woman with the bulging hips and the large feet that proved most alluring to men, and women loafed and gormandized to achieve the coveted avoirdupois. At a later period among certain groups of Russians it was the woman with the pale complexion and the slight build that proved most romantic, and women even drank ink to achieve wanness and frailty. There is nothing fixed or static about the cause of emotional responses. After all, romance is inseparable from taste and habit, and while taste and habit change, romance remains and must remain, so long as man is possessed of sex instinct and imagination with both played upon by the cultural heritages man has attained since the rise of civilization.

But whatever our opinions of the conditions in society which best promote romantic love, the outstanding fact is that the world, and America especially, is moving in the direction not of a curtailment, but an expansion of the forces which to the Keyserlings spell the death of romance. Women are advancing in the direction not of less but of greater equality with men, not of less but of greater economic independence, not of less but of more social intimacy with men; divorce is growing not less but more easy; sex is becoming not more but less mysterious and mythical; the double-standard of morality which shielded women from sex experience outside of wedlock, and which was supposed to enhance their romantic appeal, is not gaining but losing momentum.

In other words the entire world is moving not away from, but in the direction of the goal which Russia has achieved. Russia may have acted too erratically in making the leap from established conventions, what few there were in the land, and with small regard for the sensibilities of men and women. But that is the way of Revolution. Human sensibilities do not count. Besides, because of her past history, chiefly the absence of chivalry, the jar and the shock to the sensibilities of men and especially women were not, probably, as upsetting in Russia as they would have been in a western land. At any rate, in her vast social laboratory Russia is seeking to work out a new conception and a new expression of love — the one solid link left in the country to hold the family from collapse.

CHAPTER IX

FAMILY

THE NEW FAMILY

ABUSES of the new freedom in sex and marital life have been rampant in Russia. Court records shriek with them. So do news columns and editorials in the daily press and resolutions of Party and Soviet conferences. In several cities men have told me of abuses to which they are subject which are truly novel. Servant girls who find themselves with babies on their hands often fix responsibility for fatherhood on the men who employ them, and only because, if the girls win, they obtain a higher allowance from their employers than from the guilty parties, who may be only proletarians. That is why men prefer older women as servants. They may be spies of the dreaded GPU, but they cannot set alimony traps for them.

Now and again a woman will bring suit against a man for the support of a child, and the man will prove by reliable witnesses that other men have had associations with her, and that under no circumstances can he be considered the true father of the child. The court, baffled by the testimony adduced, will often make all the men charged with guilt shoulder the burden of supporting the child, and thus inadvertently foist on it a multiple father or fatherhood. There are women in Russia who make a practice of inveigling high-salaried men into cohabitation so that they can receive fat allowances for the child, and when they have snared several such men, they are assured of a good income and their worries are over. There are men in Russia who marry and get divorced more often than they buy a new suit of clothes. I met such a man once in the South, and he confessed that he had been wedded and divorced a dozen times and he had not yet attained his thirty-first birthday. Last year a man was tried in a Russian city for his failure to pay alimony to the three wives he had divorced, each of whom had a baby. When he appeared before the court he frankly stated that he had quit working for the simple reason that if he was to pay one third of his income to each of his former three wives he would have nothing left for himself. Why then, he asked, should he be working at all? He had not learned that the law allowed him half of his earnings, no matter how many women and children might be entitled to alimony from him.

Indeed, this attempt to reforge sex morality and family relations, not with palliatives but with a drastic discard of old standards and old sanctities, old fears and old shames, old restraints and old taboos, has whirled to the surface of Russian life a host of monstrosities. Tragedy and travesty follow hard on one another, and darken more often than they illumine the inner nature of man.

There are forces in Russia incident to our time and to the past of the race that severely aggravate the possibility for abuse. There was the war, and the Revolution, more destructive to inner composure than the war, especially as it was accompanied by a deathly famine. The pressure was too severe. There is also the quality of the human soil on which the new agonies and new ideas, the new freedom and new audacities have fallen — this mass of dark-minded Russian humanity, held for ages in cruel ignorance, and only now acquiring a sense of self-esteem and social responsibility. Who can estimate the amount of evil-doing that is a sheer outpouring of the innate beastliness of the Russian, especially the muzhik, this magnificent savage who can sing and dance and wail and plead with an abandon that rouses hope and ecstasy, and who can wreck and murder with a frenzy that stirs now terror, and now despair?

Meanwhile the old roots of the family have been violently shaken and in places plucked up. True, the weight of the ages still presses on it, especially in the village. But how long will it continue to do so? What of the future? I am not speaking of that distant future of which the Communists dream, when, with the triumph of communism, the family will, at best, constitute only a mere cell of the new society with but a feeble independent existence. That time may never come. Yet something new and stupendous is destined to happen to the family in Russia, is already happening to it, communism or no communism. Marriage certainly is ceasing to have any sanctity or even any vital significance. In a legal sense it hardly exists at all, and this condition would not change appreciably even if registration of unions were made compulsory again. It could not change so long as mating and separation are unbound by any hindrances.

If the Russian family is to persist it must do so in spite of the decay of marriage, and in spite of the host of other disruptive forces discussed in preceding chapters. It must hold together primarily through the bond of love between men and women and this bond, the Communists assure themselves, will gain in firmness when property has passed from private to social control. Only then, argue they, will the process of selection be purged of economic considerations which now so often debauch and subvert true love.

Given utter freedom of selection, and their system of social control and education, men and women, they maintain, will be living in worlds that do not mutually exclude one another as so often happens now. They will attain a more rational form of love than the world has ever known, for they will be drawn to each other not by mere physiological, but by a host of historic, intellectual, social and personal bonds of sympathy. There may be less sentiment in such a love, though that is not at all certain, but there will be more comradeship, more sheer human good fellowship. Since both men and women will be economically independent, irritations due to money demands will vanish. Likewise, since household cares, including the rearing of children, will be largely lifted from women, annoyances arising from this source will also wane. In other words, in their society, the Russians say, there will be a series of new conditions which, they are certain, will intensify the feeling of attachment of men and women for one another. Temptations for fresh liaisons will not disappear, not as long as men and women are creatures of impulse, and victims of flitting surges of emotion. But that does not disturb the Russians. Let men and women, they submit, sunder their associations. The essential thing is to protect the child and the woman against economic, social, and other forms of ill-usage and discomfort. As for the rest, anything is better than forced or involuntary maintenance of partnerships.

For the present, despite removal of a host of ancient pillars of support, the family in Russia has not fallen into ruins. Even divorce has not reached alarming proportions, save in Moscow and a few other cities where political tension, high prices, housing shortage, have unnerved people, made them severely irritable and thereby swelled divorce records. According to the statistical data I have obtained in the Central Statistical Bureau, in European Russia, where live one hundred and fifteen million people, and where divorce is most marked, there were in 1926 only 1.6 divorces to every ten marriages. This does not take into account the unregistered separations nor of course the unregistered marriages.

But divorce to the Russian does not imply family break-up, and for the simple reason that divorced people do remate, sometimes even with each other, and establish new families. Indeed, men of science assure us, now with bare facts and figures, and now with bursts of eloquent rhetoric, that whatever the structure of human society, the family, though changing in form, must always persist. "Love and the whole family," says L. T. Hobhouse, "have an instinctive basis, that is to say, they rest upon tendencies inherited within brain and nerve." Havelock Ellis repeats the same thought in his most recent pronouncement on the family. "Its existence," says he, "may even be said to be woven into the texture of the species."

On the face of it these pronouncements seem beyond

dispute. As long as men and women thrill to each other's presence and reach out for each other's companionship and affection, they will enter into unions and maintain some kind of family. Love, after all, implies privacy — an individual place of residence and a sundering from the outside society. Besides, there are occasions when man wants to be away from the madding crowd, when he yearns to retire into himself, into his own little nook to take counsel with his own soul, and with those in intimate touch with him. His parental instinct likewise will continue to make its demands. These innate urges or tendencies in man will of themselves create a need for occasional segregation from the outside world — that is for family life.

The Russian family then will be a union of lovers, with a place for them to give to each other the joys that love affords. This place will be a home. It will be a small place — big homes or large apartments are impossible in the new Russian society. Husband and wife may be living together constantly or may separate from each other for more or less lengthy intervals. Their children may stay with them nights and during the days of their leisure, or may come only for occasional visits. For the rest of their life husband and wife will look to the outside society. They will, of course, have utter freedom of movement, limited only by their regard for each other's wishes and feelings. In all of their relations with each other they will be governed chiefly, not by their objective, but by their subjective dependence on each other.

Such is to be the family in Russia. Such it is already in process of becoming, outside of the village, and especially in the industrial community. The family is no longer a sanctuary, a little kingdom, a whole world of its own, wrapped up in itself, its exclusive joys and sorrows, its own profits and comforts, and sundered from outside society by a formidable array of fortifications. It has lost its physical and geographic importance, and it is being continually stripped of social functions and spiritual stimulations. The family is persisting in Russia, but it is in the process of becoming a mere shadow or skeleton of the old family!

PART II

PEOPLE

CHAPTER X

PEASANT

ON my first trip to Russia since the Revolution, soon after my arrival in the country, I happened to be spending a week-end in a village off the banks of the Volga. A backward village it was, surrounded by rivers of mud, isolated it seemed from the outside world, and from all possible contact with the surge of thought and emotion that the Revolution had unleashed. On Sunday the chairman of the local Soviet called a mass-meeting. He had sent word around the countryside that an *inostranetz* (foreigner) would be present and urged everybody to come. Come they did, despite mud and rain, on foot and in cart, youths and bearded old men, girls and grandmothers. Glowing with pride the youthful chairman proceeded to expatiate for my benefit on the achievements of the local administration, and on its ambitious plans for the future. He was a fervent orator, and the crowd listened with rapt interest as Russians always do to a good speaker.

Of a sudden somewhere from the fringe of the audience there boomed out a deep voice as startling as a thunderclap. " Words, words, words, only words! " It was an elderly muzhik speaking. Barefooted, bare-headed, with a flowing beard and in a soiled linen shirt, he raised his arms high as though to quiet the murmur of protest that his interruption had called forth. " All for the benefit of the foreign visitor," he drawled

mockingly. " Showing off. Look at me, *inostranetz*,"
and he pounded his fists on his bulging chest, " I am
the truth, the sole putrid truth in this beastly land."
Denunciations hailed on him from every direction but
he paid no heed to them. " I am sixty-five years of age.
The Soviets did give me land, but what shall I do with
it? Can I eat land? Can I? I have no horse and what
can I do on land without a horse? " The chairman himself and several of his associates sought to quiet him
but he raced on unperturbed. " In the old days," he
shouted, raising his voice above the tumult that had
broken out, " we had a Czar, landlords, exploiters, and
yet I could always buy a horse if mine died, and boots
too, and all the calico I could pay for. And now there is
no Czar, there are no landlords, there are no exploiters,
and yet — no horse, no boots, no calico, nothing. Remember that, stranger."

I stared at the muzhik, at the disturbed chairman,
at the heaving mob. It seemed so unbelievable that
anyone in Russia would dare lift his voice in such
haughty disdain, in such flaming defiance of the proletarian dictators — least of all a muzhik. I remembered
him so well in the old days, this lowly miserable creature of a muzhik! How meek he seemed in the presence
of officials. How humbly he would bow before a man
in a uniform, or sometimes only in city clothes. With
what alacrity he would remove his hat before anyone
he deemed his superior. Shy he was, this unwashed,
hairy, big-boned muzhik, and cautious in his choice of
words, in voicing a grievance, lest he give offence to
the man representing *pravitelstvo* — government, —
and when he noted in the expression of the official's

face a sign of annoyance or disapproval he shrank
back, apologized, begged for forgiveness. In his heart
he may have cherished only hate for the official, but
when face to face with him he was all meekness and
docility.

But now in this desolate village I witnessed the
extraordinary spectacle of a bedraggled, mud-spattered
muzhik, actually denouncing and haranguing officials
— all government — with no more restraint or compunction than as if he were scolding his son or whipping his horse! It seemed so terribly unreal, so unbe-
lievably heroic!

At first I thought that this was just an exceptional
outburst of fury, a dash of gall on a surging billow of
despair. But further experiences in villages dispelled
the supposition swiftly enough. It was the same everywhere I travelled. On trains, on highways, in market
places, in Soviet offices, everywhere, I heard the muzhik thunder his laments and protests with a violence
and an abandon that was almost terrifying. It seemed
as if the Revolution had unlocked not only his mouth
but his heart, and all the wrath and anguish that had
gathered there in the ages was boiling out of him in
hot and fierce torrents. He seemed a law unto himself,
this ageless and unaging muzhik, a fact all his own, the
most startling and the most meaningful in the land of
the Soviets, if not in the world!

It would be impossible to overestimate the significance of this burst of audacity in the peasant. It implies
many things, chief of all an awareness of self which
was alien to him in the pre-revolutionary era. Clearly
the Revolution has been blasting his passivity

out of him and battering him into a pride, a self-respect, a dignity which he never had manifested in the old days. Yes, the peasant is conscious now of being somebody, not merely *a* soul, as he was for statistical purposes labelled in former times, a blank impersonal object, but a man, an individual *with* a soul and a personality all his own. The peasant has discovered himself.

He could hardly have done otherwise. The Revolution had made him the hero in the village. It had elevated him as much as the proletarian into a symbol of a new glory and a new day. At every step he was assured and reassured with fiery vehemence that he was the equal of everybody, aye more, the superior of the men who had ruled over him. He, toiler and producer, was vaunted as the pick and king of men, the salt of the earth, the flower of the human race, entitled as no one else to all its joys and blessings. From all directions flatteries, appreciations, sublimations hailed on him and soaked into him like rain into parched soil.

Besides, for the first time in history he has actually been a conqueror. He has triumphed over the landlord. He has become the possessor of the earth. Rivers, forests, lakes, meadows, pastures, wheat-lands, rye-fields — all these have been wrested from the landlord, and the landlord himself, once so formidable and all powerful, has been banished from the scene. Not a shadow of him has remained to darken the landscape, to remind a new generation of his former power and glory. He the muzhik has become sole lord of the countryside. True, officials and Party men are seeking to squeeze

him into a new social mold — are scolding and harass-
ing him and levelling new burdens on him, but after
all he is the supreme figure on the land. It is his now.
There is no one else left to dispute his right to it. There
is no one lying in ambush to hurtle him out of his new
possession. A complete victory this has been over an
ancient foe, and the consciousness of triumph has only
heightened his estimate of himself.

The rise of a new self-esteem in the peasant has had
far-reaching consequences. It has helped kill his ancient dread of government. He no longer regards government with the terror and dismay of the old days.
It is no longer an invincible force, above and aloof
and beyond human control. Now government is something earthly, close to life, his life, his village, his everyday burdens and needs, something that will and must
yield to pressure, his pressure. Now he can reach out
with his hand and touch it in the very flesh, shake it,
aye, slap it in the face.

The changed structure and forms of government have
only accentuated his sense of nearness and familiarity
with government. Gone are its external trappings, vanished is its external glitter. It has become a very simple,
informal affair, like the village cooperative, the village
mass-meeting. Men in government no longer wear
gaudy and awe-inspiring uniforms and seldom, save
for the police, do they bear arms. In the villages they
dress like muzhiks, talk like muzhiks, live like muzhiks.
They are mainly muzhiks. There is nothing about them,
their appearance, their manner, to command special
recognition, respect, fear. Nor do they have to be ad-
dressed as Your Lordship, Your Gloriousness, Your

Highness, not even as Mister, neither the local chairman of the Soviet nor of the highest Soviet in the province, nor anyone anywhere. They are all now *grazhdanin* — citizen, just like any muzhik, any layman. Government dwells no longer above, in some mysterious and awesome haze, but below, right on this earth, at one's very feet and it can even be stepped upon. One only has to enter a village Soviet and note the ease, the frankness, sometimes the violence, with which the peasant addresses officials to realize how utterly lacking he is in that mystic dread of government which in the old days was so conspicuous and pathetic a part of him.

Unafraid of authority and aware of his own individuality, the peasant has become the most demanding individual in Russia. The " fruits of the Revolution," which he had so long and so eloquently been promised he now wants to enjoy, and not at all vicariously. In some instances his standard of living has risen appreciably since the advent of the new regime or rather since its stabilization. The peasant simply does not take to market as readily as he once did his eggs and butter, his ham and cheese or even his rye and wheat, much to the consternation of Communist leaders. He has no special inducement to dispose of these products. He cannot obtain payment in gold since its circulation is prohibited and paper money, even the *chervonetz*, does not interest him — not now at any rate, though thus far it has bravely weathered the storms that have threatened to toss it into disuse. Besides, owing to the never-ending disparity in prices between farm products and manufactured goods he re-

ceives little in return for his produce. Why then should he sell?

Nor has he any real inducement to save money. Land-hungry, he would in the old days put away every copeck he could lay his hands on for the purchase of an additional strip of land. Land was by far the most consuming passion of his life. Now he can buy no land. None is on sale. Of course he could buy another horse or cow. But then he would run the risk of being labelled a *kulak* and invite on himself a fresh swing of the tax-gatherer's axe. So instead of taking to market as much as he can spare of his products, he sells as little as he must and consumes more himself. That is why, save when he suffers from a crop failure, the peasant is the best nourished individual in Russia.

In one other respect has the life of the peasant grown richer. He has a more abundant variety of social diversions than he ever had in the old days. Theatricals, for example, were scarcely known in the Russian village in the pre-revolutionary times. They are widespread now. Wherever there is a village with a schoolhouse there one is likely to find a little theatre. In villages far removed from centers of civilization I came on clubhouses equipped with extraordinary stage paraphernalia. I witnessed once in a village the performance of Gorki's " Children of the Sun " in which all actors were ordinary muzhiks, two of them utterly illiterate, and it was a most creditable performance. Amateur theatricals are an outstanding contribution of the Revolution to the village. So are motion pictures, radios (loud speakers) in the public squares. So are clubhouses, reading halls, parades, picnics, sport carnivals.

But the peasant is reaching out for more than an additional mouthful of bread and an occasional laugh. He wants boots, as he never wanted them in all his history. He is growing weary of his bark-sandals. He has an eye on city-made clothes which have always been a mark of distinction in the village. He is demanding textiles as he never had in the pre-revolutionary times. He wants to rebuild his houses, his barns, his wagons. He has seen pictures of new agricultural implements and has heard lecturers tell him so much of their benefits that he wants them. Hedonist and materialist that he is, he wants to live in full his everyday life. He wants to, but he cannot.

Soviet plants do not churn out goods in sufficient quantities to meet his demand, and because of financial stringency the government is importing insignificant amounts of such goods. It promises the peasant eventual satisfaction of his needs. It pleads with him to be patient and wait until new factories have been erected and put into operation. It almost supplicates him to forget present deprivations and wait until its industrialization program has been realized. But the peasant never did and does not now think in futures. Eventually means nothing to him. He was promised cheap goods, lots of it — nails, iron, steel, dry-goods, implements, and he wants the promise fulfilled at least in part. He does not understand and does not really want to understand the reason for this cruel shortage of goods — goods which in the days of the *pomieshtchiks* and the Czar he could always buy if he had the price. Now everywhere endless quest, and sometimes, after hours of patient waiting, yes even in rain and mud and snow, a clerk will step forth with the announcement that nothing more is left in the cooperative, not a yard of calico, not a nail, not a bolt! And so he roars with rage.

Time will only continue to fan the new consciousness of the peasant and spur him into ever-increasing self-assertiveness and make him constantly more demanding. It cannot be otherwise. The stage in Russia is set for just such a result. Paradoxically enough, forces fostered by the Communists themselves are contributing toward this epochal end. Harsh, for example, as is the proletarian dictatorship, within its own limits it allows the peasant an astonishing measure of political self-expression. The Communists are in fact seeking with all the resources at their command to expand the peasant's political consciousness. Through lectures, motion pictures, posters, pageants, theatricals, above all through the pre-election campaigns they are seeking to cultivate his understanding and his capacity for political action.

At one time they rode rough-shod over village elections, whether to the Soviets or the cooperatives. They would present their own nominee to the peasant, and by the simple expedient of asking the assembled voters who opposed their man, would put him into office. The peasant did not know what to make of such a procedure. He sickened of elections and stayed away from them. The Communists were perplexed. Some of them grew alarmed. The peasant was slumping into his old apathy. He was nourishing his ancient hostility to government. That was dangerous. They remembered Lenine's words that the Revolution will be a failure if

the masses, including kitchen-maids, did not learn
and did not exercise the functions if not the prerogatives of government. So they changed front. Since 1924
they have been permitting the peasant to make his own
nominations and to indulge in all the discussion, violent
and vituperative, that he chooses. Of course they are
still vigilant. They are still not averse to exercising
pressure — but through indirect channels, usually by
organizing the poorer peasantry and pitting them
against the group they wish to defeat or discipline.
Over-zealous Communists do occasionally bring into
play their old dictatorial methods. I have been in villages where they have done so. But if the peasant lodges
a complaint against such imposition, the elections are
nullified, new ones are ordered, and the over-ardent
Partymen do not always go unrebuked. Sometimes they
are severely disciplined.

Nowhere however can one observe the budding of
the new political consciousness, of the new personality
in the peasant as at the *skhod* (mass-meeting). There
the face and the mind of the muzhik in all their lights
and shadows lie as if reflected in a mirror. What a
mighty institution it is, this ancient and turbulent
skhod, as ancient as peasant society itself and far more
formidable! In the old days it was mostly an anarchic
assemblage, usually without a chairman, with discussions unregulated, with men talking as and when they
pleased, one at a time, many at a time, all at once. Often
it would end in a free-for-all brawl with men leaping
at one another to settle problems and weather grievances with rocklike fists. Women were barred from
participation. Now the *skhod* has been largely purged

of its wonted chaos. There is always a chairman present who seeks to observe the amenities of good behavior, and women are admitted on the same basis as
men.

In importance the *skhod* transcends every other institution in the village. It is a barometer of peasant disposition. It is there that the peasants, young and old,
unfold themselves in all their primitive amplitude and
with all their elemental earnestness and passion. It is
there one hears words, so stern and audacious, that one
actually forgets the dictatorship and the GPU and all
the other agencies of repression which have cast such a
pall of gloom over the Russian city. It is there that the
peasant uncovers not only his mind but his soul, for
the whole world to see, to judge and perhaps to beware.
It is there that one sees the emergence of a new man,
on the Russian scene, a man of unmeasured proportions,
with untried powers, yet with a new fervor, a new
hope, a new insolence, above all a new determination to
make himself heard and heeded.

A people's tribune, a school, a court, above all a
battle-ground of ideas and viewpoints — such is the
village *skhod!*

Simultaneously with this political awakening and
partly as a result of it, the peasant is also undergoing
a virile intellectual ferment. Never before has he seemed
so eager to know the world about him and his own
relation to it. I do not recall a single visit I made to a
village, whether in European or Asiatic Russia, but no
sooner would my presence become known than I was
surrounded by mobs of muzhiks, especially youths,
teeming with curiosity and deluging me with endless

queries as to life and work, ideas and ideals in the outside world. Wherever I went these mobs would follow me as if eager to catch every word that passed between me and the men and women I would interview.

The World War and even more the Revolution has cloven open the peasant's mind and stocked it with a fund of ideas, which has only whetted his curiosity for more and more knowledge. Through a host of visible and invisible channels new information on a host of subjects — hygiene, scientific agriculture, geology, and of course Marxism, keep pouring into the village. Newspapers and books come there regularly now. Soldiers are constantly returning from the army bringing with them tales of their experiences, their adventures, their learnings. Posters, flamboyant and expressive, convey their special messages. So do motion pictures, and lecturers keep circulating through the villages almost as freely as fish in a pond. Then there are those endless peasant delegations going off to some city or to the capital on prolonged excursions. Guests of the national government, a trade union or a factory, they visit museums, universities, industrial plants, theatres, exhibitions, parks, carnivals and other show places, always accompanied by loquacious guides, and on their return home they have stories of their own, packed with fresh information, to tell to their neighbors. New schools are also springing up in the villages. However inadequately equipped or incompetently manned they do offer some education, even if rudimentary, to about one half of the peasant children. And peasant boys and girls are greedy to learn. In every village there are youths who pore assiduously over books in the hope of some day going to the university. Its doors are now wide open to the muzhik and he makes up at least one fifth of the students in the higher institutions of learning, in itself an unheard of event in Russian history. Indeed, the peasant is developing his own intelligentsia, out of which may come a new peasant leadership. Who can tell what will happen in Russia when this leadership becomes of age? For example, will it tolerate the amusing spectacle of three million industrial workers outvoting one hundred and twenty million peasants in national elections?

The village roars with new thoughts and new ideas — political, social, economic and also moral. I am not using the word moral in an emotional sense only, though in this respect changes likewise have been in evidence. Never a puritan the peasant — man and woman — has always been outspoken on the subject of sex. Men have demanded virginity in their brides even as they have demanded dowries, though the single standard of morality never was as deeply intrenched among them as among townfolk. Public opinion visited opprobrium on men who indulged in irregularities almost as much as on women. It is with reference to morality in its larger sense as applied to man's everyday behavior, his relations to his fellow men and to the outside world that the change is especially significant.

Sadly enough did the peasant need a shaking up of this morality. Profane and inebriate he had never made truth-telling a virtue. He lied to escape taxes, fines, floggings, jailings. He lied to the official, to the landlord. He lied to his neighbor. He lied when he sold. He lied when he bought. He lied when he courted a bride, he lied when he married her. If he could cheat a buyer in the market place — well and good. His conscience remained unperturbed. The market place belonged to the outside world which was alien to him, his enemy, and which he always regarded with suspicion and sometimes with acrimony. I told once a group of university students that in America people very often leave their letters and parcels on the outside of a letter-box and no one bothers to steal them. They would not believe it. It seemed so utterly incredible to them that people anywhere could be so honest! A university student on reading once in a report that in Denmark no one steals the milk cans that farmers leave on stands on the highways for the trucks to gather, wrote to a newspaper saying that he had read much fiction in his young life and this story about Denmark was about as true as the tales of Jules Verne and Captain Maine Read!

I was once on a drive with the manager of one of the largest government sugar-farms in the Ukraine. As we were passing villages and fields, we saw little straw tents in gardens, orchards, melon-patches. Guards stayed in these, especially at night, to watch for thieves. My companion asked me if in America it was equally necessary to have guards and dogs in gardens and orchards. When I told him that, as far as I knew, it was not, he was beside himself with surprise. He could hardly believe me. How was it possible, he asked? Did not neighbors steal all the vegetables and fruit? Were people really so honest in America? Later, on our arrival at his home, he gathered all of his foremen and managers and other associates, introduced me to them and, with the fervor of a man who had made an epoch-making discovery, informed them that in America farmers did not guard their gardens and orchards and people did not steal from one another. They, too, regarded the statement as incredible. How was it possible? Why were folk so honest on American farms? Why were Russians such thieves? Beastly Russians!

Keeping track of my baggage was my biggest problem when I travelled on Russian trains. It is unsafe to leave anything unguarded in one's seat, even for a brief enough period to buy a newspaper or an apple from a peddler at a station. I have never been on a train in Russia or in a depot or on a boat where there were no robberies. I never dared lie down for the night on my bunk without first buckling to my arm a chain attached to my typewriter and suitcase so as to be jerked into wakefulness in the event of an attempt to haul them off. . . .

The muzhik somehow had never learned to cherish regard for the rights and possessions of others. Kind, hospitable, eloquent, song-loving, he has a streak of depravity in him. He is not a bandit, but he is a petty thief. Oddly enough he himself will be the last person in the world to deny this charge. How often have I heard older peasants proclaim in the open with the passion for self-chastisement which in old Russia was a habit, almost a virtue, that the muzhik is after all the beastliest of men!

The revolutionary leaders however are making strenuous efforts to wean him from his ancient vices. They are seeking to inculcate into him a new morality. They are preaching to him the virtues of truth-telling, honesty, respect for the rights of others. They have laws in Russia now prohibiting parents from whipping their children and men from beating up their wives. Let a peasant while on a visit to a Soviet office engage in profane language or spit on the floor and someone will jump up and deliver a lecture on the impropriety and indecency of the practice. Again and again, as I watched young peasant leaders in Soviet offices explain to mu-zhiks the errors of their ways and their manners I had the illusion that I was in a kindergarten where grown men and women were taught not world revolution or Marxism, or even (alas!) the villainies of British diplomats, but the sheer fundamentals of human decency.

Yet nothing else that has happened since the coming of the Soviets is of such staggering significance to the peasant and to Russia as is the movement of collective farming. The phrase has an academic ring, but the movement is anything but academic. It is a stormy real-ity, more upsetting to established ways of life and thought, more shattering to the structure of peasant society and to the civilization of old Russia than any-thing that the Bolsheviks have yet undertaken. Its effects on fundamental institutions — religion, morality, family, home and on relations of man to man, man to society, man and woman toward each other and even of Russia to the outside world, — are beyond calculation.

The very suddenness and magnitude of the movement are breath-taking. In the summer of 1928 I attended a meeting in the Moscow Peasant Home of writers who were to start for villages to make studies of collective farming. At that time no more than two per cent of the peasantry had been drawn into the scheme, and the meeting was called to whip up the enthusiasm of the writers so that through their reports they would help rouse public sentiment in its favor. Impassioned speeches were delivered. Cocksure prophecies were made. But there was little genuine enthusiasm. Writer after writer with whom I discussed the prospects of the venture was in a skeptical mood. Peasants who were staying in the Moscow Home and dropped in on the meeting laughed at it as at some silly caper of a spoiled child.

Yet only a year later in June 1929 more than one million peasant households had been merged into collective farms. By February, 1930, about one-third of such households were absorbed. The movement is sweeping the land like a prairie fire on and on over fresh and ever increasing areas.

Let not the reader conclude from the extent of the movement that the peasant is flocking to it of his own accord. Were the project left to him for decision he would bury it with loud acclaim. He is essentially an individualist, accustomed to land of his own, a horse of his own, a cow of his own, a way of his own. Age-old tradition and all-pervading everyday contacts have inculcated this individualism in him. But the *kolkhoz* or collective farm implies the abandonment of individualism. The mass of peasants therefore do not like it. I have met peasants again and again living in the vicinity of a successful *kolkhoz*, who if left to themselves would not readily part from individual land-holding. Never in all my wanderings in Russian villages have I heard so much expression of doubt, of alarm, of disappointment, so much prophecy of doom as in the summer of 1929, when the new movement had attained sweeping proportions. Older muzhiks are frantic with dismay and wrath. They see in the *kolkhoz* almost the end of the world. The whole thing is so new, so contrary to all their experiences, habits, aims, ambitions, all that they had ever heard or dreamed of.

Viewed objectively, however, the scheme, though without parallel in history, is not without economic merit. It has had its birth in political theory, but it is being nurtured in economic necessity. Russian agriculture has come to a sharp crisis. With the arrival of the Soviets the estates of landlords were divided and the holdings of *kulacks* — well-to-do peasants — were cut up. Landless peasants got land, and peasants with small allotments had their acreage increased. Young people, especially women, under the spur of the new freedom rebelled against the custom of living with father-in-law, which led to further land divisions. Between 1917 and 1929 the number of individual farms in Russia increased from seventeen to twenty-five millions, and the area of the average farm dropped to from twelve to fourteen acres.

This process of parcellization under Russian conditions carried with it disastrous consequences. Eight million acres of fine land were rendered nonproductive — used up by the new farms for the buildings and yards. In Russia also one parcel of land is separated from another by a ridge or furrow and the combined area of these, if properly worked, so a Russian economist reckons, would yield enough grain to supply half the need of the cities. Peasant stock — swine, cattle, horses, sheep — are of inferior breeds and under a system of millions of small and ever-diminishing land-holdings, scattered over vast territories with wretched transpor-- tation facilities, it is difficult to improve these. No more is it easy, in spite of constant agitation, to introduce on a nationwide scale proper rotation of crops, machinery, select seeds, fertilization and other features of scientific farming. Then, because of the policies of the Soviets, taxation of peasants with surplus produce, inability to supply the village with manufactured goods, interfer- ence with the sale of grain to private dealers, the peas- ant began to cut down his grain-sown acreage and his livestock. According to a report in the *Izvestia* of Sep- tember 22, 1929, between 1926 and 1929 there was a de- cline of ten million cattle, fifteen million swine, seven million sheep. Production, therefore, of meat and bread, the two staples in the Russian diet, had slumped heavily. The export of grain had ceased. The city was receiving food in ever-diminishing quantities. Hunger was thrusting its shadow over the town.

To avert a catastrophe the Communists proceeded to make forcible collections of grain as in the period of the civil war, only now they paid regular prices. The peas- ant grew alarmed. Had not he been promised at the time of the coming of the *nep,* that never again would his produce be forcibly taken from him? What was hap- pening? What was becoming of all this talk of *smychka* — union — between city and village? He protested. He shrieked defiance. He hurried delegations to Kalinin, Rykov and others in Moscow who would listen to his pleas. He deluged his sons in the army with letters de-- nouncing grain collections and urging them to bring

these to the attention of the military authorities. Russia
heaved with unrest, under the spur of which the Communists hastened to halt collections of grain and to issue
assurances to the peasant that these would never again
be repeated.

But the fundamental difficulty remained unsolved.
There was enough bread on hand to last until the next
harvest. And then what? How could the peasant be
made to increase his grain acreage and to sell his surplus to the state at its own fixed prices? Appeals to his
social consciousness were futile. He laughed at such appeals. He was surly and recalcitrant. He regarded himself the victim of a great wrong. What could the Communists do to placate him, to bring him to terms? He
was a mighty force and he was fighting the Revolution
with weapons which the revolutionaries could not
match. And there was no time to lose. The town had to
be assured of bread. Action swift, decisive, drastic, had
to be taken, and so the fifteenth Communist congress
resolved that collective farming was the only way out
of the dilemma.

It was an audacious decision, a stupendous gamble!
Those of us who were in Russia at the time waited with
bated breath for developments. The mass of the people
had no confidence in the new scheme. They were afraid
of the muzhik, this hard-headed century-old individualist with his deep-rooted urge for private property and
his newly acquired spirit of independence. Would he
submit without a battle? If not what would happen?
What would the army do, made up as it was mainly
of peasants? Of course if opposition proved threatening
the Communists could always retreat, but if so what

would happen to their fantastic social program and to their grandiose scheme of industrializing the land? Would the Revolution move forward to the left or backward to the right? Russia was seething with rumor, excitement, speculation.

The Communists, however, once they came to a decision proceeded to translate it into action. It was a question of life and death and they would take no chances. There was no time to lose. They loosened a flow of fresh energies into the village — the best they commanded. The peasant gave vent to violent laments and protests. Now and then he killed an organizer, set a Soviet building on fire. But he indulged in no mass rebellion. There were no mob uprisings.

Of course the method of approach is calculated to beat down resistance. An organizer comes to a village and calls a mass-meeting. Always eager to hear something new from an outside visitor the peasant turns out *en masse*. Often, however, if he knows beforehand that the purpose of the meeting is launching of a *kolkhoz* he will stay away. I was once with an organizer in a village where mass-meetings were called seven times and only the youth of the community turned out. The organizer had to resort to shrewd tactics to bring the older people together.

It is always this way. When the peasants assemble the organizer proceeds to " sell " to them the idea of collectivization. He assures them that if they pool their resources in land and in energy, human and animal, the government will help them with tractors and other machinery, with seeds, expert advice, new houses, new barns, bath-houses, nurseries, children's homes, full-blooded stock, radios, medical service, club-houses, schools. Debates follow for days, weeks, months. Finally volunteers are called for. The first ones are the hardest to recruit, but the more the peasant thinks of what is in store for him, if he remains an individual farmer, the more likely he is to join the *kolkhoz*. With the new laws and policies in force he cannot help realizing that the odds are heavily against success in individual farming. The moment he shows signs of prosperity the tax-gatherer's axe falls heavily on him and so does the wrath of the Communist rulers. He is in fact constantly warned that if he engages in sabotage against their policies, if he withholds grain from the market; sells it to private dealers at inflated prices; practices any form of exploitation, hires labor — except in time of sickness or some other unforeseen misfortune — for more than a certain number of days; lends grain, fodder, money to a neighbor on interest however low; rents a strip of land from someone, or does anything else which may be construed as exploitation — a most elastic word in Russia — he need expect no mercy. The law will crush him, confiscate his property, shut the doors of high schools and colleges to his children, bar them even from jobs in factories.

In village after village I have seen these benighted kulacks, stripped of possessions, ostracized politically, damned socially. They are alone in the world, marked men, with the badge of shame pinned to their very brows, with no friends to take their part, with no power to bring back the old holdings and the old standing in the community. They cry and storm defiance. But neither their tears nor their curses avail them. The Communists do not want a successful individual farmer, and if such a farmer falls within the category of a kulack they are determined to exterminate him. He may be a good manager, a man of enterprise and initiative, but as long as he exercises his talents for his own benefit, for the benefit of individualism, he is a great danger, a great enemy and must be wiped out.

Are not the Communists pushing the *kolkhoz* too strenuously? Do not they run the risk of rousing too much hostility in the village? Is there not real danger of mass-uprisings of the more well-to-do individual farmers? Have the Soviets the economic resources adequately to provide the new farms with machinery, seeds, stock? Where will they recruit the armies of leaders — mechanics, engineers, agricultural experts, social workers, political guides? Moreover, collectivization is making a proletarian out of the peasant (though the Communists insist they are converting him merely into a free laboring citizen). He will have the same economic and social status as the city proletarian. May it not be that in time with his increasing political power and his amazing new organization, he will pit himself against the city worker and wrest supremacy from him? These and other questions beat incessantly at the mind of the outside spectator of this amazing Russian drama. But the Communists are not bothered. They think of aims and not of difficulties. Collectivization offers them the one opportunity to industrialize agriculture and once for all to remove the question of food for export and for home consumption from their catalogue of worries. Besides, the realization of the scheme carries with it death to private property in the village, to religion, to the old individualistic family and to a host of other bulwarks of the old civilization. It clears the road to the Communist millennium.

The recent abatement in the collectivization crusade is decisive evidence that the Communists have come to appreciate the dangers of too rapid and too reckless a process of change. They seem resolved not to be as disregardful of peasant sensibilities and peasant social aims and customs as they were wont to be, and to allow him time and opportunity to achieve the momentous shift of position with some degree of immediate satisfaction to himself. But they have not abandoned the idea itself nor even its pursuit. They are merely planning to be more cautious and more sure of their social bearings. Indeed, they can no more unscramble the collectivization movement than they can dissolve their Soviets. To push the millions of peasants already sucked into it back to individualistic land-holding would be almost suicidal.

Meanwhile peasant Russia is seething with perplexity and expectation.

CHAPTER XI

PROLETARIAN

CONSIDER the Russian proletarian as he was in pre-revolutionary days. At best he was only briefly removed from the village. Often he was merely a half peasant spending only his winter in the city and in summer returning to his land. He smelled of the soil, and he never loved the city. He was in it but not of it. His voice did not count. His needs were neglected. He was the dweller of the slums, the step-son of civilization. The world of culture — opera, ballets, art theatres, museums, universities, were not for him. Still mere contact with the city had made him more individualized than the muzhik, more worldly, more decisive and often offered him the opportunity to become literate.

He was an elementary man of simple tastes, simple thoughts, simple manners, and he was not overly diligent. You saw him at work in a shop or factory and you perceived instantly why it was that Russia had given birth to such sayings as " work loves a fool," " work is no wolf, it will not run away to the woods." He had not the German or Swedish workingman's ingrained sense of duty or honesty. He dallied when he could. He loafed when he dared.

Vodka was one of his greatest joys. You visited the taverns or you walked through the streets in the proletarian districts in the evening, on a Sunday or holiday and you saw men everywhere reeling and tumbling from intoxication. Possessed of more ready cash than the peasant and always within easy reach of a tavern or a government vodka shop, the proletarian imbibed more profusely than did the muzhik. Alcoholism was as much, if not more, a disease with him as it was with the peasant.

He was a desperate fellow always. He asked for no quarter and gave none. He never shrank from battle, and when he fought he hit above the belt, below the belt, he scratched, he bit, he kicked. He fought to hurt, to bleed, to overpower. He followed no rules save those of his immediate wrath, and he could receive blows as well as deal them. Down on the ground, face scratched, clothes tattered, gasping with impotence, he would not admit defeat and would not plead for mercy. He was a Gibraltar for punishment.

Proletarianism was not an ideal with him, yet it was his life destiny. Seldom did he seek deliverance from his job in an enterprise of his own. Seldom could he find the opportunity for such deliverance. If he did save money it was for the purpose of investing it in a little house or in a strip of land somewhere in a suburb. Less than any other proletarian in Europe was he actuated by a hope to be his own master at some future time. His job was his life and his life swerved round his job.

He was a man without political experience. He lived under a burden of disabilities which prevented the acquisition of such experience and the development of political acumen. Not only his lack of education, but his social antecedents militated against his rise to prominence in political life. He could be an *uriadnik* —

constable — in a small town or a policeman or some other minor official. Hardly anything higher. Through the revolutionary propaganda disseminated in his midst he learned more than a peasant of the importance of political action, but his experience was no greater and he had a peasant's innate hostility toward all government.

He was, it is clear, a man without background, without culture, without breeding, without political experience, without a social tradition and with a body of not especially laudable personal habits. Yet now he is the master of Russia! Officially it is the Communist Party that rules, but the proletarian is more than half of the Party, and while the Party is his leader it is also his servant. He is to the Party what fuel is to an engine, what the sun is to vegetation. Without him it ceases to be.

In the sheer task of ruling he has risen to a position of supremacy, which in itself makes Russia either the great miracle or the great scandal of the ages. I do not recall ever having met a single chairman of an important Soviet, a position corresponding to that of mayor of a city, or governor of a state in this country, who was not of proletarian origin — recruited for the office from the rank and file of factory laborers. In the judiciary, in industry, in the co-operatives, in the school system — everywhere the proletarian has been lifted to heights of authority of which he never had dreamed in the old days. The very word " proletarian " has become the symbol of the good, the proper, the true. Proletarian dictatorship, proletarian culture, proletarian conscience, proletarian art, proletarian civilization, proletarian justice— at every step these phrases glare and beat at the visitor. Not Christian, not Russian, but proletarian! Power, glory, eminence — all are his!

Why, the reader will ask, such exultation and sublimation of this rough-spoken, unmannered, uncultivated creature? Why make him the base and the ideal of the coming and the common brotherhood of man? Because he, and only he, says the Communist, possesses the attributes out of which the collectivist society and the new humanity can be built. He is the natural revolutionary. He is the man without private property or with very little of it. He has no interest in a bourgeois society. He has no vested claim in a private property civilization. He has not developed a passion for personal acquisition of material goods. Besides, he is the natural materialist. He is always in contact with matter. He lives in a world of matter. He sees ore, clay, lumber, rock fashioned into machines, into tools and objects of use, through scientific methods and scientifically perfected instruments. He feels the reality of matter, so the Communists insist, with his hands, his muscles, his very soul. For him it is easy to grasp the materialist philosophy of life which is the very cornerstone of the collectivist society.

He is, furthermore, the producer. The crux of the whole Marxian theory is that labor produces all wealth and is, therefore, entitled to the control of its distribution. And the very nature of his work predisposes him to Communist thinking. His is a communistic job. Unlike the farmer or the artisan he does not turn out the finished article with his own hands. Others co-operate with him in the task. He is a participator in a collective scheme of production. His work is a link in a chain, he himself becomes, therefore, a link in a social chain.

Since he is a man without private property, with wages as his sole means of sustenance, he commands a homogeneity of interest and feeling which make possible his distinctive class consciousness. He can be unified, organized, aroused and pitted effectively against the property-owning group. He can be held together by a common purpose for a common destiny. He is, therefore, the natural carrier of the class struggle, the ideal builder of the new society. His backwardness imposes a severe handicap on him in the task of reforging the world. But a change of environment, an opportunity to study, to unfold himself, to shoulder responsibility, will ripen him for his mission. He is to change his own image and in doing so change the image of all mankind. Such is Communist theory.

Meanwhile, he reaps the richest rewards, material and cultural, of any group in Russia. His standard of living, despite constant shortage of necessaries, has risen visibly since the pre-war days. It is not an American standard of living. The five and ten cent stores alone make possible satisfactions to the American proletarian, of which the Russian worker is hardly aware. It would be absurd to compare the Russian worker's standard of living with that of the American worker. Only when one compares it with what it was in the pre-war days does one realize how high it has risen since the coming of the Revolution.

I asked once a group of proletarian housewives in

the city of Ivano-Voznesensk what was the one condition in their present day life which spoke for improve-
ment over the pre-war days. Without hesitation and
with astonishing unanimity they replied that it was
the absence of a need to fill their houses with boarders.
Boarders, they emphasized, were the bane of the proletarian housewife in the old days. They would sleep on
benches, on the table, on the floor, in two or three
shifts, on payment of one or two roubles a month. But
now while proletarians might still take in boarders,
it was not in droves as in former times.

This of course is not true of every industrial section.
There are still communities where boarders fill every
available space in barracks or boarding houses and
sleep in two and even three shifts without decent bed-
ding and in the vilest air in the world. Slums still infest industrial towns in Russia — alas what slums!
But the process of tearing them down, however slow,
has already begun. Besides, an ever-increasing portion
of proletarians are moving into the best homes in the
land, homes of the former bourgeoisie and the new
houses that are being built. Of course there is terrific
overcrowding, especially in the cities. Many large families live in one room and share a lavatory and kitchen
with several other families. But crowded quarters are
nothing new to the Russian proletarian. What is new
is running water, electric lights, a private bath, even if
shared with several other families. Go to Ivano-
Voznesensk, Baku, Shakhta, Stalingrad, the suburbs
of Moscow and other industrial centers, and you will
see townships already built or in process of construction
with modern streets, modern houses of wood, stone,

brick, with large windows, spacious rooms, running
water, sewage systems, very often with private bath
for each family, with electric lights and sometimes with
steam heat, and these are proletarian townships. Most
of the houses built in Russia since the Revolution in
industrial communities have been for proletarian occupancy. In housing accommodations no group, with the
possible exception of officials of high standing, has been
so assiduously favored as have the proletarians.

Go to the parks in any of these communities on a
Saturday evening or on a holiday and you will see
proletarians sporting around in modern suits of clothes,
in modern shirts usually with collar attached, and with
ties. I shall never forget the surprise that came over
me when, on my arrival in the city of Sverdlovsk in
the Ural Mountains, I went for a stroll in one of the
local parks. It was Saturday evening. Lanes and boule-
vards were jammed with proletarians, masses of them
attired in the modern European manner, even in low
shoes, and when in boots, with the trousers outside instead of inside the leggings.

I could not help recalling with amusement that it
was only a few years previous that the proletarian saw
in the modern suit of clothes, and especially in the
collar and tie, the symbol of capitalist greed and capitalist bestiality. How many men in the fierce days of
the proletarian battle for power were dragged to jail
and had their noses battered merely because they were
seen with collars and ties? Indeed, it was a revolution
against the man with the collar and tie, by the man who
never had worn either. In the old days the proletarian
was content enough even on Sundays to don his boots

and his blouse and always tuck the trousers inside of the leggings. Now not only his scruple against collar and tie has vanished, but these have become the fashion and I suspect also the pride of the proletarian.

What a multitude of other privileges have poured on him! When I was in Irkutsk, this fine old city in Siberia, I invited a Danish official of the Danish Telegraph Company to go rowing with me one day in the local river. When we reached the boat-house the attendant asked us if we were members of a trade union, and when we told her that we were not, she informed us, with an expression of regret, that she could not rent us a boat. She felt sure, however, that inasmuch as we were foreigners an exception would be made in our behalf, if we would apply to the local trade union authorities. We were not in the mood to go back to town and so had to forego the pleasure of rowing in a proletarian boat, while armies of proletarians, floating red banners, playing accordions and singing lustily, were gliding merrily up and down the river.

Go to any industrial city in Russia and you will discover that not only boat-houses, but parks, amusement places, sometimes opera-houses, theatres, motion picture halls, are in control of the trade unions, and through them the proletarian obtains admission privileges which no other group enjoys.

In matters of education, again, everything is open to the proletarian as to no one else in Russia. No proletarian with enough credits to enter a university need ever worry about a vacancy, nor even about expenses during his years of study. If the central government has exhausted its allotted number of stipends, his particular trade union will furnish him with one, so that he can continue his studies unharassed by material want. Nor need he have any anxiety about securing a position when he is finished with his university course. He will not be required to waste a single day in search of a situation. He will be automatically absorbed into some phase of his particular specialty by one of the large government enterprises, and if he shows the least promise he will be rapidly promoted to a position of high command.

Medical service, the best in the land, is his for the asking. Hospital care, the choicest in the country, is his at no cost to himself. Social insurance provides him with a living in the event of physical disability. Every enterprise pays seventeen per cent of the amount of its wages to a social insurance fund, out of which come the means, though still inadequate, for support of the sick, the disabled, the aged. If he is a consumptive, he is sent to the very best of sanitariums, again at no expense to himself. If he is nerve-wrecked and exhausted and requires a change of climate and special medical attention he need have no worry. All will be provided for him. The best of the old sanitariums and a number of new ones built since the advent of the new government are held exclusively for members of trade unions.

His hours of work are being constantly shortened. In some industries like coal the hours for the men who work underground are now reduced to six a day, and in others which involve no special hazard to health they are being rapidly cut from eight to seven. By 1933 the seven-hour day, if present plans materialize, will become universal. The proletarian also enjoys vacations of two weeks annually on full pay. Often he spends his vacation again at no cost to himself in a special summer resort.

Looking from whichever angle you will, the proletarian has made mammoth gains since the coming of the Revolution. He is the most privileged person in Russia. He has more ample security than others and he is garnering an ever-increasing measure of comfort. The best in the land in education, amusement, living quarters, above all in social prestige, is his. When a Russian makes out an application for admission to a trade union, a university, a military academy, he is asked of what social origin he is. If of proletarian origin the application is immediately acted on. Otherwise it is liable to be held up for months, for years and then possibly rejected. In a court of law the judge always seeks to ascertain the social origin of the defendant, and again if of proletarian or related to proletarian origin, the sentence is milder than it otherwise would have been. The very word proletarian is the highest badge of honor in the land.

Standard bearer, the proletarian is also standard maker in the new society. I once asked two working girls in the city of Tula why, since they were earning good wages, they were not wearing hats. " Because," replied one of them, " if we did, and if we ever had to stand in a queue, we would be pushed out and told to get to the end." The fact that they themselves were proletarians did not matter, for the reason that few proletarian women in Tula had reached the hat-wearing stage, and they would be so conspicuous that they would

be labelled *bourzhuis*. " Why," I once asked another
working girl, " don't you wear the fur coat which you
have inherited from your mother? "

" Because," came the reply, " if I did, I'd lose my
job. I'd be regarded as a *bourzhui*. I have to wait until
proletarian women begin to wear fur coats."

Precisely. Men may now be wearing the once execrable collar and tie, because the proletarian is wearing
them. Women may be properly wearing hats, silk
stockings, fur coats, when the mass of proletarian
women have come to them. In the large cities where
the proletarian merges himself in the mass of the population, this tyranny of his over personal taste loses
its sharp edge. But in distinctively industrial communities it is wiser not to push one's standard of living too
perceptibly above the level of the proletarian. The
word *bourzhui* still carries its lacerating barb. I doubt
if there are more than one hundred privately owned
automobiles in the whole of Russia, and most of these
are taxis fit more for the junk-pile than for service.
Ownership of an automobile is still a mark of bourgeois mendacity, though the motor cycle has already
become respectable, and only because, as a means of
fostering good road-building, proletarians have been
encouraged to buy motor-cycles. There is hope, remarked a Communist editor to me, that some day they
will be encouraged to buy Ford cars, and then of course
the badge of disgrace will be lifted from automobile
ownership.

I met once a young Russian journalist who, while
vacationing in the suburbs of a factory district, had
purchased a saddle horse and would take long rides

every afternoon. He was reported to the GPU, the state political police, and after a prolonged investigation he was exonerated of any wrong-doing. To avoid further unpleasantness he disposed of his horse. In everything one does in Russia, particularly in a proletarian community, one has to be on one's guard. The eyes of the proletarian are always wide-open and his mouth is ever ready to thunder forth imprecations and anathemas.

Few have been the classes in history who have had such power of sanction or veto over personal habits and social usages as the proletarian in Russia. The results, while cheering in some respects, are saddening in others, not alone because the individual must always be conscious of the repressive hand of the proletarian mass. There is no outward finesse in Russia and but scanty courtesy, save toward foreigners, who are treated always with special consideration. Efforts are being made to infuse refinement into the proletarian, and he is not an inept pupil. But he has so much to unlearn. He cannot recast his soul overnight. He cannot brush away old habits like lumps of mud on a garment. He is still woefully lacking in the rudiments of good behavior. He is still addicted to the vilest language in the world and to alcoholism. Alas, what a ghoulish drinker he is! He still has no respect, not to say reverence, for human individuality. He is still rough and callous and reckless in his treatment of others, especially non-proletarians. Where else in the world is there, for example, such constant arguing and wrangling as in Russia? In street cars, in shops, in offices, everywhere, with the exception of places in

command of the old intelligentsia, there is incessant
bickering and brandishing of fists. Even Gorki when
he visited Russia in the summer of 1928 was openly
chagrined at the spirit of sullenness he observed in the
land, as though the proletarian were perpetually out
of humor. Much of this surliness in Russian life is an
incident of the class-struggle, which is ever aflame, but
even more is it the result of the domination of the
proletarian who, after all, is a man without breeding.

Yet directly and indirectly he is master of his world
and he is fiercely jealous of his mastery. His class
consciousness and his fighting spirit are ever inflated to
a point of explosion. He is easily roused to wrath
and desperation. He has quaffed deep of power and
privilege and he will fight to death against efforts to
deprive him of either. Let there be no mistake on this
score. Now that he has a personal stake, a vested interest, in the new society, he will give freely of his
blood to fight off all invaders.

Collective control of the means of production may
yet steer Russia into an economic bog, out of which
only private enterprise can retrieve her, and the proletarian, to save himself from ruin, may yet be compelled to make generous concessions to individual economic effort. But it will not be at the price of a heavy
curtailment of the privileges and prerogatives he has
won since the coming of the new regime. Even if the
Communist Party were to be ousted from control of
the Russian nation, he would have to be reckoned with
in any final readjustment of the nation's affairs. He
may lose his political sovereignty. Someday the peasant
may snatch it away from him, but to dislodge him from

a voice in the control of industry will be no less easy than to drive the peasant from the land.

Whatever the fate of collectivism or the Communist Party in Russia the proletarian henceforth will remain one of the supreme masters of Russia's destiny.

CHAPTER XII

COMMUNIST

"HIS letter I did not finish reading, for before my eyes there rose a big muzhik with his red goatish beard and his beastly walk." Thus writes a peasant girl, a Young Communist, and the man she writes of is her own father! Involuntarily the reader asks himself whether such a burst of scorn for a father is not the invention of a sententious writer rather than the expression of genuine feeling of a human being, and involuntarily there comes to mind the instance of Tolstoy's "Anna Karenina."

This lady of great charm is wooed and won and wed by a gentleman of note. She lives with him in peace and plenty for over a decade, bears him a son of whom she is inexpressibly fond. A quarrel of her brother with his wife takes her to the latter's estate, and while there she meets a most gallant young man, an officer in the army. She is desperately smitten with love for this young man, and on the train, while on her way home, she is convulsed with a tempestuous emotion. St. Petersburg! Her husband, austere, proper, devoted, meets her at the station, and on sight of him she exclaims to herself, "Oh! oh, *mon Dieu!* why have his ears grown so long!" This exclamation has made the rounds of the world, eliciting everywhere high praise for the author, for his devastating insight into human reactions. What has happened to Anna? Not much and yet everything. During all the years of courtship and married life she never had noticed the size, shape, texture of her husband's ears. Only after she is overpowered with an emotion for another man does she observe them at all, and she shivers with disgust.

An emotional convulsion does often enough affect our intellectual attitudes. In Russia at any rate you will find everywhere sons and daughters who, through the deluge of revolutionary fervor that has swept over them, have become so sternly estranged from their fathers that they have perceived in them their " goatish beard and their beastly walk," and often enough nothing else.

Will I ever forget the bony Ukrainian youth with the sloping cheek-bones and the Tartar slit in his eyes whom I met once in a cooperative store in an Ukrainian village? He had once been a coachman for a rich landlord. When the Revolution broke out he joined the Red forces and became commander of a military unit. One night in winter he was galloping about the steppes when a squad of his men had haled before him fifteen peasants, all armed with rifles. They had done no shooting, but they bore arms and they were not Reds. One of them was his own uncle. By his own testimony, this uncle was a kindly man, the father of seven children. His soldiers asked what they were to do with their captives. " Shoot," was his reply. " My uncle," he continued his narrative, " burst into a wail. But I did not wait to hear his plea. I spurred my horse and dashed away to my next position." He spoke without a tremor — without a trace of sorrow or regret.

" That alone that you are captured with my help,"

says the Communist Seryozha in the novel " Cement,"
" gives me great joy . . . I shall myself lead you away
with my own gun over you." And the reader knows
that Seryozha will not flinch, that he will be as good
as his word. . . . " My mother came," says the hero
of another Russian novel, " and wept before me, begging me to intercede in behalf of her brother under
arrest by the *cheka,* but frankly her tears were re-
pulsive to me. . . . They were tears of bourgeois sentimentality, tears of bondage. . . . She knew her brother
had been a speculator, said so, but insisted that after
all I was his nephew, and how could I see him shot? "
Still he did not see why this uncle of his should be
spared, when others in his position were turned over to
the firing squad.

And so this mother Klara Andreyevna cannot help
feeling that her son is no longer blood of her blood,
flesh of her flesh. She makes another attempt to stir
his filial affections. She is beyond everything else a
mother. She wants him back, to embrace him, to caress
him, to hear him say at least one word of tenderness.
She begs him to restore the things that officials had
confiscated from her, to obtain the release of a friend
of his boyhood days, whose only offence was that he
was a *menshevik,* and to help his younger brother find
something to do, somewhere. . . . She reminds him that
he has influence — power. Is not he a Party man, an
official of parts, high in the councils of the new regime?
But her words only rasp his ears. They sound so per-
verse. He is a man of culture. He is polite. He will not
intentionally hurt his mother. After all she is a widow
now, impoverished and in misery. The best he does is

ask her to present to him a written memorandum of her requests, and the reader knows that he will never even glance at the writing, that he will merely crumple up the paper and cast it into the waste basket. . . .

Long ago Turgenev's master nihilist Bazarov in speaking to his friend, Arkadii, remarked, " You have no audacity and no malice." And Bazarov, be it known, is the spiritual grandfather of the Bolshevik, the Russian Communist. Audacity and malice! A roar of fiery voices seems to be echoing and re-echoing these words. Audacity and malice! Without these, charges the Communist, you do not count in a Revolution. You are worse than an encumbrance — you are a deadly menace. You indulge your sentiments and release a foe who may smite you in the heart and ruin you and your cause. Audacity and malice . . . in time of battle, vows the Communist, these are more pressing than food, are indeed as vital as air.

" To be born a second time," says another Russian character in a recent novel, " is just as terrible as to die." Aye, far more terrible. For to be born a second time you must die first, die as completely as though you never had lived — die slowly, lingeringly, with terrible pain. Then you are a new man. Reborn. You are an alien to those who had not been with you in those hours of deathly transformation. Then you can see the goatish beard of your father and his beastly walk. You can run away from the pleas of your uncle whom you have condemned to die. You can see in your broken-hearted mother a symbol of bourgeois sentimentality . . . tears of bondage. You can experience a burst of glee at the capture of your own one-armed brother who

is your enemy and whom you will help put to death. . . .
You can turn against your father, mother, brother,
against the comrade with whom you had once trudged
the snowy wastes of Siberia and shared the same filthy
cell in an out of the way jail. Aye, if you are as stormy
a personage as a cossack, you can even help hack to
death your own father as does Senka in Babel's terrific
short story "The Letter." "You must learn to look
at the sun and at blood alike without winking an eye-
lash," says still another character in a recent piece
of Russian fiction. "You must not fear that the sun
will burn your eyes or that blood will poison your
soul." No, you must not, or you are lost beyond hope
of recovery. You must have audacity and malice. You
must steel yourself against everything but your fiery
conviction, your cause, and when you have done so, life
will remove qualms, doubts, hesitations. You will be
stronger than others. You will be invincible!

It is hardness that distinguishes the Russian Communist from other radicals and revolutionaries in the
world. To him nothing must matter but the cause.
Everything else — personal welfare, life itself — are of
no account. It is always a choice between the cause and
other things, and the cause must not suffer. " You understand," says the Communist Tkatcheyev to his comrade Zudin in the poignant story "Chocolate," "not
we but our cause . . . don't imagine that we have
made this decision (to shoot you) out of a feeling of
hate or vengeance — there is no other way out." When
Tkatcheyev leaves Zudin, knowing well he will never
see him again, his parting words are " Don't be angry,
brother, . . . be brave! " Be brave in the face of

death to which I have helped condemn you, because the cause demands it! No, the hardness of the Communist is not the consequence of an innate sternness, of an absence of feeling, but rather the contrary — because of an overflow of emotion, a deluge of passion, so high, so tumultuous that it drowns out habit, comradeship, tradition, your whole past consciousness, and makes you fit for the pursuit of the one and only Purpose, the one and only Battle!

A unique personage he is, this Russian Communist. He has quaffed so deep of agony and ecstasy that nothing holds any terror for him, nor even surprise. He has been through such a baptism of fire and blood that, like Mephistopheles, he laughs at life and nature, and deems himself both invincible and invulnerable. He is the most supremely self-confident man in the world, overcome with something that is akin to omniscience. Let the great minds of the world — scientists, philosophers, statesmen — doubt the wisdom of his thought and the justice of his ways. Let them prophesy his doom. Let them scorch him with invectives. Let churchmen hurl their anathemas at him. He is sure that in the end they will succumb to his onslaught — the flame of his ardor or of his wrath will consume them. When I introduced Professor John Dewey to a Young Communist in a colony for former street waifs, the first question the lad asked was not what achievements Columbia's famous teacher was noted for, but whether or not he was a Communist. He was perplexed, indeed mortified, when I replied that Professor Dewey was no Communist. How, he argued, could a really great man remain outside of the fold of the greatest cause in the world? To the Bolshevik, young and old, any man who fails to perceive the truth and the grandeur of his mission is either a dolt or a scoundrel.

He sees himself and only himself as the true captain of the forces of history. There is no use arguing with him that conditions in England or America, for example, are so different from what they were in old Russia that attempts at Revolution in these lands must result in failure. It is of no avail to tell him that a proletarian who can drive to his job in his own automobile, even if a battered one, and who can afford pie for his dinner is much more interested in baseball scores than in historical materialism or the proletarian dictatorship. It is futile to seek to convince him that there may be other more pacific ways of achieving the collectivist control of property — than the one he advocates. He will tolerate no difference of opinion. He will not be doubted.

Yet opinionated and stubborn as he is, he is no egotist. There is little place for egotism in his world. There is so much action and interaction of the group on the individual that egotistical proclivities, however intense, remain subdued. When they do not, they are ground out of a man ruthlessly without regard for the amount of blood-letting the process may require. That is why there is hardly a leader in the Party and Soviet Government but shuns the limelight. There is no country in the world where it is so difficult to obtain interviews with leaders as in Russia. They simply will not speak for publication, save when some fortuitous event compels public utterance. Journalists, especially American, fume and fulminate; but of no avail. Doors remain closed. The supreme self-confidence of the Russian Communist is almost impersonal, yet is so conspicuous and powerful a part of him that it goads and spurs him into deeds most desperate and most cruel.

Hence also his double standard of morality. What is right for him, is wrong for others, and vice-versa. "When our men kill a counter-revolutionary," said to me once a prominent secretary of the Party, "we applaud him; when your capitalists slay a member of our Party we pronounce a curse on them." Exactly. When you German Socialists vote for the building of a cruiser for the German Navy, you are the world's champion scoundrels, but when you workers of some Red factory give your last pennies to build a tank for the Red Army, you are revolutionary saints. When you, Judge Thayer, evince bias toward a Sacco and Vanzetti you are the world's supreme villain, but when you, Krylenko, demand the death sentence not only for engineers who are palpably guilty of misdeeds, but of those who to the minds of the entire foreign press, yes, and of the Russian journalists in attendance at the trial, are no more guilty of the charges against them than is the presiding judge or you yourself, you are — if not a hero at least a true soldier of the cause. No one will speak ill of you. No worker will reprimand you. No Party leader will accuse you of having been injudicious or over-zealous. You remain irreproachable. And only because you represent righteousness, and the Thayers do not and cannot. Their motives do not count. Their sincerity does not matter. They are in the service of Baal and not of the one and only true god.

Is it any wonder that the Bolshevik is so flamingly

intolerant? However honest a Scheidemann or a Ramsay MacDonald may be, they are to him scoundrels, soul-wreckers, and only because they dare deviate from his prescribed mode of social behavior. Either you are with him or you are against him. Either you accept his formula of human salvation, or you are his enemy. Either you see the ultimate redemption of man through a bloody class struggle or you do not belong. You are fit only for the garbage heap of history. If you are in the way, you must be removed through open trial, secret trial, no trial at all, through merely administrative process. It all depends on the nature of your offence, and the particular revolutionary tension of the moment. Even if you are a Trotzky and have by sheer force of your genius and personality welded together an anarchic army into a victorious fighting force, and thereby brought triumph to the cause, you are not to be spared if you fail to toe the prescribed mark. You are to be shoved off into a hamlet in Central Asia, far from anyone and everything of consequence. Your writings are not to be printed. Your allowance is to be limited. You are to remain there to expiate your heresy in solitude. You are to acknowledge the error of your ways, or else languish away perhaps even until death. If you dare protest against the treatment accorded to you or continue the defence of your heresies, you are to be cast into a foreign land and allowed to shift for yourself as best you can, and to use your own wits to escape the knife or the bullet of some exiled countryman who thirsts to settle an ancient grudge against you.

Even if you are a Radeck with a pen as sharp as a

surgeon's scalpel and the courage of a Napoleon, once you are out of the line of march, you too are to be packed off into some far-away nook in Siberia to read, to write, to ruminate, but never to lift your voice in criticism or indignation. No matter your past achievement, your potential virtues, the need of the moment for just the type of talent and personality you possess. As a non-conformist you have in you the power to undermine the unity of the movement, the single-mindedness of the Party. Therefore, away with you, unless like a Kamenev and Zinovyev you come back on bended knees with a heart full of repentance and promise to obey and follow. No one shall be spared. When the cause demands cruelty to anyone within or without its ranks, cruelty is to ride rough shod over him.

On first contact, the Russian Communist seems a curious paradox. He has made the cause of the under-dog the basis of his mission. His whole attitude toward life is molded by a wish to lift the underdog to a plane of equality with other groups, more — to super-impose him on others. If the new Russian art, which he has inspired, whether of the drama, fiction, ballet, has any value at all, it is precisely because of the vehemence with which it pictures the submergence of the underdog and his desperate struggle to rise to the surface of life, to a position of command. Who that has seen " Roar China " in the Myerhold Theatre can forget the sweep of woe that overcomes the mob of bedraggled coolies when they assemble to select by lot the man who is at the behest of the white naval commander to forfeit his life? Who that has seen the film, " Woman of Rya-

zan " can ever blot out of his mind the horror and the
awesomeness in the life of those Russian muzhiks?
Not even Tolstoy in his " Power of Darkness " has
given us scenes so weighted with agony and degradation as is this most unforgettable motion picture.
When you see such a play as the " Armored Train "
mounted with riotous magnificence by Stanislavsky,
you do not bother to ask yourself whether it is great
art or great literature, you so overflow with flaming
pity for these wretched mud-crusted muzhiks that you
feel as though you ought to join in the bloody crusade
on which they have embarked to avenge the orgy of
violence their enemies had perpetrated on them. Not
even Vereshtchagin's painting *Victory* — that pyramid
of scowling skulls — conveys so poignantly the anguish
and horror of war, as does Pudovkin in his memorable
" The End of Saint Petersburg." Like some Diogenes
the Russian Bolshevik, lantern in hand, struts about
the Russian scene, uncovering everywhere and with
a ferocious zest the brutalities and agonies, the degra-
dations and adulteries in which the underdog wallowed
in the old days.

You are stirred and appalled. You overflow with
sympathy for the man so brutally weighted down with
barbarities. But the Communist himself shows no tenderness. He seems almost as void of compassion as an
executioner. He is always so cool, so deliberate. Only
when he talks of children does he grow mellow. Hence
such slogans as " Children are the flowers of Life,"
" Children are the joy of Life." Otherwise there seems
to be no glow of sympathy in him. The emotion that
seems to rule him is not tenderness for those in whose

behalf he is defying the world, but hate for those whom he has risen to overthrow and destroy. " His creative work," says a Russian critic in speaking of the novelist Nikiforov, " is to generate a great love for a great hate." Nikiforov himself makes one of his heros say, " Often I see a man who would purify this earth with the power of a great hate so as to prepare it for the cultivation of a new civilization and a new life." With especial emphasis do these words apply to the Communist. If love for a new humanity is his end, then most assuredly hate is one of his chief methods of achieving this end. He will never concede redeeming features to an enemy. Is he lacking in a sense of sportsmanship? The capitalist is always to him a pariah whose soul reeks with filth. His church, his religion, his humanitarianism are sodden in iniquity. He has no virtues as a human being which the proletarian need respect.

The Communist is the real ruler of Russia. In conference, national and local, he decides the policies and principles not only of the Soviet Government, but of the trade unions, the schools, the press, industry, trade. Hardly an aspect of life escapes his attention or his control, complete or partial. He is everywhere deciding, dictating, dominating.

Such a position of command confers on him a multitude of privileges. Next to the proletarian he is the most favored person in Russia. He need never worry for lack of a job. The machinery of the Party, the trade unions, the Soviet Government, are at his disposal, or rather he is at their command. He is sucked into some activity swiftly enough. Being the trusted man of the land he is promoted over the heads of others. Like the proletarian he is given preferences in schools, in rest homes, in trips to far away places or abroad. His enemies in Russia speak of him as the new *dvoryanin* — nobleman — the man who allocates unto himself rights and enjoyments that he withholds from others. Often there is a Communist who does not hesitate to use his privileged position to settle personal grudges with present or former rivals or enemies, or to extort for himself benefits at the expense of others. My mind, even as I write, teems with a host of abuses that Party men for one motive or another have perpetrated on non-partizans, through the power their privileged conditions afford them.

Yet since all that glitters is not gold, the advantages that the Communist enjoys are not without their dark underlining. I doubt if there is any man in the world who is subject to such severe discipline as he. He is never his own master. He is always under the behest of the Party. And first and foremost, the Party is death on material aggrandizement. He may be holding the most responsible position in the country, but materially it is not the most lucrative. He is always limited in his earnings. Two hundred and twenty-five roubles a month, or about one hundred and ten dollars is the maximum he is allowed to receive. That is all Litvinov and Chicherin are paid. That is all Stalin receives. That was all Trotzky, Lenine, Zinovyev, in the height of their glory and power, commanded. Recently there have been some exceptions made to this rule. Engineers, for example, may draw as much as four hundred roubles a month and skilled laborers even more. Like-

wise literary men are paid according to the amount of
their output, and sometimes on a royalty basis without any limitations as to the total sum they may earn.
Some writers command handsome incomes. But —

The Party has an axe that chops into these incomes
with neither pity nor let-up. A Communist receiving
fifty roubles a month pays to the Party treasury one-
half per cent of this sum; on one hundred roubles a
month, the levy is one per cent; on one hundred and
fifty, it is two per cent; on incomes higher than this
sum the levy is three per cent. Since literary people
are the ones that are liable to earn the handsomest
salaries, they pay into the Party coffers one fourth of
the sum or sums they receive over and above the established minimum of two hundred and twenty-five
roubles a month. These official levies however do not
exhaust the obligations that are constantly being made
on the Party man. A monument is to be built to Lenine,
a tank or an aeroplane is to be presented to the Red
Army, a piano is to be donated to a village schoolhouse, an oven is to be erected in a peasant club-house,
a motion picture machine is to be presented to an or-
phan asylum, a subscription is to be raised for an in-
valid comrade in a foreign land, a subsidy is to be
gathered for strikers in some place outside of Russia,
a home is to be opened for street waifs — endless are
the demands and calls for special contributions or for
special levies. A Communist simply must live from
hand to mouth, no matter how high the sums he earns.
He cannot accumulate an estate, even if it were morally
just for him to do so, which, of course, it is not. The
Party is most exacting on this score. It will tolerate no

deviations. It will accept no excuses and it will deal
mercilessly with falsifiers. When a Communist manager
of a factory, whom I knew, had with the consent of
the factory committee dispensed with the automobile
placed at his disposal, and instead drew for his trans-
portation an extra one hundred roubles a month, which
he kept for himself with the knowledge of his committee, he not only lost his position, but his membership ticket in the Party, and he is now a finished
man. Never again will he rise to a place of prominence and importance. He has committed the most
grievous of all sins — yielded to the lure of material
aggrandizement!

What burdens of work and duties the Party fastens
on the Communist! His real labors begin when others
have finished theirs. He must always be a social worker,
devote his leisure to a multitude of unpaid social tasks
that the Party imposes on him. He must teach, study,
lecture, investigate, watch. Portfolio in hand, he is constantly flitting about from place to place, job to job.
He is always overwhelmed with calls to meetings, conferences, and he never knows where he will be tomorrow. The Party hurls him around hither and thither
almost like a beast of burden. Today he is in one city,
tomorrow in another. Today he is in Moscow, tomorrow
on his way to some Buryat settlement deep in the heart
of Siberia. Today he is in the tropics of Central Asia,
tomorrow in the Arctic North of Asia or Europe. Today
he is factory manager, tomorrow only an office clerk.
He is the most over-ordered person in the world.
He is always at the beck and call of the Party, and
there are no refusals. He must be ever ready to obey,

no matter who he is; and if he does not, he is cast out and disgraced.

His personal life does not escape scrutiny and control. The Party compels him to be always on his best behavior. He may be abusing the privileges it confers on him, squeeze a non-partisan out of a job he may covet for himself or a friend of his, manipulate the eviction of a non-partisan from an apartment he wishes for himself or a friend. When the Party learns of such procedures and discovers malice or spite or search for material comfort as the exciting cause or motive, it deals mercilessly with the offender. On criminal charges again it is the Communist who receives the severest sentences. Woe to the Communist who accepts or solicits a bribe! A non-partisan may for such an offence escape with a heavy jail sentence, but not a Communist. It depends, of course, on the extent of the bribe and the resulting damage to the cause. If these in the eyes of the judge and his two jurymen loom momentous, the penalty invariably is death.

In his private life the Communist must follow a rigorous code. He must indulge in no luxuries. Not that luxury in itself is a sin. It is not. But — at this stage of the Revolution, there are few enough luxuries to be had, and the Communist must not be the one to seek them. He must not over-indulge in gayeties. His time is too valuable — and so are his energies. Both he must devote mainly to the cause. He may take a drink of vodka, but a conspicuously immoderate amount of imbibing is most improper for him. It may ruin his health and evoke disdain and mockery from the non-partizan or others outside of the Party fold. He must not gamble. He must stay away from all gambling resorts, and if he does not, the hand of the controlling commission will fall heavy on him. Dancing in itself is not necessarily improper. But he can devote his time to more useful pursuits. He certainly must not overdo it, even in his own club-house, and as for attending a dance in such places as the Bolshaya Moskovskaya in Moscow or the Hotel Europe in Leningrad — he had better beware! These are resorts for nepmen and foreigners, not for him. The very air there is tainted. He must, of course, divorce himself from all religious practices and all church associations. If his father and mother are of the bourgeois group, he must break with them, write himself out of his family, and preferably change his name. He must disown his old world and all those living in it, no matter how intimately he is bound to them by bonds of blood. All these limitations as to earnings, personal behavior he must observe, and he need never regard himself free from the eye of the controlling commission. Sooner or later he will be discovered in his trespasses, if he indulges in them, and then he must expect no mercy. . . .

Above all he must be prepared for a crisis, either on the home front or on the international scene. He must ever be ready to bring all the sacrifice of which he is humanly capable — not only time, talent, health, but even life. I have often thought that fundamentally what distinguishes a Communist from other revolutionaries is his readiness to kill and to be killed. He must show no mercy to others or to himself. He cannot compromise, and he knows that his enemies, when they lay hands on him, will make no compromise with him.

Many a prominent Russian Communist, when sent
abroad on some mission is never sure he will return
home alive. Too many are the enemies in foreign lands
lying in ambush ready to strike him down. In time of
war, which he is convinced he cannot escape, he will
be the one to hold the most dangerous positions, and
he knows that when he is captured by the enemy he
is lost, perhaps killed at once, or perhaps tortured
fiendishly. He knows that he is no ordinary enemy, that
on him his foes, especially if they are of the same race
as he, will loosen their most fierce rage. He has had
experience enough during the civil war when he battled
for power. He knows what peasants, Cossacks, White
generals have done to his fellow Communists — how
they have strung them up on trees, buried them alive,
often making them dig their own graves, or hurled
them head down into the deep and arid wells of the
desert. He knows the terrors and agonies that await
him in time of war.

No wonder that so many folk in Russia, proletarians
and intellectuals, though Communists by conviction
and socially qualified to membership in the Party, remain without. They would rather forego the privileges
the Party confers, than assume all the obligations it
exacts. They know that when a man is a Communist,
a member of the Party, he is not master of himself.
The Party becomes his mother and also his father, his
servant but even more his master, controlling his job,
his leisure, his education, his relaxation, his whole life
and sometimes the very hour of his death. . . .

Yet spiritually the Communist is perhaps the most
satisfied man in the world. Principle, Passion, Power,

Triumph rule his life. These are his chief pillars of support. On them he has hung his heart, his soul, his life, his whole future. He never doubts ultimate triumph. No religion the world has ever known has inculcated in man a sense of predestination more sturdy than the Communist harbors. He is sure that his cause will win over all foes, no matter what the set-backs it may suffer again and again. Bourgeois nations may seek to undermine his Revolution, may set scientists and militarists to devising new and deadly weapons of attack on him and his Revolution. Outbreaks of proletarians in Java, China, Hungary, Austria, and other places may be washed out in blood. The Soviet Government itself may be pounced upon, battered into dust; his leaders may be seized, shot down, strung up on telephone poles. Yet eventually victory for his cause, like water seeking its level, will rise to the surface. Of this he is as fervently convinced as is the Fundamentalist of a hereafter and of a paradise to come.

That is why, I must emphasize, the Communist is really a happy man. No despair for him. No doubt. No disappointments with Versailles treaties, Polish Corridors, League of Nations, Franco-British naval pacts, entangling alliances, military combinations, Fascist dictatorships. All of the things which wring forth wails of sorrow from a " New Republic," a " Nation," a " Manchester Guardian," give him no qualms. All the doubts and perplexities that assault the minds of a Spengler, a Keyserling, a Bertrand Russell, leave him unmoved. He expects nothing from liberalism, nor from the men in whom liberals repose faith. He derides their appeals to human goodness and social justice just as ferociously as he mocks the churchman's call to Christian service and Christian charity. He has only contempt for the capitalist and his order of society, and is never annoyed or worried or saddened by anything that happens within its bounds. Two worlds exist for him — his own and that of those outside his ranks. He can see no middle world — nor a middle way of bridging the gap between these two. " If you want peace of mind," says he, " freedom from spiritual stress, come into my fold, because where you are, and no matter where you are, you will and you must be subject to constant or periodic torment and perplexity. I and I alone can guarantee you peace of heart and soul."

He is a new man not on the Russian scene alone. Decisive, impassioned, impudent, at times ruthless to himself and his own even more than to outsiders, he would if necessary ruin everything in his way so as to build anew in his own manner, and in complete disregard of the chivalries, the graces, the traditions, the social habits, the amenities of the existing world. Gone from him is the old Russian spirit of doubt, self-reproach, resignation. Gone from him is the soul of Oblomov, Rudin, Lavretsky, Raskolikov and the vast coterie of Russian intellectuals, who on the pages of Russian literature and on the highways of Russian life have through their irresoluteness and self-castigation tormented themselves and others to ennui, distraction, madness and even death, sometimes by their own hands. Gone are Turgenev's Lizas who, when frustrated in love, bid the world farewell and bury themselves in the cloistered walls of a convent resigned to a life of solitude, self-abnegation and unhealed agony. Gone are Chekhov's "Cherry Orchards," "Uncle Vanyas" "Three Sisters," — who sob so beautifully, suffer so nobly and so uselessly.

A terrible destroyer, the Russian Communist has this to his credit — he has infused a new will into the Russian man, a new energy, a new impudence. He is hardening the very fibre of the Russian soul. Blunderer and wrecker that he is, he never looks back on his errors save only with the thought of never repeating them. He may fail in his ultimate goal. Property may never become the possession of the collective society. He may be swept off the Russian stage, indeed the stage of history, by a fury more mighty than he had unleashed when he swooped on old Russia with the resolve to whip her into submission. But it will not be by the Kerenskys and Milyukovs, by men "sicklied o'er with the pale cast of thought" and with eloquence as their chief weapon of combat. It will be by a new man, forged by the Communist himself in his own crucible of Passion, Principle, Power, Triumph, a man mightier than he not only in thought, but in will and in deed, as ready to wreck as he, but with far more ample capacity to build and to conquer!

CHAPTER XIII

YOUTH

"IT is the year one hundred and seven," exclaims a character in one of Alexey Tolstoy's recent stories, and the reader perceives instantly that both author and speaker do not mean one hundred and seven A.D. or B.C. but A.O. — after October, the month of the Bolshevik Revolution. How dramatically these words coincide with the remark of a Russian girl, a student in Moscow University, who in response to a query of mine as to what was the key to the spiritual life of the revolutionary youth, replied, " Always remember that to us the world is just beginning."

The world just beginning! Outside of science all that had happened in Russia and in other countries in the pre-October days was not of much account. Man groped, blundered, brutalized and deluded himself with chimeras and utopias. He had no sense of true reality. Science had opened to him new vistas of knowledge and brought him into closer harmony with his sternest foe, Nature. But the achievements of science, however glorious and heroic, man had subordinated to the perpetuation of inequalities in possession and enjoyment. The one effort to usher in real enlightenment and righteousness — the French Revolution — was smothered in blood. The proletarian, the real " hero of our times " was unfree, had not yet come into possession of the means of production. Man, therefore, was weighted down with injustices and the whole past was a maze of horror and gloom, riven now and then by a flash of revolutionary lightning.

Consider the immense implications of such an approach to life. Consider the deliberateness with which Russian youth has dammed up the stream of spiritual nourishment that flows into the very soul of the youth in other lands. Religion, morality, family, nationalism, social justice, all these, as understood in the outside world, mean little, if anything, furnish neither inspiration nor guidance. The standards, traditions, sublimations, exaltations, that have clustered about them, the Russian youth has cast aside almost like so much cluttering garbage. Despite Lenine's admonition that the new man must assimilate the useful cultural heritages of the former bourgeoisie, youth has no reverence and hardly any respect for the past or for those habituated to its ways of life and thought.

Hence the boisterous conflict between youth and age in Russia, between fathers and children is the harshest Russia, or perhaps the world, has ever witnessed. The barbaric thrusts at elders of a Bazarov in Turgenev's " Fathers and Sons " are a warm caress compared to the deluge of blows that modern youth has been leveling at its elders. The so-called revolt of the younger generation in America and in Europe is a good-humored caprice, almost a childish jest compared to the passionate defiance of age on the part of Russia's revolutionary youth. No two worlds could be further apart in spirit and in manner than are youth and age in Russia. The two may be living in the same home, eat at the same table, sleep under the same roof, perhaps in the same bed, as so often happens in Russia, yet they are separated by a chasm which it would be hopeless to attempt to bridge. Never have I been in a Russian home, in city or in village, but there was evidence of a continuous battle between fathers and children. Well, indeed, might Russian youth boast, as did one of its leaders, that this era of the proletarian conquest, of the Red October, is a challenge and a battle to the end against the civilization of the Ten Commandments and of the Golden Rule.

I am speaking, of course, of the youth that has been won over heart and soul to the new gospel. This youth dominates the life of the young generation, but does not embrace all of it. Outside of its fold are two groups of youths that must be mentioned here, even if briefly, for they are both a problem and a tragedy which thus far has eluded solution. In social and cultural antecedents these two groups are quite unlike one another. Yet both find themselves, one by choice, the other by compulsion, stranded in a no-man's land. They have lost their roots in the old civilization and have struck none in the new. Both accept the new regime as something that is and must be, yet socially and spiritually they are alienated from it. Both drift about, one seeking and failing to find an anchorage, and the other scorning attachment to a definite social base.

It is this latter youth that yields chiefly the hosts of hooligans that infest the Russian community, principally the city, and who now and then perpetrate an atrocity, like mass assault on a woman, that convulses the nation with rage and horror. The one thing it has copied from the revolutionary youth is group life, but it behaves like a wolf-pack. It attacks in unison. I have before me a stack of books discussing the outrages this youth has, during the past few years, been perpetrating, and they make ghastly reading. This youth is not only beyond the reach of home, school, church, but of revolutionary public opinion. It swims along on a wave of immediate impulse, recognizing no responsibility, no restraint. In every land there is, of course, such an anti-social youth, but it is to all appearances more conspicuous in Russia than elsewhere, and possibly because of the very obliteration of the old world and its steadying bulwarks.

This youth is impervious to public opinion, and for that reason it is, in its own way, happy. It lives with and for itself. More tragic is the fate of the other group of non-conformist youth, if only because it is oversensitive to the reactions of the outside world. It has a sense of social responsibility, and it is the unhappiest youth in Russia, if not in the world. It is wondering where its perplexities will end. It accepts the Revolution as a finality. It would fain make friends with it, but it is held on the sidelines. It is refused a place in the procession. It is not regarded chaste enough. Its antecedents, in the eyes of the revolutionary, are tainted. It is largely of the intelligentsia and of the former propertied and professional class, and to the revolutionary it has been somewhat " spoiled and softened " by its home environment, a charge not entirely unwarranted. This youth, even if at variance with its elders intellectually, has not broken ties with them. It has too much fear and too much reverence for life to take it into its hands and break it as one would a withered limb off a tree.

It responds to the woes and perplexities of its elders with warmth, suffers with and for them. This youth has intellect, ambition, imagination. It aspires to make something of itself. It seeks the choice fleshpots perhaps more assiduously than does the revolutionary group, but even more does it want to develop its capacities. But it finds the bars up. It does not belong. It would fain flee to a foreign land, but it has not the material means and it is not always allowed exit abroad. When it is admitted to the higher institutions of learning it feels itself as if in exile, at any rate as a stranger. The revolutionary organizations keep it out from their inner life. It is thrown on its own resources, its own inner reserves and sometimes its patience ebbs, its courage snaps. It becomes introspective. Its sensitiveness feeds on itself, morbidity sets in and " there is nothing good to live for." The result is suicide, by shooting, by poisoning, seldom, incidentally, by hanging.

However, it is of the revolutionary youth that I wish to speak in this chapter; of the youth that is an integral and boisterous part of the Revolution. This is the creative youth of the land. It is to be the future ruler of Russia, and knows it. It is, in fact, to an astonishing degree already a part of the governing apparatus of the land. Not the least impressive feature of present-day Russia is the amazing rise of youth to power. In no land in the world, hardly even in Nationalist China, has youth been elevated to such a position of responsibility in the judicial, administrative and economic functions of the state, as in Russia. The policy that other nations follow in putting into places of command persons of mature age, because of their supposed experience and ripeness of judgment, is precisely the one that the Russians have discarded. They will have none of the " ripeness of judgment " of persons reared in the old days, save in the purely technical fields of effort. They would rather take chances with inexperienced youth, which at least possesses a feeling for the spirit of the Revolution.

This Russian youth is a world all its own, compactly organized, sternly disciplined and boisterously articulate. There is the Komsomol (Young Communist) for youths between sixteen and twenty-four. There are the Pioneers, for youths between seven and sixteen. There are the Octobrists, for youths under seven. The Komsomol, being made up of the oldest youth, is the leader of all youth. Everywhere it has its own quarters, libraries, schools, club-houses, sporting fields, little theatres, parks, and at times its own honor courts. It has its own press, far-flung, deep-rooted, virile. Its daily organ in Moscow, the *Komsomolskaya Pravda*, is the most lively, the most audacious, the most indelicate and the most enjoyable journal in Russia. It is the only journal with a sense of humor. Its monthly journal, *The Young Guard*, fairly spills with challenge and aggressiveness. Its book publishing houses have turned out the most sensational novels of the Revolution, all dealing with the problems and vagaries of youth.

Through these many-sided literary avenues, and through discussion at its meetings this youth bares itself to the outside world, its hopes and despairs, its achievements and even more its failures. Its voice is the loudest, the clearest in Russia — and the most intriguing.

The chief purpose of the revolutionary youth is to prepare itself for life in a Communist society. It is, therefore, seeking to habituate itself to manners and standards that will fit such a society. First and foremost it is endeavoring to saturate itself with the new political faith. This faith is always in the foreground of its life, its guide and inspiration, its avocation and its adventure. That is why political education is so outstanding a feature of all Russian education. Everything is political in the Russian schools, especially in the lower ones, even lessons in geography, geology, biology. In no country in the world, not even in Fascist Italy, is youth so continually deluged with political ideas and political enthusiasms, as in Russia. I doubt if there ever was a religious movement in the world which sought to inculcate in youth its tenets more or even as assiduously as the Communist Party is doing in Russia. Youth is made not only to believe in the new political faith, but to thrill to it, to be ready to fight and to die for it.

With their innate love of drama, the Russians have linked this faith to everyday life, have woven it into the very fabric of everyday experiences. They have made it not merely a philosophy, an abstraction, an idea, but a guide and an inspiration, a body of sanctions and usages. It is to them, not merely a wave on the ocean, but the ocean itself, constantly heaving up new waves, new storms that overwhelm, submerge and transform. . . . Where else in the world, for example, is youth being reared in a spirit of internationalmindedness, as in Russia? The Ukrainian boy speaks his own language, knows he is an Ukranian. The Georgian girl knows that she is Georgian. The Buryat youth knows he is a Buryat. But they all are brought up to feel that first and foremost they are internationalists; they are to draw no line against any person because of race, color or nationality. They are to join hands with the African, the Mongol, the Hindu, the Turk, as readily as with the German, the Englishman, the American or any other white person. An earthquake in Japan? A strike in Johannesburg? An uprising in Java? They are to contribute their copecks to provide succor for the struggling and suffering mass . . . because they themselves are a spiritual part of this mass, are one with it, and must always be for it. Watch a parade of revolutionary youth in Russia and you instantly perceive the boisterous, the almost terrific quality of this spirit of international-mindedness. No national assertiveness. No national banners. No national songs. Nowhere a sign of race or color discrimination. All tribes and peoples in Russia and other lands, principally Asia, in their native garb and with their native slouch, marching arm in arm, boys and girls always together, all under the same red banners, wrapped in the same red bunting, striding to the same red tune, singing the same *International!*

I cannot help wondering, however, especially as Sovietism fails to spread in other lands, if someday this international-mindedness will not crystallize into a new and rabid nationalism? Color line may play no part in it, nor race. But then the Russian has never shared the Anglo-Saxon's sense of superiority toward other peoples. Racially he always has been rather humble-minded and humble-mannered, save toward Jews, in

which respect he is far from having shed his ancient
coat-of-arms. Anti-semitism, despite vigorous propaganda against it, is still deep-rooted in the Russian
soul, even among the proletarians. Let us remember,
however, that at present this Russian international-
mindedness means mainly, perhaps solely, loyalty to
Sovietism. Supposing Sovietism remains intrenched in
Russia and spreads no farther. Supposing Sovietism remains synonymous with Russia. It matters not that the
word Russia no longer is in use, has given place to the
euphonious " Soviet Union." After all it is a geographic
and political entity. Will not this new passion for the
proletarian cause become localized, center itself on
Russia, or what was Russia?

Communists dismiss with a flitting laugh any suggestion that Russia is developing a new and robust
nationalism. But it is not at all a matter to be lightly
dismissed. Russia may yet become the most rabidly
nationalistic land in the world, especially as the youth is
growing up with the notion, which in Russia remains
undisputed, that the Soviet Union is in the vanguard
of mankind, the champion of the holiest principle and
the holiest cause the world has ever known. In the past
there have been nations who, though spurred on by
sets of motives alien to those animating modern Russia, have set themselves up as superiors to other nations, and we know how this *idée fixée* of theirs has disturbed and exasperated their neighbors. May not
history repeat itself? There are voices in Russia, still
feeble, that do now and then express misgiving lest
such be the outcome in the Soviet Union. Certainly the
older Russian revolutionaries who cherish their inter-

nationalism as though it were a new divinity, have before them, among all the other tasks that are wracking their minds, this one of keeping the tide of internationalist sentiment from bursting into a distinctively nationalist direction!

At best, however, the internationalism which Russian youth is espousing does not imply social tolerance. Just the contrary. It implies a flagrant social intolerance. It could not be otherwise, with the notion of the class struggle so much in the forefront of the intellectual and emotional life of the people. From its earliest days youth is reared in the belief that mankind is divided into a class of proletarians and a class of bourgeoisie, who are at constant war with each other. The history it studies in schools is not the history of nations, but of classes and their struggle against one another. The Bible and religion it approaches as documents and products of this class struggle. That author is most eminent who through his art has perceived the class struggle most lucidly and has bestowed his tenderest sympathy on the submerged mass. Tolstoy, Turgenev, Dostoyevski, Anatole France, Dickens, all are subjected to this test, and all receive praise or censure, according to the measure or the intensity of the sympathy they manifest toward the struggling class. All civilization, in short, is a matter of class struggle. Often when I would tell Russian youths that I was a writer they would immediately ask what was my political *napravlenie* — orientation. What they really meant was whether I was for or against the class struggle. They could not conceive of a writer being apolitical and indifferent to political viewpoints. To them

the class struggle is a magic wand and a Holy
Grail.

It is in the purely human aspects of its life that the
revolutionary youth of Russia presents such a dramatic
spectacle. Nowhere in the world is youth so independent of parental authority or of the guidance of elders.
Nowhere is it so militant and so militarized, nowhere
so habituated to the notion of sex equality and sex
freedom, to a repudiation of religion, to the conception
of social service as a motive and a goal in life, to aversion to personal acquisitiveness, to group action, to exaltation of labor. Labor is not merely a source of livelihood, it is a part of livelihood. It is not merely a means
to an end, but an end in itself. Is there a grist mill or a
fishery in the neighborhood? Youth must familiarize
itself with the methods and purposes of the enterprise,
and with the contribution these are making to the social self-sufficiency of the community. Is there a farming region specializing in cotton, corn, horticulture,
stock-raising? Youth through its schools must learn to
appreciate their economic and social value and how to
enhance both. Is there a textile factory, a hardware
store, a coal mine, an electric project in process of construction? Youth must know what it is all about, learn
to appreciate its social, political and economic implications. All education is related to some type of labor,
to some constructive effort.

It is in the application of principle to conduct that
Russian youth encounters its chief perplexities, and
receives its chief schooling and incidentally unfolds a
most dramatic aspect of the Revolution.

A member of a collective commits suicide. He was a

loyal worker, but he is a suicide. He believed in the right to die, and a revolutionary must only believe in the right to live. How is he to be buried with honors, speeches, a parade, red flags? Can revolutionary youth recognize the merits of the man, independent of his lack of revolutionary stamina? What is to be done?

A girl has gone through an abortion, without consulting her immediate group. Abortions, of course, are legalized. But a revolutionary must think of the obligation to the new society. An abortion weakens the health and renders a woman less capable of doing the best work for the cause. Besides, the Revolution demands that women give birth to children. So again what is to be done?

A youth is in love with a girl. He is an atheist. She is not. He loves her desperately. He is sure that in time after marriage he will win her away from her faith. Meanwhile she is stubborn. She will marry him only if he consents to a church wedding. Has he a right to yield to her? And supposing he has, without consulting his collective, gone through with a church ceremony — has, as one youth expressed himself, " compromised with his atheism for no more than two hours." What is the collective to do? Expel him and lose an active worker for the Revolution, or pardon him and compromise with " the power of darkness." What is to be done?

A youth has married, and has been coming to the collective meeting alone, very seldom with his wife. Is he pursuing the right attitude toward her and the cause? What is going to become of the principle of equality of sexes if she is going to slump into domesticity and wrap her life in mere household tasks, and

in children? What should and what can the collective
do in such a case?

A Gentile youth has made an insulting remark to a
Jewish girl, just because she refuses to be his sweetheart. How is such a youth to be regenerated, to be
drained of the ancient taint of race hate?

A youth has been hobnobbing with the son of a nepman. That in itself is no misdemeanor. The son of a
nepman may someday become a fervid revolutionary
and it behooves a class-conscious revolutionary youth
to associate with him and to propagate to him the new
gospel. But the revolutionary youth has been visiting
the nepman's home too often, has accepted gifts from
his friend's father — a gold chain, which he has been
flaunting before his comrades and rousing the envy of
some and the scorn of others. Was it proper for him to
accept this gift? Is it ever proper for a revolutionary
youth to accept a gift from a nepman, and if so what
sort of a gift, and where is the limit to be drawn?

Endless are the problems that youth is facing in its
daily life, and always it is obliged to seek solutions in
its own heart. It can hardly seek them anywhere else. It
will not heed the counsel of its elders, who, even when
of the ranks of the revolutionaries, are not entirely free
from old notions and standards. Party men likewise,
if of adult age with the fires of youth and the passions of
adolescence burned out of them or held in the background, can suggest answers to perplexing questions,
but not always with the touch of life in them. Consider,
for example, such a mite of counsel as the inveterate
Zalkind once offered when in all earnestness he ad-
monished youth that it is just as fitting for a revolu-

tionary to marry a daughter of the bourgeoisie as to marry a gorilla! Youth will listen to older Party men, but it often feels bound to smile at their words of guidance. For a gratifying solution of its dilemmas it must take counsel with itself, experiment, suffer, discard, select and stick!

Yet it is a happy youth, perhaps the happiest on earth. It has its failings, too obtrusive and too pathetic not to be noticed by the most casual observer. It is boisterously self-assertive. It is insolent. It is so cocksure of itself, its aims, ideas, prejudices, that it regards the rest of mankind as still living in some dark age. Of course, it has no way of learning to understand the outside world. It has no personal contact with it, and the sources of information at its disposal are trimmed to suit the political purposes of the ruling Party. It is almost savage in its lack of compassion for a foe. Like the proletarian it still has much, very much to learn about the sheer worth of human individuality. It still has to discover the value, if not the beauty of respect for human personality. It still has a whole world to unlock, explore, admire and emulate.

Yet in its own rights and by its own lights it is as happy as only youth can be. The civil war, the famine, the Party conflicts, the international crises have hardened it to obloquy and privation. It has made a virtue not of self-denial, but of indifference to material enjoyment. It does not complain if it has to share a room in a dormitory with three, four or even six other persons. It does not grumble if it must sole and resole its tattered boots. It is content enough to eat black bread and cabbage soup every day. It lives with its loyalties

— not to home, not to parents, not to elders, not to any church, not to the past, but only to the Revolution and to the future. It has none of the skepticism of Scott Fitzgerald's " Sad Young Men," or Ernest Hemingway's and Aldous Huxley's desolate folk. It is bursting with faith and an eagerness to live and to struggle. " Do you see how the sun is trying hard to shine? " remarks a character in a new Russian novel. " It is all for us, for our sake." Yes, the sun and all nature seem to Russian revolutionary youth to be in alliance with it in its battle for a new world. " To live," says another character in the same novel, " so that every nerve, every muscle might participate in this big struggle, in this big construction." Which is precisely how revolutionary youth wants to live.

Someday a wave of disillusionment may sweep over Russia and dissolve youth's overpowering faith in itself and in its cause. If that time ever comes Russia will witness a suicide epidemic, the like of which the world probably has never known. For the present this faith, like a full moon, shines bright and high.

CHAPTER XIV

INTELLIGENTSIA

PEASANT, proletarian, Communist, youth! To them the Revolution has meant havoc but also hope, frustration but also fulfillment. Above all it has meant expansion of personality, social and intellectual ascent. But what shall, what can, be said of the *intelligentsia* (intellectuals)? To them the Revolution has brought havoc and hardly any hope, frustration with but little fulfillment. It has meant not expansion but contraction of personality, not social ascent but descent. It has been almost a holocaust.

Intelligentsia!

What a hallowed word it was in Russia in the pre-Bolshevik days!

What nobility it symbolized, what reverence it inspired!

Coined in Russia the word had made the rounds of the world, but nowhere had it attained the distinction and distinctness that it had in the land of its birth. Everywhere in Russia it roused respect and adoration. The peasant might fear the official, but not the intellectual. The proletarian might snarl at the capitalist, but not at the intellectual. The Czarist might howl at the rebel, but in his heart he cherished a sneaking admiration, colored often with envy, for the intellectual. The intellectual himself might be an official, a rebel, a capitalist, but as an intellectual he was the symbol of something noble and indispensable, transcending age, politics, institutions, personalities, classes, something related in a warm and intimate way to life, to the very soul of man.

The intellectual was the soul of Russia. The very word " intelligentsia " brings to mind Gogol, Pushkin, Chernyshevsky, Herzen, Byelinsky, Dobroliubov, Turgenev, Tolstoy, Dostoyevski and other literary luminaries who were not only the soul but the conscience and the glory of Russia. Skeptic and sufferer, the intellectual was also the great discoverer and the great builder, the great humanitarian and the great lover of the dark people. He it was who had made the name of Russia revered in the outside world. All that Russia has given to mankind in literature, art, music, science, social movements he had created. " A king in the realm of ideas," as one Russian writer makes one of his characters express himself of the intellectual, " and," one might add, " without any living king daring to dispute his right to his throne." He, if anybody, lived in a kingdom that was not of this earth — a kingdom of dreams and illusions, of hopes and even more of despairs.

The Revolution itself is largely his creation. Long before there ever was a proletarian in Russia he had dreamed of the Revolution, had actually built barricades and had fought behind them and was hanged for doing it. Witness the Decembrist Revolution in 1825. Where would this much-vaunted proletarian, this roistering self-annointed master of Russia's destiny be, if the intellectual had not lavished on him his sympathies, his talents, his very soul? Omnipotent and all-righteous as the proletarian may now deem himself, he was only a

semi-savage peasant when he first appeared on the
Russian scene. Illiterate, suspicious, somewhat afraid
of the outside world, he was interested not in ideas, not
in humanity, not in a new civilization, not even in revolution, but only in himself, his own slothful little
world. He cared for nothing so much as for a few roubles with which to hie back to the folks at home in his
barbaric village and to help them buy a new plow, a
new horse, a new strip of land. What did he know of
class-struggle, of class-consciousness, of dictatorship,
of Soviets, of freedom, of culture, of personality, of
science, of *technic*, aye of Marx himself and of materialism — of the whole avalanche of ideas and terms
with which he is now so freely and exuberantly bandy-
ing about, and which so exhilarate and intoxicate him?
What did he know of anything, even himself, before
the intellectual had descended on him and like a loving
mother embraced and fondled him and washed the
sloth away from his eyes and opened them to a new
world, new ideas, new inspirations?

Yet now in the moment of triumph of the Revolution, of the conquest of the proletarian, he — teacher,
guide, inspirer — finds himself not discarded, but dis-
owned, shoved into the background, into the shadow,
to watch, to obey, never to command. His talents are
exploited, for after all he is the intellectual, the big
creative force; but he himself is mistrusted, guarded
over like an unruly child that might break discipline and
indulge in mischief.

A characteristic incident the following: I had invited
once a young engineer and his wife to join a group of
Americans in the Bolshaya Moskovskaya, one of the

leading hotels in Moscow, for supper and to dance. He shook his head and refused to come. " That is a luxury which only you foreigners can allow yourselves." I sought to argue him out of his contention. But he was steadfast. " We Russian intellectuals," he explained, " know our place. We have to." He was no Communist and, therefore, not subject to the rigid discipline of the Party. He was no nepman and, therefore, immune from the disapprobation visited on this group of cast-offs whenever they make themselves obtrusive or conspicuous. He never had been in sympathy with the counter-revolutionary movement and, therefore, beyond possible suspicion of disloyalty. He was an engineer of some prominence, faithful to his job, on the best of terms with the ruling powers. Still — " We Russian intellectuals know our place. We have to." Bitter words pregnant with tragic meaning. Doubtless he was a sensitive person. So are all intellectuals. They do often magnify possible consequences. " Fear," says a Russian proverb, " has big eyes," and the intellectual has the biggest eyes of anybody in Russia. He is abnormally anxious. He finds himself in a position of defence, almost on probation, and he cannot help being over-cautious.

Not that he is politically recalcitrant. He has long ago become reconciled to the inevitability of the new regime. He is not seeking, and most positively would not welcome, an overthrow of the Soviets. He is sick of destruction. He is tired of war. He is afraid of fresh strife. He is nerve-wrecked and wants a chance to recuperate and to pursue his labors in peace. " We are just getting started again," once remarked to me a

famous and venerable Russian archaeologist whom I
met in my wanderings in Siberia, and " now there is
talk of war with England. Do you really think there
will be a war? " He shrugged his shoulders, looked at
his tools and tears glistened in his pathetic eyes. No,
the intellectual wants no more upheavals. He dreads
further conflict. He is content to let time and destiny
fulfill the necessary readjustments.

Yet to the proletarian he still is the link to the pre-
October age, a remnant of the pre-October civilization,
a reminder of the most hectic day in his history. Whenever an incident bursts on the scene involving an intellectual, like the trial of the mining engineers in the
spring of 1928, his old wrath rises high and hot, and
must be held back by a vigorous hand to keep it from
spilling into action. The plain truth is that the proletarian's distrust of the old intelligentsia will continue as
long as there is such an intelligentsia alive. It is too
deep-seated to die out completely. It is rooted in a
mighty, historic passion.

To the proletarian and to the Communist the intellectual damned himself eternally when he failed to respond to the October Revolution. Of course, the chief
leaders of this Revolution were intellectuals. They still
are. But in the mass the intellectual not only held aloof,
but denied and defied the October Revolution.

He could hardly have done otherwise. History had
not ripened him for the event. Culturally and psychologically he was as utterly unprepared for it as a child
is for trench warfare. He was primarily a man of compassion with deep reverence for human individuality.
He was and is a " soft fellow " without " audacity and

malice." Think of Dostoyevski's Raskolnikov, who after killing with an axe the withered and rapacious pawnbroker — a " mere insect " as he had regarded her — discovers that he had really killed himself. There was much of the Raskolnikov in all Russian intellectuals.

True, in the Social Revolutionary party there were intellectuals who embarked now and then on acts of terror, hurled bombs and fired revolvers at Czars, governors, ministers, generals. But they were rare exceptions and terror was to them an act of desperation. They saw no other way of bringing tyrants to an abatement of their cruelties. Yet on the whole no person shrank from bloodshed with deeper revulsion than the Russian intellectual.

Besides, he was a child of a private property civilization. With his mind he may have been floating in a socialistic utopia, but with his body he was hugging a private property reality. Despite all his revolutionary proclivities and ardor he was a man with a middle man's tastes, a middle man's sense of caution and comfort, a middle man's revulsion against rash action, a middle man's love of compromise.

What more natural than that he should shrink away in horror and disgust when the proletarian pleaded for support in the crusade for the dictatorship? He had been with the proletarian again and again and for him, but to storm the citadels of power after the almost bloodless overthrow of the Czar, was to him the height of stupidity and madness. He saw only battle, death ahead — chaos, agony, despair, the ruin of all that he had loved and revered. The march of the proletarian for power was to him a Gethsemane. He pictured all Russia, all civilization tumbling into an irretrievable ruin.

The proletarian in power! This man without background, without culture, without tradition, without political experience, this erstwhile unwashed muzhik, with his mud-crusted boots and his black finger nails, holding in his callow hands the destiny of one hundred and fifty million people! To the intellectual it seemed like a wicked and putrid jest! He laughed with mockery, he cried with scorn. When the Bolsheviks did sweep into power he refused to be of help to them. He would not recognize them. He deserted his post in factory, office, laboratory. He went on strike. He sabotaged. He would be no partner to what he deemed as the greatest outrage, not only against himself, against Russia, but against the world. He was sure that the proletarian had only capacity to wreck, none, or very little, to build — with his own hands. He was waiting for the inevitable collapse of the Bolshevik hegemony. He was sure it would come. He wanted it to come and by all the laws of history it should have come. But it did not. The proletarian remained master. The intellectual had miscalculated his fighting capacity, his physical endurance, his mental resourcefulness, his and those of his leaders.

The proletarian rankled with resentment. In the hour of his greatest trial the intellectual had failed him. The intellectual was a traitor, a foe. At one time the very word intelligentsia was as much a term of reproach in Russia as the word *bourzhui*. But Lenine, with his amazing capacity to brush aside personal rancor and face realities, sensed the danger of crowding the intellectual to the wall. He called for a truce, for a compromise, and since the proletarian needed brains — and the intellectual needed bread, the two did reach an agreement. They joined hands for the upbuilding of Russia — hands, but hardly hearts.

Some Communists of prominence have been assuring the world that the feud between the proletarian and the intellectual has been " liquidated," that the intellectual is happy in the new society. But is he? Can he be? I am speaking, of course, here as throughout this chapter of the intellectual reared in the environment and the idealogy of the pre-October days.

Politically he is out of the picture. He has pledged his loyalty to the new regime. He has behaved with model circumspection. He has even shown signs of penitence. Still, politically he is not consulted. Not often is he even considered. If he wants to join the Communist Party, and unless he does he can exercise no influence in political life, he must be on probation for two years instead of six months like a proletarian. Positions of political responsibility, as already recorded in a preceding chapter, are seldom open to him. If he has not been deprived of his citizenship he can, at election time, cast his vote, that is raise his hand for or against a deputy to the Soviet. But this is a matter of routine, almost a mechanical act, without a breath of excitement.

His standard of living has sunk perceptibly from its former level. Salaries in some intellectual professions like teaching and medicine are markedly low. No intellectuals in Russia complain so vociferously of being

underpaid as do teachers and physicians. Often, however, the intellectual is the highest paid worker in the
land. He is after all the *spetz* — specialist, the engineer,
the architect, the chemist, the economist, the organizer.
But even then his earnings are limited, seldom rising
above four hundred dollars a month. Limited also,
strangely enough, are his spending opportunities. No
longer can he rent the apartment that he formerly occupied, with its parlors, its bedrooms, its playrooms
for children. The housing shortage, if nothing else,
makes this impossible. No longer can he subscribe, at
his will, to foreign periodicals and books. No longer
can he travel at his wish to foreign lands, see new
sights and stimulate himself with new contacts. Even
if he has enough money saved up for the trip, the state
bank, because of the financial stringency of the country, will not exchange his roubles into foreign currency,
unless, of course, he is a noted savant, and without
such currency he cannot travel in foreign parts. No
longer can he go to his favorite tailor and order an overcoat, a suit of clothes from choice English cloth. There
is no such cloth in the country, save what smugglers
haul in, and that is prohibitive in price. As for dinner
jackets and dress suits — he does not bother — he has
almost forgotten that there are such things in the world.
He has no occasion to wear them anyway, save possibly at a banquet to a distinguished foreign visitor,
and even then he feels more comfortable mentally in
his everyday clothes.

Worst of all is the sense of insecurity that preys on
him — sheer economic insecurity. The engineer, the
architect, the chemist, the *spetz*, or specialist, need have

no anxiety of losing his job. The state will seek to make him reasonably comfortable, so that he can do his best work. After all he cannot be easily replaced. But the intellectual of lesser distinction, the manager of a drug store, director of a hospital, superintendent of a co-operative, principal of a school, men, in other words, in the so-called secondary intellectual pursuits are in constant dread of dismissal. Journalists from one end of the country to the other, who are not members of the Communist Party are always fearful lest they make some slip which will invoke on them the displeasure of their chiefs and result in dismissal. The same is true of clerks, of all non-partisan office workers, in industry as well as in government. With the passage of time this condition will not improve but will grow progressively worse.

It can hardly be otherwise. The Communists complain that the old time intellectual is too highly individualized, too conscious of his superiority, and not heartily interested in the social Revolution. He may be a more adept worker than the Party man, but he has not saturated himself with the new social spirit, and under the best circumstances he cannot infuse this spirit into his work. He must, therefore, be supplanted by men who will work not for themselves, but for the cause. He must give way to Party men. A good enough reason for the Communist, but it does not mitigate the tragedy of the intellectual. With a quaking heart he is constantly casting eyes upward to see if the political axe is descending on him. I once asked a group of literary folk in Moscow why they spurn offers of lucrative editorial positions from the state and cooperative publishing house. " Why should we not? " replied one of them. " The moment our assistants, who will, of course, be Party men, learn from us how to edit books, they get into our places and we get the gate." So the feud persists, invisible and irrepressible.

Gone also for the intellectual is his old social world — a mere cracked shell it is now. The physical surroundings of his every-day life and his economic position do not permit of social expansiveness. Besides, there is always the danger of becoming conspicuous. He gathers, of course, at scientific conferences, at meetings of his professional group. But the old social outlet with its amplitude, its cheer, its abandon is now a thing of the past.

To add to his discomfiture there is the problem of cultural readjustment. The values in which he has grown up, in which he exulted, do not fit the new society. He has retested and recast them, but the flavour of the old civilization persists, which is not at all to the liking of the new rulers. They are constantly censuring him for his failure to adopt and to promote the new proletarian cultural values. To him of course, these new values are still in a state of flux. He insists that cultural values, unlike clay dolls, cannot be made to order over night. Time, he insists, effort, tradition, social mood, sentiment, must distill the ingredients out of which to mold them, and if he dared be more frank with his rulers, if not with himself, he would bluntly inform them that the spirit of these new cultural values are not to his tastes. They lack the aesthetic finesse, the social delicacy of the old values. But however annoyed he may feel he says nothing or little in reply.

Terrific, indeed, has been the ordeal of the Russian intellectual since the coming of the new regime. It has meant trial and turbulence, tears and pain, self-denial and even self-abasement. Gone is his old comfort, often enough his security. Gone is his old prestige. The peasant, the proletarian, the Communist, the youth — each in his own way has been made conscious of a new self-respect, a new dignity. They have discovered or recovered their I. But the intellectual has had to shove his I into the background, to keep it from public view. It has no standing in the new society and hardly any value. As a matter of sheer psychology his has been an excruciating task. It is never easy to break off a habit, and he has had to wrench himself loose from an entire set of habits or else find himself ground between the wheels of the Revolution.

Still, if the Revolution has severely narrowed outlets for economic, social, cultural, political self-expression and advancement it has not been without its positive contribution. It has meant torture but also purgation. It may not have brought new happiness but it has opened up founts of new wisdom, or at least understanding. Despite his humanitarianism and his professed love for the dark masses, the intellectual had not, save in theory, cherished respect for labour. He would not soil his hands with menial toil. Now when he looks back at his old attitude toward labour he laughs at himself. " It did seem silly," one of the most famous scientists of the land confessed to me. Now it no longer hurts his conscience if his neighbours see him carrying a sack of flour on his back or a load of wood in his arms. Now he has no sense of inner incongruity or perturbation when he has to wash his own windows, mend his own shoes or repair his own stove. " Yes, I am late today," announced a popular professor of literature, to his class once, in Moscow University, " because I had company last night and not being able to afford a maid, I had to wash my own dishes." The students roared with delight.

As never before the intellectual is also beginning to appreciate the value of decisiveness and action. His ancient Hamletism is not dead, but it is no longer in the foreground of his consciousness. Life in revolutionary Russia, like water in a mill-dam, rushes swiftly on and on sweeping people along with it, and the intellectual cannot and dare not pause to look back or to immerse himself in speculation and self-scrutiny.

Best of all he has remained at home. He has escaped the cruel fate of the emigré intellectuals. Scattered they are over all corners of the globe. Unhardened, unsophisticated, over-sensitive, Russians that they are, they cannot acclimate themselves to an alien civilization. They cannot strike roots in an alien soil or only very few of them. They shake fists and shriek defiance; they threaten and they boast, but these are mere gestures of despair, and perhaps of folly. They drift along with the winds of chance and circumstance. They still live with the inspiration of old Russia, the Russia that is no more, save in their own memory. Lonely folk they are, the loneliest in the world and they are rapidly growing sterile. Their souls are wilting. Merezhkovsky, Hippius, Kuprin, Amfiteatrov, Milyukov, world figures once — now withering in ever-deepening obscurity — ghosts fumbling for light and never finding it!

The intellectual who has remained in Russia, however disappointed and aggrieved he may feel, has his roots in his native soil. Nourishment flows freely to these roots. He has tasted his fill of agony and sordidness — and will until the end of his days — but he has his delights, and at times even inspirations. Cut off from physical contact with the outside world he can yet roam at will over his own vast variegated and boisterous land. He can write, sing, dream, if not of the new social gospel, at least of the things he has always loved and still loves — of the muzhik, the steppe, the birch forests, the Volga, the Caucasus, the Russian sky, his own yesterday and even of the soul of Russia. Russia still is his homeland, his immense, brooding, ever-stirring little mother.

He cannot help realizing, of course, that his end is coming — that is, the end of his old dreams and illusions, his whole old world with its pathos and beauty, its unrest and promise, its yearning and its frustration. He must smile now perhaps with gall, but certainly with amusement when he reads the words of Chekhov's Baron Tuzenbach that " not only after two or three hundred but in millions of years life will still be as it is." He knows how pathetically deceiving are these words. He could cry out their falsity until his heart burst. People may eat, drink, sleep, fight as they have always done, but they will seek new purposes, new adaptations, new exaltations, new desperations, aye, new follies. They have done that in Russia, and he knows that for good or for evil they have not failed. . . . The proof, too living to be denied or misjudged, is the new intellectual!

He has not the social background of the old intelligentsia. He comes from the earth itself, from the masses. He has no soulfulness, no delicacy, no artistry. He has not even the competence of his predecessors. He is unkempt, uncouth, unshaven, with calloused hands, but with an insatiable hunger for knowledge and conquest. He smells of dirt, of coal dust, of oil and also of wind and rain. He revels, not in Nadson, in Pushkin, in Lermontov and other similar poets, but in Marx, in Lenine, in Ford, in Edison, in Taylor. When he invites his fair one for a walk or a ride in a canoe he does not, like intellectuals of a former generation, declaim love lyrics to her. He does not even ask her whether she has read Pushkin's Onyegin, but talks on endlessly and with passion of smoke-stacks, tractors, engines, dynamos, cities, machines, factories; and the fair one listens and glows with as much ecstasy and far less heartache than did fair ones in other days when, in a sobbing voice, men recited to them Tatyana's letter to Onyegin.

In the twilight of their history well might the old intelligentsia greet the new with the words of Turgenev's Lavretsky: " Play on, make merry, grow on, young forces. Life lies before you and it will be easier for you to live. You will not be compelled, as we have been, to seek your road, to struggle, to fall and to rise to your feet again amid the gloom. We have given ourselves great trouble that we might remain whole and how many of us have failed! But you must now work, perform deeds, and the blessings of the old fellows, like me, be upon you."

CHAPTER XV

COSSACK

HERE I was in a *stanitsa* — settlement — in the Kuban, famous Cossack stronghold in southern Russia. It was a Sunday morning, bright and hot with a slight breeze stirring playfully the outward layer of leaves on the trees. Church-bells were ringing with that booming clang so peculiarly Russian that bursts sharp on the ears and lingers long and plaintively in the air like the wail of a lonely animal. Kerchiefed women, young and old, sturdy and sunburned, with babies in their arms and with tots about them, were on their way to church — a straggling procession — women and only rarely a man.

I strolled leisurely through the streets, so wide, so ancient, without sidewalks or pavements, with ruts and hollows, with only the whitewash on the little cottages and the flourishing fruit-trees in the yards giving colour and freshness to the scene. It was a large *stanitsa* with a population of over thirty thousand, but it might have been only a peasant hamlet, so quiet and listless did it seem, with not even dogs, as you passed them, bothering, as in a peasant village, to leap at you.

It was only when I strayed into the market-place that I found myself transported into a new world. A huge crowd of Cossacks had gathered there — all men — to while away their leisure hours. And what men they were! Immense, fearsome, with massive backs, as upright as those limbless pines in Russia's northern forests, real giants in the earth, as if lifted bodily out of the pages of Grimm and Andersen. Despite the heat they wore woolens and flannels and hardly one of them, youth or grandfather, but sported a tall sheepskin hat, in which they appeared even taller than they were, and almost as awesome as some untamed beasts strutting at ease in their native haunts. Their faces etched themselves on the mind like burning metal. Broad, swarthy faces, with heavy jaws, with now and then that upward slope of the cheek-bones, that sharp slit in the brow which denote Turk or Tartar or some other Asiatic heritage, and always with a profusion of hair, brows, moustaches, beards — as gorgeous as grass in rich well-watered soil. Massive faces, seasoned to wind, rain, sun, as of men defiant of trial, of battle, of death. Faces with callous self-assurance and with hardly a trace of mellowness, except in the *stariks* — the older men who were as if of a race apart. Big men — no sunken chests, no bent backs, no paunchy figures. Upright, lean, supple men, with the deep-cut wrinkles losing themselves in immense beards like rivulets in a big stream, with the light of wisdom in their gleaming eyes, above all with an air of prepossession and conceit that invested them with a grace no less than a terror. To see such a crowd of Cossacks in their native setting for the first time in one's life is an experience ever to be cherished.

There was a mass-meeting in the *stanitsa* that morning — the most important mass-meeting of the year, if not of the entire post-revolutionary period. A host of important personages had arrived to attend it — the

editorial staff of the newspaper in Krasnodar, the capital of the region, Party workers, men from the commissary of agriculture and finance and even the prosecuting attorney. They had all come to give the floor
to the Cossack and not only to allow, but to coax and
goad him into free expression of opinion on anything
and everything that perplexed or grieved him — even
to the point of denouncing local officials, any officials
anywhere. It was to be a meeting of that *samo-kritika*
— self-criticism — which the Communist Party had
loosened like a tornado over the country, and which
had blasted to the surface heaps of abuses that a stiff
and implacable bureaucracy had held under cover.
" Talk, talk," said a tall stately woman with roseate
cheeks, the associate editor of the newspaper and one
of the most gifted orators of the region, " nobody will
interfere or molest you. Here is the prosecuting attorney in person not only to defend you, but to press your
charges against any and all evil-doers in your midst."

The Cossacks took the orator at her word and burst
into a storm of complaints. Hours and hours of oratory,
charges and countercharges. The heat scorched and
baked. I squeezed out of the crowd and strolled off into
the shade under a mammoth apple tree. A slice of the
mass-meeting had as if peeled off and wound around
me. They would talk to an American now — learn
something of the country of which they had heard so
much. Then an old man queried how I liked Cossacks?
" They do seem like beasts, don't they? " he remarked.
" But you have not seen us when we are aroused. We
are the worst of beasts then — real tigers."

" Yes, they are that," came a woman's voice, " ti-

gers, and what tigers. . . ." She was of middle age
with shrewd grey eyes and a chin as massive almost
as a man's. There was vigour in her voice and an utter
self-confidence in her manner — a real Cossack woman,
she was never afraid to hold her ground against any
man or any crowd of men, " O, how they could hurt
people with their whips and their swords! "

" Whom did we hurt? " indignantly protested a
patriarch with a flowing beard.

" Whom? You know, uncle — *nu,* students for example, and Jews."

" Don't lie, you witch; there are no Jews here."

" I didn't say here," retorted the woman sharply.

" Where then? " he inquired with equal sharpness.

" Do I have to tell you? O, you innocent soul! In
the cities — *pogroms,* don't you remember? Think of
your yesterday? "

" I didn't take part in any such affairs."

" You didn't, eh? " pursued the woman relentlessly.
" Other Cossacks did. I have seen them, the brutes.
Ekh, the Soviets ought to thrash you all a little, then
you'd know how your victims felt when you snapped
the lash over them. . . ."

" *Nu, baba,* stop," interrupted the patriarch with a
gesture of disgust, " or the American will think you
are a damned fool."

" Aye," she chuckled, " let him think what he will,
but I am telling the truth, and you know it, you bearded
devil."

He motioned violently with his hand and spat with
contempt in the direction of the woman, not once but
three times. The crowd roared with amusement. Then

someone asked me if men ever beat their wives in America, and before I had time to reply a girl with a kerchief round her head and flaming with radiance broke in with the story of a neighbour of theirs, a man of sixty-five who had thrashed his wife who was seventy-two, because she had flirted with another man. "He even threatened to kill her," she finished with a touch of gravity in her voice.

"And you women," chided the patriarch again, "are saints, you never beat your husbands."

"Of course we do," several women responded in unison, "and why shouldn't we when they deserve it?"

"I saw a woman only the other day turn her fists on her man," someone else volunteered, "until he shrank together like a cat cornered by a dog."

It was instructive to hear the Cossacks jest so merrily. It was good to discover one of their own tribe, a woman at that, remind them trenchantly of their past offences, which history will neither dismiss nor pardon. Above all it was cheering to hear them voice their grievances in an open mass-meeting with such vigour and audacity. All this gave one a chance to take the measure of their manhood, and, alas, I must confess that the Cossack is a crushed man and crushed, I think, forever. If he ever does emerge from his ordeal, it will not be as Cossack. Never. His Cossackdom is as much a memory now as the regime which it had served.

His very protests at the mass-meeting were unmistakable proof of defeat if not capitulation. Think of a Cossack having to complain of anything, especially of taxes, of which he knew nothing in the old days, as he had none to pay, or of land apportionments, when formerly he received all that he, or rather his women folk, could till. Think of a Cossack being obliged to stand in a queue to obtain calico, when in the old days people brushed out of his way when he entered a shop, and not only calico but woolens, silks, satins, velvets, were his in whatever quantity he wished! The very appearance of the Cossack nowadays speaks with pathetic eloquence of his downfall. Not even on Sundays does he sport his broad trousers with the flaming stripes, his *cherkeska* — flowing cloak — with the row of silver-headed cartridges across the breast, the inevitable sword swung from his side and the bayonets flung from his belt.

Once on a Sunday I wanted to take a picture of a group of Cossacks in their tribal regalia. But in the entire *stanitsa* of thirty-five thousand there were only three men who could boast of uniforms, and even they had neither sword nor dagger any longer!

So this Cossack who had always thought himself superior and invincible, as if above all law of man and nature — has actually been bowed, if not cowed, by the Revolution. He cannot flee from it. With a multitude of invisible whips this Revolution is lashing him in body and mind. It is compelling him, against his will, to abandon, and abandon forever, his old habits, as well as his old faiths and to gird himself as best he can to a new life and a new world. Well indeed might that Cossack whom I met once before an open fire on the steppes outside of the city of Tzaritizin, now Stalingrad, chant of the dismal fate of his tribe. . . . A Cossack, ran his ditty, is no longer a *voyak*, a warrior, a man of power and importance in the world, with a fiery steed as mindful as a wife, with a shiny saddle and a gaudy uniform and with money in his pocket for boots and vodka. No, a Cossack was like an old woman now with an apron round her waist.

Apron— symbol of toil, docility, monotony, which the Cossack always despised! History is settling its score with the Cossack. It is sweeping him with brutal energy into unredeemable oblivion. . . .

And yet what a boisterous and romantic part he has played in the making of history! With what desperation he had slashed through forest and mountain, swamp and river, and planted the Russian flag over new and boundless territories! Who knows what Russia, what Europe, what the world would have been like if it had not been for him, his ever surging lust for new adventure, new battles? It was he who had conquered almost unaided the whole of Siberia — a land twice the size of the United States. It was he who had penetrated Turkestan and Central Asia, who had scaled the mountains of the Caucasus, who had followed Napoleon out of Moscow, who had played a decisive role in every war and every advance Russia had made in the last two hundred years. He was not only the reconnoiterer, the killer, the conqueror, he was also the frontiersman, the colonizer. He it was who was always sent to stand watch over a new territory, to plant himself in the soil there. Only he could be trusted with such a task, for no matter where he was or what his condition, he could be relied upon to remain loyal — to flout seditious ideas and to cleave the very heart of the man uttering them.

He was the eternal suppressor of rebellion. Hardly

a city but had its scores and hundreds of his tribe to hurl themselves with deadly fire on all enemies of living rulers. The very Cossacks in the Kuban who were discoursing with such gloom of their fate were the most ardent defendants of the old order. They were the most heroic of their tribe. It was they who made up the personal guard of the Czar. *Kubantsui* —those superb giants who inspired wonder and terror in foreign visitors, and who seemed a symbol of the invincibility of Czardom.

Cossack! What a fearsome word it had become, not only in the Russian but in all languages. What savagery it suggested, what tyranny it spelled, what terror it inspired! Turk, Tartar, German, Pole — in battles with Russia they always quaked at a personal encounter with the Cossack. They knew his parts. No warrior was more doughty, or more savage. Even now in every *stanitsa* there are men who, while dashing about on horseback can, with one stroke of the sword, cleave an adversary in twain. The Cossack asked for no quarter and gave none. Cause did not matter. He raised no questions. He cherished no doubts. Scruples did not trouble him. He did not wait and did not want explanations. His horse and sword were always ready and so was he. He loved the smell of blood. The sight of men in death or in agony never annoyed him. His hand was firm and his heart joyous — always. He could fling himself with song at an adversary or gasp out his last breath likewise with a song. He bothered not whom he was sent against — foreign foe or his own brother, Jew, student, proletarian, or only wretched muzhiks. He was ready for slaughter . . . always.

Yet it was not so in old days. Not at all. History has played a sinister caper with the Cossack. It had ushered him on the scene not as a defender but as a hater of tyranny. In old days he was both a child and a symbol of freedom. His very name implies a person in search of liberty. He always preferred death to subjection. He was, in fact, the earliest Russian revolutionary.

He first emerges in history as an adventurer, chiefly of peasant stock, who had tired of the monotony of village life, especially as landlords were acquiring more and more power over him. He fled south, where the climate was mild, game and fish abundant, vegetation rich, the forests thick and above all, no rulers and no law. He fished, he hunted, he battled, now with Turk, now with Tartar, now with Circassian. He plundered merchants and travellers, especially on the treks along which passed the interminable caravans from Asia to Russia.

In the sixteenth century his numbers swelled. Landlords and princes in Russia were gaining ascendancy. Wealth in the form of cattle, implements, grains, as well as political power were centring in their hands. Peasants without cattle, implements, seed, would hire themselves out for a period of years, often would actually mortgage themselves for long terms, even for life. From year to year the number of these voluntary serfs increased and not all of them would or could tolerate subjection. So they fled at the first opportunity, now only to a neighbouring landlord and now, as new laws were passed forbidding landlords to offer refuge to fugitive peasants, to the wilderness in the south where the hand of the law could not reach them. They sped to the brush-covered islands and the wooded marshes of the big rivers. They swept south in two streams — one down the Don River, hence the Don Cossacks, who were mainly Great Russians, and the other down the Dnieper, and they were mainly Ukrainians and called themselves the *Saporozhtsui*. But whoever they were, wherever they hailed from — sometimes they were merchants, bandits, princes, even clergymen — their chief concern in life was freedom from tyranny. *Volnitsa* — freedom — was the staff of the Cossack's life, his very goddess!

The *sech*, literally a hewing in the forest, was the citadel of *Zaporozhtsui* Cossackdom. It became, in time, the seat of an amazing republic, military yet free, with traditions and heritages all its own, a complete world, secluded yet boisterous and fairly impregnable. It had no written law. The Cossack wanted none. He was afraid it would in time curtail his liberties, and besides he was so busy roistering about the rivers, steppes, forests, that he had no time to compose a written code. But his customs had the power of law, stern law. He elected his elders and if they abused their authority or misruled, he recalled them and often punished them cruelly and ignominiously, set them in water with their bosoms loaded with sand and with the crowd near to hurl merry quips at them. Women he barred from the *sech*. He considered them too distracting, liable to weaken his fighting prowess. If one of his clan did yield to the allurements of a woman he had to leave the *sech* and lost the esteem of his comrades.

Brigand and plunderer that he was, with his brother

Cossacks he was most upright. Woe to the man who was not! If a Cossack failed to pay his debts to a fellow-Cossack he was chained to a cannon until his friends came to his rescue and redeemed his obligations. If he was caught stealing from a fellow-Cossack, he was tied to the pillar of shame in the public square for three days or longer, unless again his friends made good his theft. Right beside this pillar lay an oaken cudgel and every passer-by was bound to pick it up and strike the offender with it as violent a blow as he chose. Vodka was sometimes given him, but only to make him " wild," so it would be more fun to wield the cudgel over him. Often the offender died on the first day of the sentence, so savage were the blows administered. Nor was it unusual for such a man to have his arms or legs broken in punishment for his transgression. Most ferocious were the Cossack death penalties. With a hook thrust through his ribs the condemned man would be hoisted up a tree and left there, until he not only died but crumbled to pieces. If a Cossack killed a chum of his, he was buried alive under the coffin of his victim.

When the Cossack was free from military duty he would loaf around in the *sech*. Labour he despised and business still more. Any man who did not pursue a life like his, that is, a life of idleness and plunder, of battle and freedom, was to him a pariah. He was an intense man in everything he did, in his fighting, his adventuring, his eating, his dancing, and above all in his drinking. What a monstrous drinker he was! During his idle days he was always inebriate, disposing often of his boots and his shirt to obtain the coveted brew.

Drinking jousts were a pastime as much as a passion with him, even more favoured than fist-fights, though usually the two went hand in hand.

It was because of his irrepressible love of freedom that it fell to the Cossack's lot to engineer some of the most sanguinary uprisings in Russian history. Consider the rebellion of Stenka Razin in 1669. He had sent out emissaries to the big estates with the message that he would liberate serfs from bondage and give them land and freedom, if they would enlist under his banner and battle to the death with landlords and officials. Peasants responded in overwhelming numbers. Stenka moved onward slaughtering enemies with terrible ferocity. Town after town succumbed to his onslaught. He had seized the rich city of Astrakhan with scarcely a battle, and only because the masses within its gates had been roused by his propaganda to a frenzy of enthusiasm for him and his cause. When he entered the city bedlam broke loose. The proletarians of the day — lackeys, janitors, serfs — seized the homes of their masters and helped themselves to anything they could lay their hands on — clothes, food, money, furnishings and sometimes the wives and daughters of the fallen nobles. Stenka had conquered the Don and Volga basins and was marching on Moscow.

The larger his army grew the more unwieldy it became. Withal he lacked war material and reliable officers. In the end he was conquered and he and his brother were captured. Weighted down with chains, the Razins were hooked to a huge wagon and led through the streets and roads in their disgrace and agony as a lesson to others of what awaited them if they dared rise in rebellion. Officials sought to wring from Stenka a confession of guilt, but in vain. He resisted all allurements to stamp himself as a traitor. He was tortured horribly and then in accordance with the custom of the day was quartered alive.

A century later another Cossack, Yemelyan Pugatchev, round whose exploits the poet Pushkin has woven an exquisite romance, led peasants in another rebellion. He had gathered an immense army and won many brilliant victories, but like Stenka Razin, in the end, because of unwieldy organization, inadequate supplies, lack of competent associates, he was conquered and like Stenka was tortured and quartered alive.

How did it come that this stormy rebel, the Cossack, whose very slogan was *volnitza* — freedom — in time became the most savage suppressor of liberty that the world had ever known? For nearly two centuries he fought wildly and desperately to preserve a system that was in utter opposition to the tenets, sentiments, traditions of his tribe. An historic anomaly this would seem. But it was not. The Cossack simply was not socially-minded. He had never conceived of freedom as an ideal or a social goal.

It is the tragedy of the Russian Cossack that he never had a leader with a bit of prophetic vision or a social consciousness, who could rise above his daily exploits and transmute his passionate urge for personal liberty into a political philosophy or a social program, and imbue his followers with zeal to make these into a reality. Lacking such leadership his fine tradition deteriorated. He never bothered about a stabilized society. He never worried about tomorrow. He cared only for his immediate self, his immediate physical appetite. Society, mankind, his own people, the world at large did not bother him. Of the needs and feelings of others he was brutally callous. He pillaged, burned, killed outsiders on the least provocation, often on none at all. Undisciplined, the tempestuous impulses of the Cossack never emerged from the bounds of physical exploit and in time degenerated into mere lust for reckless and destructive adventure.

Lacking a sense of social responsibility it was easy for him to make compromises with the Russian rulers and enter their service. The Czars could well afford to grant him privileges which would allow him full scope to express his stormy personality. Three things the Cossack required to keep him contented — freedom to pursue his tribal and communal life, ample physical excitement and economic security. All of these the Russian monarchs were in a position to gratify abundantly. Since the Cossack's urge for freedom and his local democratic usages were grounded in no subversive political theory and practice, they held in them no vestige of menace to the rule of autocracy. As for physical excitement — military service and constant warfare on the internal and external fronts — war with outside nations, suppression of Russia's subject peoples and campaigns of pacification against students, workers, peasants, yielded enough of it to gratify the urge for physical violence. Economic security likewise was no difficult matter for the Russian Czars to provide. Land was abundant, Cossack women were unexcelled workers, and this, together with the exemption from taxes and occasional subsidies, kept the Cossack free from want.

Thus it happened that the Russian Cossack who had embarked on his career as a rebel ended up by being the most brutal suppressor of rebellion.

But his picturesqueness and his prowess were only external. Sundered physically, socially and culturally from the outside world, he could not help stagnating. The age of science and enlightenment hardly penetrated into his midst. He could tyrannize and terrorize, but like the very power he was protecting he remained inwardly hollow, out of tune with the swarm of ideas that the age of science had wafted into the world.

How dismally backward he has remained, this once all-powerful Cossack! At every step in the Cossack settlements you stumble into evidence of pathetic stagnation. Not a single *stanitsa* I visited, however large the population — and sometimes it was as high as forty thousand — could boast of a public bath-house! Not in the Kuban, except among the non-Cossack inhabitants. Cossacks there do not bathe save in summer in the rivers! With the exception of the houses, which are larger than in peasant villages and always elegantly whitewashed inside and outside, the Cossack *stanitsas*, in their outward appearance, are as wretched as any peasant community — without sidewalks, without pavements, without drainage, without water-power and with the streets, after a heavy rain, turning into pools of slush. In one *stanitsa* the young people told me that it took months of desperate warfare with their elders to win them to the proposition of drilling an artesian well so that the people would have healthy, instead of dung-infested water to drink. Living in a most ideal climate and occupying the best land in the country — rich black soil that needs no fertilizer — and with abundance of rain and sunshine, the Cossack is yet raising crops which would make an Iowa farmer scream with despair. Superstition likewise has retained a firm clutch on him. Let the following incident speak for itself:

A young and brilliant agriculturist had discovered a method of growing cotton on the Kuban steppes. In a certain *stanitsa* one Cossack was especially enthusiastic over the new crop. He had tended his patch of cotton with the tenderest of care. As fate would have it there was a drouth in that region. The older men in the *stanitsa* were worried. They engaged a priest to march around with an ikon and sprinkle holy water and pray for rain, but in vain. Their crops were beginning to burn up and still no rain. They were growing desperate. Never had they had a drouth. Why were they having it now? Surely it was because the Lord was punishing them. And for what? They had not turned against Him like people in so many other places in Russia. They were bowing to ikons, and burning candles, fulfilling the fasts. Why then was He punishing them? There could be only one reason — for the violation of His will. And who could possibly be violating His will? The man who was doing things that had never before been done and that man was the Cossack who was growing cotton! God must have taken offence at that, for if He had wanted cotton to grow in their settlement, He would have Himself planted it long ago. So they held a secret meeting, the older men of the community, and decided that whatever happened they must not allow cotton to grow in their vicinity or the Lord would not abate His wrath against them. Late one night they swooped on the field of cotton in their *stanitsa* and plucked up every plant!

But a new spirit is storming the Cossack steppes. Hardly a settlement but can boast of a nucleus of youths who had been stirred into an understanding of a new life and a new world. In every *stanitsa* there are men like T—— whom I met once in the office of a newspaper. A giant of a man he was — though only twenty-three years of age — tall, with immense shoulders, a neck no less immense and a chest that bulged with muscles. He was married, the father of three children, and had come to town to hold examinations in the university. He had been studying hard at night in his home to prepare for these examinations, and if he should pass them he would, so he assured me, go through a course in the university — just so that he might become cultivated and have power to spread enlightenment among his semi-savage brother-Cossacks in the steppe.

He was no Communist. He was sure he never would be one. But the life of the Cossack was so terribly dark, soaked in superstition, barbarities, meanness. A Cossack was just a powerful beast — knew nothing and cared for nothing save his brute appetites — battles, vodka, fist-fights. The old government had given him land, exempted him from taxes, surrounded him with special privileges, pampered his vanity with glittering uniforms, armaments, decorations, but it had held science away from him, and without science men nowadays must perish, must they not?

But the Revolution, my narrator continued, was bringing science to the Cossack and that really was its chief achievement and justification. Let Communists impose heavy taxes, let them seek to press the Cossack into their political mould, let them come and gather bread as they had done the previous spring, let them resort to all the measures they choose to keep the Cossack from accumulating capital — all that paled before the benefits science would achieve. In the old days there were only thirteen agricultural advisers in the entire Kuban. They never lived on the *stanitsa*. They were officials rather than advisers. But now there were already five hundred of them, and they all lived on the *stanitsas,* and worked indefatigably to bring enlightenment to the Cossack, teaching him modern ways of growing wheat, alfalfa, cotton, sugar-beets, aye, even how to build American silos! A host of new ideas of which he had heard little or nothing in the old days had stirred the Cossack — water-power, drainage, bathhouses, nurseries, new methods of tilling the land, little theatres, museums. *Nu,* science was coming to the Cossack and in time would chasten him of his ancient dross, and make an enlightened citizen of him!

Meanwhile he is Cossack no longer save in name. His old privileges, prerogatives, distinctions, he has lost. He is making his exit from the stage of Russian history with teeth gnashed in wrath and eyes blazing with hate. The older Cossack never can forget the old days and the old glories. He sighs, and sobs, and swears for the old days, the old adventures, but there is no echo to his voice. He is a helpless man, he has nothing with which to offset the onslaught of science which the Revolution is exploiting as one of its weapons.

The movement of collective farming is further grinding his old attributes out of him. It is subjecting him to a discipline that must irk and pain, so contrary is it to his age-old traditions and practices. It is making him part of a social machine which he cannot control, and which drives him on and on to field and barn, to carpenter-shop and flour-mill — to some place where he must toil away for hours every day on a plane of equality, and perhaps in the society, of mere muzhiks. His enemies, and he has many of them, can, if they are vengefully-minded, gloat with joy at the fate that history is meting out to him.

He is not pretty in defeat, this awesome Cossack. He is really pathetic, as all strong men are when prostrate with impotence. Still, despite his depravities, his has been a heroic past. The world will ever remember that whatever his sins and iniquities, the one quality that cast a glow of romance over him was his matchless courage. He never knew fear. He never hesitated when in quest of adventure or battle. Nothing dismayed him. North, south, east, west, in the *taiga* of Siberia, in the marshes of the Ukraine, in the deserts of central Asia, in the mountains of the Caucasus, he always dared defy man, beast, even nature, and he always seemed invincible. His matchless courage and his physical exploits will continue to inspire poet and artist even as they had in the past. There are no finer tales in the Russian language than Gogol's " Taras Bulba,"

or Pushkin's " The Captain's Daughter," or Tolstoy's
" The Cossacks." Long after the world has forgotten
pogroms and pacifications it will thrill to the songs and
stories that commemorate the heroic, even if not always
commendable exploits of the Cossack, this greatest of
all Russia's, if not the world's warriors.

CHAPTER XVI

JEW

NO people in Russia have been so wrought up by
the destructive and transforming forces of the
Revolution as have the Jews, the three millions that
still live there. They, more than any other racial group
have been essentially a city people, and the Revolution
has dealt its fiercest blows to the city. In the village
the peasant could plant himself in the soil of which he
smells so pungently and with his bare fists fight back
the revolutionary avalanche. He has done it again and
again. He has won many a notable victory over the
revolutionary powers. But the city man has not the
firm ground of the peasant to stand on. He has been
stripped of all means of resistance. He has had to bow
to all the blows and all the biddings of the revolutionary
dictators.

There have been Jews, workers, intellectuals, youths,
who have marched hand in hand with the Revolution,
some of them rising to positions of supreme leadership.
But they have been in the minority. The bulk of Russian Jewry had no hand in the making of the Bolshevist
Revolution, could have had no hand in it, for in the
old days they were forbidden to live in the cities of
Leningrad and Moscow, where the Revolution had first
become entrenched and whence it hurled itself on the
remainder of the country. Besides, they were essentially middlemen. As such, they were interested in a

society that would enable them peacefully and prosper-
ously to pursue their chosen vocations. But the Bolshevist Revolution had aimed at the opposite result —
the annihilation of just such a society. It was primarily
and most emphatically a Revolution against the middleman and his world, economic as well as social and
spiritual.

That is why the Revolution has so turbulently upset
the old individual and social life of the Jew. I do not
know of any instance in the history of the Jews when
they have had to undergo so volcanic a process of
readjustment in every phase of their life and thought
as in Russia since the coming of the Soviets. Individual
and group aims, ambitions, beliefs, habits of thought
and action, which were formerly an ingrained part of
their everyday life, they have had to modify, discard,
often at cost of excruciating pain. They could no longer
take for granted their traditions, their ideals. The Revolution had ground them up and is only now slowly
piecing them together again. It is making them less
distinctive and less group-conscious, more militant and
more earthy. It is even threatening eventually to assimilate and thus destroy them as a separate people.

Something that I saw several years ago on my first
visit to Russia since I left the country as a boy, impressed me dramatically with the inner change that
the Revolution has wrought in the Russian Jew. I was
visiting the town where I had once attended school.
Across the street from the house where I was staying,
there stretched an immense garden, and in the morning,
no matter how early I arose, I could see from the
window in my room a girl at work there. She was always

barefoot like an ordinary peasant, and during the hours when the sun was not hot, also bareheaded, her glistening blond hair held in place by a red ribbon in the manner of a *Komsomolka,* a Young girl Communist. She could not have been more than seventeen or eighteen, though her face bore the stamp of that solemn maturity so common to Russian girls, especially working girls. At times, as she was hoeing, weeding, pouring water from a wooden pail over parched cucumber beds, she would sing, softly, delicately, in the manner of a person accustomed to singing to himself. She worked with such zeal and steadiness that I wondered who she might be. I could tell from her appearance that she was no peasant girl; for these rarely bob their hair or wear city-made clothes while at work, or sing in a modern style as she did. On inquiry I learned that she was the daughter of a formerly well-to-do Jewish merchant and was a student of the University of Moscow. She had come home for her summer vacation and had taken it upon herself to look after the immense family garden.

Now, to the average American, bred in the tradition of the pioneer and the self-made man, to whom work is almost a religion, it would not seem especially significant that a Jewish college student in Russia, even a girl, should engage in outdoor physical labour. But to me, with the pre-war social cleavages and conventions in that land of my boyhood still fresh in my mind, the fact was momentous. Where in Russia, in the old days, in city or village, would one encounter a Jewish university student, let alone a girl student, condescending to blister his hands with common toil?

The medieval notion of the debasing quality of physical labour, alien to America but common to countries that have not outlived the tradition of master and serf, nobleman and peasant, had bored deep into the Jewish mind in Eastern Europe. The intellectual tradition of the Jew, his worship of learning, his exaltation of the man of the book, further intensified the hold of this notion on his mentality. In the Jewish communities of Eastern Europe, with the exception now of Soviet Russia, the doctor, the lawyer, the rabbi, the teacher, the scholar, to this day command the highest respect and incidentally the highest dowries. Mothers in these communities, in reprimanding their children for slips in behaviour, are wont to tell them that they act like shoemakers, blacksmiths, horse-skinners, teamsters. These same mothers, wishing to spur sons lax in their studies to more diligent efforts, often hold forth the threat of sending them to a shop to learn a trade — a fate that even children are supposed to dread. In the pre-war days Jewish parents in Russia sought by all means at their command to keep their children from falling into the ranks of proletarians, not only because of the possibility of greater earnings in other occupations but because of the heightened social prestige that these would automatically confer.

Now what an epochal change! No longer is it a disgrace but a positive virtue for a Jewish youth, boy or girl, to engage in proletarian pursuits. In town after town I saw Jewish college youths — boys and girls — working barefoot in fields and gardens like ordinary muzhiks. I have been entertained in the homes of Jews, of the so-called middle class or of the intelligentsia,

whose children, while often unsympathetic to the Revolution, because of the adversity it had heaped on
them and their families, yet invariably confessed with
a feeling of joy that the Revolution had taught them
at least one blessed thing — the worth and the dignity
of labour — sheer physical toil. Let a Jewish mother
nowadays make a slighting reference to a proletarian,
any proletarian, as a means of shaming her son into
respectable behaviour, and it is certain the son, loving
as he may be, will rebuke her and perhaps not too
gently. The Revolution is battering out of the Jew his
one-time aversion toward physical labour.

And not only that. I was once interviewing in the
Ukraine a young Jewish woman, the presiding judge
in a Jewish court, that is a court held for and by Jews in
which Yiddish, the Germanic jargon that is the mother-
tongue of all Jewry in Eastern Europe, is the official
language. I had reported to her the remarks of a local
militiaman who was daringly outspoken in his anti-
Jewish sentiments. I asked her what the revolutionaries
were doing to combat anti-Semitism, especially among
Soviet workers and industrial proletarians. She emphasized the campaign to make people and particularly
workers think in terms not of superior and inferior
races, but of classes of workers and capitalists, and
then she drew close, pointed her finger upward, to give
emphasis to what she was about to say, and declared:
" And we don't stop with anti-Semitism, we Jewish
revolutionaries don't. Have you ever thought of the
Jewish feeling of anti-Goyism — anti-Gentilism? "
Jews, she proceeded to elucidate with vigour, had always
placed themselves on a pedestal of their own, above

the rest of humanity. They had so long been regarding themselves as God's chosen people that the idea of their superiority had been colouring not only their thinking but their behaviour. The fact, she explained, that the outside world had treated them as inferiors, only helped to heighten their estimate of themselves. Her own father, a noted Talmudic scholar, had brought her up to believe that in every way the Jew was superior to the Goy. She had grown up to esteem the very words " Goy " and " Shaigetz " — young Gentile — as terms of opprobrium. If she ever misbehaved, her mother, she confessed, would tell her that she was acting just like a Goye — a Gentile woman. As a judge in a court, she went on, she had occasion to observe that now and then there was a Jewish trader who thought lightly of treating a peasant less honourably than a Jew, all because to him the peasant was only a Goy anyway! " But we Jewish revolutionaries," she exclaimed with a sense of triumph, " are resolved to smash once for all the fiction of a Jewish superiority, and, when that is achieved, at least one cause of anti-Semitism will have been annihilated."

It is not, of course, all classes of Jews, even in Eastern Europe, who cherish the belief of the superiority of their people. Modern learning and socialist liberal teaching, which have shaken out of the Jew many an old conception and many an old taboo, have not left this idea unshattered. Still, the masses of Jews in Russia who in the pre-war days had been scarcely influenced by modern learning or socialist liberal morality are likely to continue nurturing this ancient belief. But not their children. They are growing up to regard the profession of it as a mark of intellectual inferiority and moral backwardness, which the Revolution so eloquently teaches that it is, and which the Jewish revolutionaries, who are daily gaining increased control of the spiritual life of Russian Jewry, with especial vigour hold it to be.

What is facilitating the effort of the Revolution to break down old social usages and beliefs is the collapse of the Jewish religion, in itself an astounding result of the Revolution. In town after town which I visited, synagogues have been abandoned for lack of attendance. It is seldom that one sees a young Jew at religious services even in the smaller towns which had always been strongholds of Jewish Orthodoxy. The women, especially the young, are succumbing to the wave of atheism as easily as the men. Religion with them is not even an excuse for social diversion, as it is with so many Jews in this country and so many non-Jewish infidels in Russia. Orthodox Jews have assured me that the time is not far distant when Jewish communities in Russia, should they need a rabbi, would have to send for him to Poland, Rumania or America. The Revolution is killing in the young Jew the spiritual incentive to take up rabbinical studies and is making it increasingly difficult for him to obtain the proper rabbinical training. "We'll be just like the *Goyim*," mourned a patriarchal Jewish scholar in the city of Minsk; "only we won't even believe in Jesus."

Parents with the best of intentions are helpless to stem the tide of infidelity. In the old days every Jewish boy and a good many girls, in addition to receiving a rigorous religious training in the home, attended the Jewish schools, such as the *cheder* or *Talmud-torah*. There they studied the Old Testament and other exclusively Jewish subjects, which gave them a knowledge of the Jewish religion and ancient Jewish history and stirred their so-called Jewish consciousness. Attendance at these schools stored their minds with impressions and memories that, in later life, even when they strayed away from the Jewish religious fold, often ripened into dearly cherished sentiments of group loyalty and of reverence for the Jewish religion as, though viewed in retrospect, something sacred and beautiful.

But now the *cheder*, like all other religious and semi-religious schools, Jewish and others, has been banned. The religious Jewish father and mother seek, of course, to impart religious instruction to their children. But these spend most of their active time outside of the home, in a Soviet environment, under atheistic influences, which effectively counteract the home training. If nowadays the Jewish youth in the public school does make a study of old sacred writings, it is for the purpose primarily of discrediting their teachings, or interpreting them in terms of the Communist conception of history, which is equally fatal to religious belief.

No wonder that older Jews, Orthodox and others, imbued as they are with religious convictions and with a romantic pride in Jewish exclusiveness and Jewish unity, find themselves so excruciatingly out of place in present-day Russia. They rage and wail against the tide of *Goyishness*, Gentilism, as they call it, that is engulfing the young generation. They are dismayed and bewildered but utterly helpless. They cannot persuade nor cajole nor terrify their own children into a preservation of this ancient creed, or even the ancient unity.

Not even the collapse of their religion, however, has caused the Russian Jews such earnest heart-searching and such radical departure from age-old practice, as the breakdown of their economic structures. The Czarist Government had limited their economic efforts ruthlessly enough. With the exception of merchants who held first guild licenses — that is, merchants of the first rank — university graduates and certain technical experts, all of whom constituted a tiny fraction of the Jewish population in Czarist Russia, the Jew had to make his domicile in a prescribed area, known as the "Pale of Settlement," and embracing roughly the territories of White Russia, old Russo-Poland, a section of the Ukraine and a strip of Great Russia. Within the Pale he was further restricted to town and city. From the village he was banned unless he was born there. He was forbidden to own land. He was barred from state service. He was shut from a career in the army. He was for the most part a middleman, a merchant, a peddler, a contractor, tossing about from deal to deal, job to job, eking out a living somehow by his wits.

It was on this Jew who made up the bulk of Russian Jewry that the Revolution, with its onslaught on private trade, bore hardest. It left them uprooted and desperate. Not even the Nep (New Economic Policy) with its legalization of private trade, holds forth any promise of salvation. On the contrary it has made quite clear to the Jew that under a Soviet regime the life of a middleman must always be economically precarious and politically and spiritually desolate.

Thrust into such a plight the bulk of Russian Jewry have had to seek a way out. Two avenues of escape have been opened to them — proletarianization, that is becoming industrial workers, and colonization or farming.

There were Jewish industrial workers in Russia in the old days, but their number was small. Few of them held jobs in the metallurgical industries. For one thing, they were not permitted to reside in the Ural, the Don basin, Central Russia, where these industries were chiefly located. Now Jews are entering these and other industries in increasing numbers. There is scarcely an industry in Russia into which they have not penetrated. I have met Jews of the middle-class type who have flung shame to the winds, and have cheerfully accepted jobs in shops and factories. At least one hundred and fifty thousand Jews are now employed in industries, primarily as labourers. The great cry of Jews, especially in the small towns, is that there are not enough jobs available for them. How often have I heard Jewish nepmen declare that they would be glad enough to scrap their miserable little trading enterprise and turn proletarian if only they had the opportunity. As Russia develops industrially more and more Jews will seek proletarian jobs. Why should they not, when a man no longer loses but gains caste by being a factory worker, when he is regarded not as the villain but as the hero of society and is the beneficiary of a host of advantages, not the least of which is the free education of children — always a matter of serious concern to a Jew?

The exodus to the land has caused even a louder commotion in the Jewish world in Russia than has the movement to the factory. There is something painfully and yet sublimely picturesque in these Jews, age-old city folk, many of them close to or past the meridian of life compelled to conquer anew a place for themselves in this world, and no longer with their minds alone but chiefly with their hands, in stark conflict with the forces of nature, of which they know so little.

No wonder that muzhiks, who had not been accustomed to seeing Jews work on land, asked themselves what was happening. They seemed not resentful, nor jealous, nor fearful of competition. They were merely amazed and amused. I well remember a peasant gathering in a village in the Ukraine at which the subject of Jewish colonization was under discussion. There was not a man present but prophesied utter failure for the enterprise. One elderly man expressed himself with this cryptic comparison: " You cannot keep a wolf from the woods, and no more can you keep a Jew from trading."

Yet more than twenty thousand Jewish families, embracing a population of one hundred thousand souls, have already settled on the land. Once while wandering around in Russian villages I drifted into a Jewish agricultural commune in White Russia. Not aglow with joy, the members of this colony were yet markedly more content and more hopeful than the non-proletarian Jewish city dweller, who is in despair about his future and lives in constant dread of new repressions. The men and women in this commune could work, eat, sleep, plan their future without fear of some new law upsetting their calculations. The children were an especial delight. They had their pet dogs, their pet calves, their

pet colts and they romped about the barnyards and
fields with an abandon unknown to the Jewish child in
the city. They were growing into sturdy, self-reliant
men and women, void of that haunting dread of officials, Cossacks, peasants, which in pre-war days had
been the bane of many a Jewish child. Farm life is,
indeed, infusing a fresh virility into the Jew in Russia,
is making him more steady of eye, more firm of hand,
more brave of heart.

Jews have been migrating to the farms at the rate of
six thousand families, or thirty thousand souls, a year.
Were not financial difficulties hampering the enterprise, probably twice as many would have settled annually on the land. The plan of the Soviet government
and of the Jewish agencies cooperating in the movement
is to raise the number of colonists to ten thousand
families a year, until at least a half-million Jews have
settled on farms. The lands that are at present exploited for the purpose are located in the Crimea, in
the northern Caucasus, in the Ukraine and in White
Russia. In the latter country and especially in Volhynia
there are millions of acres of swamp which can be
drained and turned into highly productive land. Jews
who have no funds of their own to migrate from
home, or who have no desire to move away from their
native habitat, have begun to reclaim some of this
swamp-land. As I watched a gang of them working in
the hot sun, barefoot and knee-deep in muck, the youths
stripped to the waist as is the fashion of Russian youths
nowadays, their bronze skins glistening with sweat, I
could not help marvelling at the epochal transformation
that the Revolution has wrought in Russian Jewry.

What Jew in the old days, however lowly in origin, would have cared to embark on the task of draining a swamp with his own hands? But now here they were, Jewish youths wielding spades and shovels with a vigour and a steadiness that would have done credit to any worker anywhere, and singing as they toiled!

Recently a new territory has been opened to Jewish colonization, farther, incidentally, from centres of Jewish life in Russia than in America. This territory is known as *Beera-Beazhan* and is slightly larger in area than the state of New Jersey. It is in Russia's Far East. It is a rich land bounded by fine rivers and crossed by the trans-Siberian railway with a native population of only twenty-seven thousand souls, mostly Cossacks. Only Jews are permitted to migrate there, and it is amazing with what eagerness Jews are applying for the opportunity to move to this far-away land deep in the heart of Asia. The plan is to settle at least a million Jews there.

I have often been asked by Jews and non-Jews if, after all, there is not something tortuously and hopelessly artificial in this movement to make a proletarian and a farmer out of the Jew. Is he not too keen-witted and too ambitious to remain content with physical labour and the returns that it may bring? All I can say in reply is that the Jew cannot be the chooser. No work is available for him in occupations that may prove more congenial and more lucrative. Emigrate? But where? The doors of America are shut, as are the doors of other modern countries in Europe and elsewhere. There remains South America, but it does not lure the Jew. He must remain in Soviet Russia and, in the present circumstances, must choose between physical labour on a farm or in a factory and starvation. There is no other course for him save suicide.

Indeed, of the three million Jews in Russia, it is only about one third who have thus far been absorbed into industry, agriculture and other so-called legitimate pursuits, such as state service, the professions and the collective trading organizations. Of the other two millions only the craftsman has of late been gaining stability and independence. He has been enfranchised and allowed as many as three apprentices without forfeiting his citizenship rights or being subject to special and excessive taxation. More than one million Jews still earn their livelihood from some form of trade. Some of them merely flit about from job to job, scraping a miserable subsistence as best they can. Others there are who earn a comfortable living, but they have no peace of mind and heart, and can have none, so long as the government and the ruling party and the new public opinion regard them as slimy social scavengers.

Incidentally, Jews of this group, the successful Jewish nepmen, have intensified anti-Semitism in Russia. They are conspicuous in all large cities. They are among the most successful of private traders, which does not escape the attention of the Russian proletarian or of the less fortunate Russian nepman. Both point to the Jewish nepman as the real gainer by the Revolution, the man who is turning the nation's agony into personal profit and pleasure. Neither of them has been far enough away from the old regime and the old social and racial prejudices to view the Jewish nepman, however successful, as an incident of the Revolution, which

Communist teachings say that he is. Personal resentment or jealousy seems to be gaining sway over the proletarian consciousness of many a Russian worker. To him and to the struggling Russian nepman, the Jewish nepman is above all else a Jew. They see his outward comfort and not his inner anguish. They point their finger of scorn at him and growl fiercely at his Jewish greed and Jewish luck.

Yet despite this new anti-Semitism, which the Communist Party and the Soviet Government are combating with all the weapons of enlightenment at their command, the Jew as a Jew has attained an equality, racially, or politically, or humanly, of which in the old days he never had dreamed. His present political status vouchsafes him all the rights and privileges that any other group is enjoying. His racial identity is neither a political nor even a social disability. It serves no longer as a barrier to a career in the army or in state service. The old Pale of Settlement, confining him to towns within a prescribed geographic area, has ceased to be. He can now move about the vast country at will and settle wherever he chooses, in city or village. He is admitted to schools and colleges, not on a basis of racial percentages as in the old days, but on terms of equality with other peoples. When he is excepted to, it is because of social not because of racial considerations. The Jewish nepman is discriminated against, but so is the Russian, the Ukrainian, the Tartar nepman — in Communist eyes they are all execrable creatures.

Under the Soviet regime the Jew has been effectively shielded against outbreaks of official anti-Semitism as well as against organized social animosities. There have

been no pogroms in Soviet territory. Reactionaries of
the old days in their efforts to embarrass the new regime have attempted to foment anti-Jewish uprisings,
but they have been hunted down, punished. Let a Jew-
hater give public utterance to his anti-Jewish sentiments and he is liable to arrest. I saw a policeman in a
market-place arrest a man for calling a Jewish peddler,
with whom he had been haggling furiously over the
price of a hat, *proklyiata zhid*, the Russian equivalent
for " damned sheeny." Not even a prominent poet like
the late Eseinin could escape censure and a trial by
literary colleagues for having indulged, while in an
inebriate state, in slurring remarks on Jews. Neither
politically nor economically does the Jew in Russia suffer because of his Jewishness. Even Orthodox Jews,
pained as they are at the attacks of the Revolution on
beliefs and institutions that they had always held as
sacred and as indispensable to the welfare of the Jewish
group, readily and gladly admit that the burden of inferiority which the Old World had forced on the Jew
has been lifted from him. The Revolution has been
draining out of the word " Jew " the infamy that Russia had so long injected into it.

As a consequence of this racial emancipation, and as
a by-product of the Revolution in general, there has
sprung into life a new and many-sided cultural awakening among the Russian Jews. They, like any other people with a language of their own, have been encouraged
to build their own schools and colleges and to develop
their cultural life as abundantly as they choose, always,
of course, in harmony with Soviet aims and purposes.

Indeed, there are even hints in the utterances of

revolutionary leaders of the possibility of launching a Jewish Soviet Republic. If there were a section of the country where the Jews formed a majority of the population, such a republic would in all likelihood already have been established. At present there is no geographic area where the Jews, however numerous, form such a majority. In time, as more and more of them settle on the land in contiguous territories, they may attain the desired preponderance in numbers, and then be ready for the formation of their own Soviet Republic. It is most likely that *Beera-Beazhan* will be the seat of this republic.

As one contemplates the new cultural and political life of Russian Jewry, with its manifold group activities, one cannot help wondering what the purpose of it all is? Is it to foster an already deep-seated separatism and to make the Jewish group a complete national entity in spirit and in body, such as it was in ancient days in Palestine? This would seem to be the purpose, but it is not. The idea that underlies the present community efforts of the Russian Jews is not nationalistic. The Jewish revolutionary groups, which dominate the Jewish scene in Russia, which mold largely the psychology of the Jewish youth, regard nationalism as a bourgeois conception which the world would do well to renounce. Jewish pride, Jewish glory, a Jewish destiny, mean nothing to them, are, so leaders have repeatedly told me, just so many hollow and baneful words. Nothing infuriates them more than the claims of Jews that the Jewish people have a mission to perform in the world — to uplift and exalt humanity in the spirit of the ancient Hebrew prophets and of

other great Jewish teachers. All the impassioned eloquence of a Ludwig Lewisohn glorifying the Jewish
spirit of peace is to them only sentimental drivel. They
will have none of Jewish superiority in any field of endeavour. All the preachments in favour of a Jewish mission and a Jewish destiny are to them only an expression of a Jewish chauvinism, which they consider as
vitiating in spirit if not in form as the chauvinism of
any other nation. In the end, they declare, it stirs only
a false loyalty in the Jewish worker, weakens his proletarian class-consciousness and his revolutionary zeal.
Zionism they vigorously denounce as a piece of bourgeois brigandage. They see no romance and no beauty
in the idea of bringing to new life the Jewish state in
the old homeland. Zionism has been outlawed in Russia. Indeed, they are taking the heart out of what is
known as Jewishness or Jewish idealism, stripping it of
all spiritual pretensions, of all romance and grandeur,
and reducing it to a bald social fact, a mere accident
of history.

I shall not indulge in prophecies as to the future of
the Jew in Russia. But one thing is already impressively evident — intermarriage, so rare in old Russia,
is a common occurrence now, not only in the city but
in the small town. The fact that the Jew marrying a
non-Jew is no longer required by law to become a
Christian, as he formerly was, and that religion, both
Jewish and Christian, is on the rapid decline, accounts
only in part for the spread of intermarriage. It is the
general new spiritual outlook of the Jews and the non-
Jews, especially of the young, that is conducive to this
result. After all, the Revolution is attacking old cleav-

ages and emphasizing new unities, even to the point of
having sublimated devotion to the Soviet idea and the
Soviet state, which does not necessarily mean communism, into a super-nationalism submerging old group
loyalties as well as group prejudices. The Jewish boy
and girl may be attending a Jewish school and may be
obtaining their education in the Jewish language under
Jewish instructors. But this education has no distinctive Jewish qualities, stirs no distinctive Jewish passion. The same is true of the non-Jewish boy and girl.
Both are reared in the Soviet idea, which dismisses
racial differences as unimportant if not artificial, and
which emphasizes the common purpose and the common destiny of the working folk of all races. It is not
a question of whether these purposes and this destiny,
judged by American standards and in the light of
American traditions, are worthy of emulation or even
toleration. Good or bad, base or noble, there they are
in Russia, a flaming reality that is burning itself into
the mind and heart of youths of school age and of
others too.

There is, to be sure, the new anti-Semitism, a force
that always makes the Jew shrink into himself and
away from the outside world. It is a most earnest problem in Soviet Russia and its magnitude is on the rise
and not on the wane. There are, however, the counteracting forces — the Communist Party, the Soviet Government, the trade unions, the public schools, the press,
each in its own way battling against racial ill feeling.

Jewish colonization, which implies the compact settlement of Jews in communities of their own, may in
time give rise to a new group spirit, a tribal pride if

you will, especially if the Jewish republic is established, which will stiffen Jewish resistance to intermarriage. But this resistance never can possess the force of the old opposition; for under Sovietism it never can develop into a religious precept or a tribal taboo. Besides, only a portion of the Jews will settle eventually on the land, perhaps about a fourth, certainly not more than a third of them. The majority will continue to live outside of Jewish colonies. They will move about the country and settle in different regions and mingle more and more freely with the outside world. What forces, physical or spiritual, will hold them back from intermarriage? I, for one, can see none. The very notion, so widely cherished by the Jews in America, that marrying outside of the race is not the proper or advisable thing to do, is increasingly losing its force or appeal in Russia. I cannot, therefore, escape the conclusion that unless the Soviet government collapses or anti-Semitism reaches the magnitude of a national epidemic the bulk of Russian Jewry is destined to assimilation.

CHAPTER XVII

WOMAN

IT was a small photograph and an old one, set in a black frame somewhat battered with age. It hung inconspicuously in the revolutionary room of the museum in far away Chita, deep in the heart of Siberia amidst rows of other photographs, mostly of persons long since dead, martyrs all to the cause of liberation. When I read the name, Maria Volkonskaya, I paused with a flutter of emotion for closer scrutiny. A small head resting on pretty shoulders; dark hair combed loosely back in tresses that brushed airily over the temples; big eyes, round and even-browed, not joyous nor especially sad; a delicate face, not too thin nor yet too full and not at all arresting on first sight, but gaining in appeal as one continued gazing at it, mellow with compassion and expressive more of self-possession than resignation, a face that does not haunt yet somehow lingers in the mind.

Ask the modern revolutionary in Russia what he thinks of Maria Volkonskaya and most likely he will dismiss her with a gesture of indifference. Implacable champion of the class struggle he sees in her no figure of outstanding challenge or heroism. She had not taken part in the war of the classes, not directly, though she had lived in one of the dreariest periods of Russian history, in the day of Nicholas the First, when serfdom in force for nearly a century and a half had already wrought its wreckage in Russian humanity, a day depicted now with hilarious mockery and now with poignant woe in Gogol's " Inspector General " and " Dead Souls." The daughter of a wealthy landlord, a hero of the Napoleonic wars, she had been closely sheltered from personal contact with the squalid realities of Russian life. Her husband, likewise a hero of the Napoleonic wars, never had drawn her into his inner life, never had conveyed to her the least intimation of the conspiracy he and other military men had been heading to overthrow the Emperor and make of Russia a constitutional nation patterned after the American Republic. Only after the insurrection, known as the Decembrist Revolution had failed, and Volkonsky was arrested did she hear of his political disaffection. Several of the conspirators, including the poet Ryleev, were hanged and about ninety others, including Volkonsky, men of rank and distinction in social and military life, were banished to remote parts of Siberia, with the avowed aim of wiping out, not only their influence but their names, the mere mention of which caused the impetuous Nicholas to explode into torrents of rage.

The true historian, however, will accord to Maria Volkonskaya no mean place of honour in the annals of Russian social advance. She is a landmark in woman's tortuous search for liberation in Russia. She was only in her early twenties, of ill health, the mother of a newly born son. Her husband was in disgrace. Society and officialdom would have applauded her, had she turned her back on him. Had he not besmirched the name he bore and outraged all existing rules of social

decency, of political decorum? Had he not slapped the
Emperor, the court, society, her very self in the face?
But Maria Volkonskaya thought differently. Her husband was a sufferer, a martyr, doomed to a life of
torture and isolation in a land thought of then as a living tomb. So she resolved to cast in her lot with his. She
would follow him to Siberia.

Society and officialdom were staggered at her decision and sought to frustrate its realization. Indeed,
right beside the photograph at which I was gazing, set
likewise in a little black frame, was a letter written in
longhand by a high official and said to have been inspired by the Emperor himself, picturing to Maria with
terrifying vividness the hazards in store for her on her
contemplated journey. But she would not be swerved
from her decision. And so, like Ibsen's Nora, she
slammed the door on all that she had grown to revere,
on society, officialdom, respectability, comfort, and sallied forth into a world far more bleak and uncertain
than Ibsen's heroine could possibly have faced, and not
in search of a miracle but resolved to perform one herself — to live her life in accord with the promptings of
her own inner spirit. In sledge and in cart she made the
arduous journey to the penal settlement where her husband was a prisoner. When she reached him and beheld
him unwashed, unkempt, in an ugly prison garb and
manacled, she knelt down and kissed his chains. It was
this kissing of the chains, or perhaps Nekrasov's dramatic recital of it in his " Russian Women," that has
made her the outstanding heroine of the period. After
all there were seven other women, wives and sisters of
the Decembrist rebels, who, like Volkonskaya, trekked

their way to the lonely Siberian outposts of civilization to share exile with the men they loved.

However, the action of Maria Volkonskaya and these other women marks a new epoch, when women in serf-ridden semi-patriarchal Russia no longer blindly follow the iron-clad mandates of society, when they begin to ask questions, issue protests, make decisions of their own and defy the forces of man and nature that bar fulfillment of their desires. They are precursors and inspirers of that generation of women of whom Turgenev wrote with such melancholy exaltation, women who could lose themselves with thrilling abandon in the passion of a great love or a great cause. More, they are the forerunners of that galaxy of women who but less than half a century later amazed and thrilled the world with their exploits in the revolutionary movement. No wonder that Nekrasov, Russia's most tearful poet, in his " Russian Women," chants of Volkonskaya and the other Decembrist women with an adulation that exalts and saddens even more.

Not that a spirit of independence was alien always to Russian women. It most certainly was not in pagan times when women were under law and custom almost the equal of men. They could rule estates and the wives of princes could receive foreign emissaries and conduct diplomatic negotiations. There were princesses who maintained their own communities and built their own armies. The widowed mother was practically the ruler of the household. In marriage women were not mere subjects of parental authority. They could choose their own husbands, and in the Ukraine, according to the testimony of the French writer Beauplan, " Contrary to the usages of all other nations the husbands did not select their wives, but were themselves selected by their future consorts." After marriage a woman might lose certain privileges she held as a girl, but she never became man's slave. Nor was she barred from a voice in the *vetche* — the community council. She was often a contender for honours even in the realm of physical prowess. Epic songs still abound in certain sections of the country picturing women of the pagan day as mighty *bogatyrs,* warriors, capable at times of administering defeat to the best of men fighters. The *polyanitza,* Amazon women, figures with especial prominence in these old ballads. Even Illya Murometz, Russia's most loved *bogatyr,* fell once before the onslaught of a *polyanitza* who proved to be his own daughter. Women did not even shrink from taking up arms in times of war.

Thus in pagan Russia women of high and low rank, before and after marriage, lived on a basis of equality with men. They suffered little from strictures on their spirit of independence. Often they rose to positions of high rank. They were regarded as specially gifted with supernatural powers. They were at any rate the best healers and conjurers.

In time, however, new forces appeared on the scene and swept away the ancient freedom and equality that women had enjoyed. The patriarchal family with its emphasis on the power of man; the new religion, Byzantine Christianity, with its stress of the debasing nature of women; the Tatar invasion lasting for nearly two centuries with its brutalizing effect on all humanity; the rise of political despotism with its suppression of personal liberty, all these forged a new code of social usage and brought to naught the ancient prerogatives of women. Education, social life, politics — women were barred from all these. They fell into so low a state that they became mere playthings, something more, perhaps, than objects of sensual appeasement, but certainly no companions and no helpmates to the men they married. Removed from open life and locked in a *terem,* the attic or back partition of the house, they ate and drank and grew fat. They gossipped, intrigued, loafed and grew fatter and fatter, so as to make themselves more seductive to men. They were reduced to the mere status of animality and held in such status for several centuries.

The change came with the rise to power of Peter the Great. In his resolve to make Russia a modern nation he scrapped the *terem* and released women from secluded bondage. He compelled them to mingle with men in public and to attend social functions. The Moscow nobles fumed at the innovation. In their hearts they invoked curses on the perfidious " anti-Christ " who ruled the land. Oppose him, however, they dared not, lest they find themselves behind prison doors. After Peter came the Empress Elizabeth, distinguished for her abolition of capital punishment. Not a vigorous person, superstitious and so ignorant that she did not know England was an insular country, she yet encouraged the new spirit of tolerance toward women unleashed by Peter, and thus paved the way for the reforms of Catherine the Great, chief of which was the promotion of education for women. Women began to study, to read books, above all to learn new manners.

In fact the chief emphasis in the schools for women was laid on external behavior, on drawing-room virtues, the art of social accomplishment, of pleasing men and feeling at home in the society of foreign visitors of distinction. It was not until the coming of the Decembrist Revolution and the train of new ideas it wafted into the land, and the example of Maria Volkonskaya and the other women who followed their brothers and husbands to their Siberian exile, that a new woman made her appearance on the Russian scene, a woman of initiative, self-reliance, aware of her personality, with the will and the courage to break through the wall of convention and legal restriction, and dash forth into the big world to make her own conquests in accord with her own inner spirit.

And here is the most significant aspect in this struggle of the Russian women for emancipation. They did not, as in other lands, have to wage their battle single-handed. Men, intellectual, literary, in other words the Russian intelligentsia, took up the cudgels on their behalf, in fact sought with energy and fervour to spur them into an ever-growing urge to rise above their accepted position in the world, to strive for rehabilitation of their flesh, as well as their spirit. When the question of higher education for women arose in Russia, these men with but extremely rare exceptions were among the most brilliant champions of the movement. When young women shut from the Russian universities journeyed abroad in search of higher learning, these men again encouraged and aided them, and to facilitate their migration to a foreign country often entered into fictitious marriages with them. When women in protest against the inferiorities and disabilities visited on them by government and society, began as early as the sixties of the past century to bob their hair, wear simple dresses and low-heeled shoes, these men again applauded them with vigour and joy.

Finally when the revolutionary movement sprouted into life, women from the first were welcomed to its ranks as, in every way, the equals of men, and they acted true to this trust in them. They accepted any positions offered to them, anywhere, everywhere, no matter how odious or how risky, if only they could be of use to the cause of liberation. Not a few of them, but hundreds, thousands. They demanded no distinctions and no favours. They were ready for anything, even death. They were followers, they were leaders. They were spies, they were bomb-throwers. They shared everything alike with men. They lived together with men, planned, plotted together with them, together marched to goals and penal settlements in Siberia, together ascended the gallows.

I can think of no other movement in history where men and women lived on such terms of intimacy and camaraderie, of mutual respect and trust, and worked with such sublime selflessness for a common purpose. There were no discriminations or rivalries between the sexes. Women not only became a vital part of the movement, they rose to positions of highest command. Consider Sofya Perovskaya, the daughter of a nobleman, after many vain attempts finally carrying out the assassination of Alexander the Second. The letter that she wrote to her mother just before she was hanged remains to this day a momentous document of pure devotion to a cause. Consider the other women in the movement — Beshkovskaya, Figner, Zassulitch, Spiridonova — world-celebrities all, hallowed names in the Russian revolutionary crusade.

Under such circumstances feminism in Russia never could assume the narrow form that it did in other lands — that is a battle against the domination of men. Women in Russia were not fighting for the mere right of suffrage, higher education, opportunity to hold office or enter the professions. Men and women were waging together a war to death for the same cause — the liberation of the Russian mass with equal rights for both sexes. This equality was not a mere abstraction. It was a passion with men and women. There was never any question as to any discrimination against women in the event of the triumph of the Revolution. Never. Women would enjoy the fruits of victory as much as men, no more but no less, and that regardless of the party that might ascend to power. Menshevik, Bolshevik, Social-Revolutionary or even liberal Cadet — all were pledged to the fulfillment of this exalted heritage of the Revolution.

Well, the Revolution has triumphed. It matters not for purposes of this discussion that the Party in power happens to be out of accord with the fundamental tenets of western civilization. It matters not that it is a fierce dictatorship. After all even under a dictatorship, however brutal, there are rights and opportunities for men and women within the camps of the ruled and even more within the camp of the ruling. To what extent then has the revolutionary heritage of equality of women been fulfilled? How is woman faring in the Russian society, and what is the social and spiritual import of her new position in life? Though in preceding chapters I have already discussed this aspect of Russian life in some detail, it will bear further and more detailed scrutiny, if only because the condition of woman in the new Russia is in itself an epochal social revolution.

In one respect, in her outward appearance, the Russian woman presents the sorriest spectacle of any woman in Europe. In such lands as Poland and Germany one stumbles often enough into shabbiness of attire among women. But there, side by side with the woman in home-spun and cotton jeans and coarse boots, there parades the woman in silks and velvets. Not so in Russia. The fashionably dressed woman has practically disappeared from the scene. Nowhere is there any semblance of elegance, any display of gorgeousness, any show of style in woman's dress. It is all so drab, almost sordid, to the western eyes. To this day the majority of women do not wear hats, not even on the Nevsky in Leningrad and on the Tverskaya in Moscow. The kerchief has displaced the hat, and of late in some parts of the country especially in Siberia the boy cap has been striving for supremacy among the young girls and particularly the college students. Neither at the opera nor the ballet, nor the theatre is there a glitter of jewelry, or a shimmer of gowns to dazzle the eye, as in other lands. Fashion magazines are slowly creeping back to life, but the fashionably-gowned woman is still a memory of the past.

In other ways extraordinary things have been happening to the Russian woman. She is undergoing an

inner revolution, so violent that it must stir a repercus-
sion in other lands. She is working out her destiny in
a manner to make her already distinct in mental attributes and daily pursuits from the woman in Europe
or America. She has lost not a little but she has gained
much. If she is discriminated against it is not as a
woman, but as a member of a group that is for one
reason or another in disfavor with the dictatorship.
Prejudices, taboos, conventions, especially in the village
and among Asiatic peoples have not entirely lost their
sway, but new forces are at work everywhere attacking these with relentless persistency and seeking their
ultimate and utter annihilation. There is something big,
challenging, disturbing, in this recreation of the Russian
woman, something that must be honestly and search-
ingly considered.

Of primary significance is the fact that through the
Revolution the *Russian woman has attained complete
political equality with man*. She has the right not only
to vote but to hold any office for which she is fitted. I
do not mean to imply that the exercise of suffrage is as
free in Russia as it is in this country. It most manifestly is not, excepting in the village. Pressure is ex-
erted now openly, now secretly and drastically to swing
or suppress support of this or that candidate for office
to the Soviet, the trade union or any other governing
body. But such pressure is directed against men with
no less force than against women. Sex, I again must
emphasize, is neither a deciding nor a decisive influence. In the matter of holding office the right is not
merely a legal abstraction. In this respect the contrast
between even America, where women have achieved

distinction and success in public office, and Russia is noteworthy. There have been two women governors in America and nine congressmen and they have all become national figures, only because their election to such offices proved so novel a thing that it commanded front page space in the newspapers. But in Russia, within the limits of the dictatorship, of course, women in high office are too common to command more than passing notice in the press.

Everywhere one goes one sees women in high command. Eight per cent of the members in the all-Russian Soviet, the chief governing body of the nation, are women. Scores of women have been chosen to the chairmanship of town and city Soviets, that is to positions corresponding to mayors in this country. In more than twenty states in America women are still barred from jury duty. Nowhere in Russia are they barred from such duty. In the judiciary in Russia women are gradually attaining immense prominence.

In 1926 in the part known in the old days as Great Russia there were one hundred and forty-six women judges and about a score of women prosecuting attorneys. For the first time in history a woman has been ambassador in a foreign land, a Russian woman, just as in the preceding century, it was a Russian woman, Sofya Kovalevskaya, an outstanding mathematician of her day, who was the first woman in Europe to be professor in a man's university, not, however, in Russia, but in Norway. While no woman has as yet reached the position of a commissary — a member of the Cabinet — women in all commissaries have risen to posts of high responsibility. In the Commissary of Education two women, Yakovleva and Krupskaya, are in rank only second to Lunacharsky and in achievement, perhaps, transcending him.

The significant aspect of the new political equality in Russia is the attitude of the men. " In America," says Mrs. Franklin Roosevelt, " women are frozen out from any intrinsic shade of influence in their parties. . . . Beneath the veneer of courtesy and outward show of consideration universally accorded women, there is a widespread male hostility — age-old perhaps — against charging them with any actual control. . . . In these circles which decide the affairs of the nation's politics women have no voice or power whatever." In Russia on the other hand, excepting among the older folk in the villages, woman's entrance into political life is never treated with pusillanimity as though it were merely another caprice which men must tolerate. There is no attempt to be merely polite to her. Of course, there is only one political party in Russia, but within its ranks women do enjoy " an intrinsic share of influence," and sometimes a decisive one. With all the power at its command the new society, whatever our feeling against it, is seeking to fan woman's political consciousness and to encourage her to seek everywhere in government positions of trust and responsibility. Likewise the idea, deep-rooted in some parts of this globe, that it is a reflection on men to be governed by women, or that if allowed free reign in government, women will, in time, impose their domination on men, has never invoked any anxiety in Russian manhood. They just do not think in terms of the domination of sexes. Possibly because of the old revolutionary notion that women are not competitors, but merely companions of men in the affairs of the world.

The Russian woman, through the Revolution, has attained complete legal equality with man. In no sphere of life are men accorded privileges from which women are barred. A man cannot, for example, impose his name or his nationality on the woman he marries. She may retain her own name if she so chooses. Nor can the man impose his place of residence on her. She does not have to follow him in his migrations if she does not wish to. When she leaves his bed and board he cannot advertise that he will not be responsible for her debts, unless, of course, he obtains a divorce. In the matter of property rights the law again nowhere discriminates against the woman. Nor on the other hand does it assume the attitude that she is the weaker or inferior party in society and must therefore be accorded special protection. The jilted woman cannot sue a man for breach of promise, nor can she ever seek compensation for so-called alienation of affection. The woman bandit or counter-revolutionary, unless she is pregnant, is dealt with as summarily as the man — she is turned over to the firing squad.

The Russian woman, through the Revolution, has attained complete social equality with man. There are no exclusive men's clubs in Russia unless it be in walks of life in which women do not care to enter. Nor are there any exclusive men's schools or colleges. Even in the sporting organizations the membership is mixed. There are nowhere in Russia exclusive hotels for men or women, or restaurants with signs " tables specially reserved for ladies." In the trade unions, in the Com-

munist Party women are welcomed on the same terms
as men, and are as much responsible for the principles
guiding the practices of both. There is no field of effort
in which sterner social demands are made on women
than on men, not even in the teaching profession.
Women teachers may have their associations with men
as freely as other women without invoking suspicion or
criticism and possibly dismissal from work by the ruling
authorities.

Women may and do smoke in the streets, on the
campus of a university, in the smoking compartments
on trains, in the lobbies of the theatres, anywhere and
everywhere that men enjoy the privilege. Smoking, of
course, may not be a healthful or aesthetic or dignified
practice, but the notion that it is less so for women than
men, has received no approbation in Russia. Nor is
there anything left of taboos that limit woman's sphere
of locomotion or subject her to special restrictions. I
know of no place in Russia where women must enter
a building through the side and not the front door as,
for example, in the Union Building of one of our most
progressive western universities, nor where they are permitted to use the library only during certain specified
periods of the day, and then under special regulations,
as in Harvard. Women are nowhere made to feel that
they need distinct social treatment. They can go alone
and unescorted to taverns, to dance clubs, to hotels, to
restaurants with as much freedom as men, and without
invoking on themselves suspicion or criticism or opprobrium. Women are thrown on their own responsibility and on their own good behaviour on a par with
men. The Russians may have carried the idea of social

equality too far, as when they sell tickets to men and women in the same compartments in sleeping cars. From an American standpoint such a practice is neither of good taste nor of good morals. But somehow the Russian public does not protest.

The Russian woman, through the Revolution, has been attaining cultural equality with man. Educational opportunities in and out of schools are as open to her as to men. Nor is she debarred from so-called men's professions, such as medicine, engineering, law. Women enter these professions in ever-increasing numbers. About one half of the students in the medical schools are women. About one fifth of the students in the engineering colleges are women, and this includes not only civil but mining and electrical engineering.

There are women students in the military academies — though not many, and for obvious biological reasons. Yet in the widespread campaign for war preparedness that has swept Russia since England's break of relations with the Soviet Government, women have been almost as conspicuous as men in the parades and often on the training grounds. I am sure that in an emergency women would go to the front in one capacity or another even more so than they did during the civil war when they became commissaries in the army and operated machine guns and poison gas tanks. Even now there are several women with the rank of general in the Red Army.

Here again with reference to the cultural equality of the sexes the attitude of the men in Russia differs from that of men in other lands. I have before me an item culled from a dispatch from a European city with

significant bearing on this issue. Women medical students, according to this dispatch, have been barred
from five hospitals. The men objected to their presence
because "the two sexes cannot mix in the study of
medicine. . . . Their presence interferes with ath-
letics. . . . They distract men from their studies. . . .
Women are not successes as doctors. . . ." Such an
act of discrimination would be impossible in present-
day Russia. The mere presentation of such a petition by
men students would be unthinkable, and if it ever did
take place, the signatories to the document would be
branded as traitors to the revolutionary spirit and to
the heritages the revolutionary movement has be-
queathed to the youth of the land.

*The Russian woman, through the Revolution, has
been achieving economic equality with man.* Now the
Communist, with his worship of economic determinism,
lays the disabilities from which women have suffered
throughout the ages primarily to one cause — economic dependence on men. In all Communist, in all
Marxian writings, the point is always emphasized that
the spiritual liberation of woman is conditioned on her
economic emancipation. Women must be workers. They
must do something to contribute to the economic gain
of the nation and to win their own economic independence. The old notion that work is debasing, especially
to women, has lost all its force, has in fact, given way
to the new notion that to be idle is no less degrading to
women than to men.

The new law has dealt harshly with taboos, usages,
and economic policies that fostered discrimination
against women. In all pursuits whether industrial, cleri-

cal, educational, women receive equal pay with men for equal work. In all collective agreements between trade unions and industrial enterprises nothing is said of women workers. Terms and conditions apply to all members regardless of sex. Likewise the conception that a woman works for pin-money only and that she is an intruder in man's sphere of activity, his competitor and a dangerous one, has received no support. Such attacks as were directed on women barbers by the Journey-man Barbers' Union in this country as recently as 1924, when women who took up barbering and sought admission to the Union, were described as unmoral, as scabs and worse, are inconceivable in present-day Russia. Discrimination such as some unions in America and England still practice in barring women from skilled jobs is likewise unthinkable in Russia. If women are debarred from certain jobs in so-called heavy industries it is not because of a wish to protect man's hold on these jobs, but because of the physical unfitness of women to perform the tasks required.

Nor is there ever any discrimination against married women. They too can hold whatever jobs they are fitted to perform, whether in the teaching, medical, engineering professions or in industry. Neither a school board nor a factory manager nor anyone in charge of hiring workers has a right to refuse a woman applicant a position just because she is married, or even if she is pregnant. Work in all fields of human effort is made compatible with motherhood. In fact factory regulations and insurance laws giving pregnant women a leave of absence of from one to two months prior to and after birth, with full pay, are intended primarily to encourage married women to seek economic independence. In industries, such as the textile, in which women predominate, a network of nurseries has been established so as to make possible the proper care of babies during work-hours, and the mother is allowed certain periods during the work day to visit the baby without deduction in wages.

Of course, on the whole women are among the lower paid workers in industry, and that is not because they are women, but because they have not yet made much headway in the skilled occupations, and even in Bolshevik Russia the unskilled are paid less than the skilled workers.

The Russian woman, through the Revolution, has been winning equality in a phase of life in which she has for centuries been discriminated against with especial cruelty. I am referring to the matter of sex. In this respect Russia is an astonishing contrast to the rest of the western world, and the outsider, after a protracted stay there, particularly if with a knowledge of the language he has been able to draw close to the people, finds himself, on reaching a western land, both surprised and perplexed. This, at any rate, was my experience after one of my recent visits to Russia. I had gone from Siberia to Harbin, the northern city in Manchuria. Hungry for American reading matter I picked up in a bookshop a copy of a freshly received American magazine in which appeared a story by Theodore Dreiser under the title "The Woman Pays." The story was as hackneyed as the title. A girl in a small town falls in love with a boy, who after winning her to his desires discards her. Overcome with dismay over the

disgrace she would bring on herself and her family if
a child came outside of wedlock, she grows desperate
and when the boy repulses her plea to marry her she
shoots him and then drowns herself. Fresh with impressions of Russia this story seemed to me desperately
unreal. I could not help asking myself if tragedies like
that did actually happen in the world? They seemed so
alien to the new social atmosphere of Russia. A woman
disappointed in love may resort to desperation to
avenge an unfulfilled promise, — but the inciting motive save possibly in the village would not be mere dread
of social scorn. It could not be, for the woman with a
child outside of wedlock is, in present-day Russia, not
necessarily an object or subject of public obloquy.
Neighbours and friends do not necessarily regard her as
debased. Nor does the law bear down on her with
acrimony. On the contrary it holds her on the same
level of respectability as other women. The child has
the same legal standing as any child born in regular
marriage. The very word illegitimate has been expunged
from the legal vocabulary of the nation. The father is
a father, and the mother is a mother, and both must
meet their obligation to each other and even more to
the child.

Of course, as in everything else in Russia one must
speak of this subject with reservations. There is a body
of public opinion reared in the old social habits and
sanctities that repudiates the new standards in this, as
in other phases of human relations. But it is without
power to make itself seriously felt, and therefore, can
hardly impede the spread of the new gospel, including
the insistence on the single standard in sex. Indeed, the

very phrase " the woman pays " has an odious ring in
Russia. The woman does pay, biologically perhaps more
than the man, but socially, or to the extent that it is
within power of man to control things, hardly more
than he.

Surely changes in the position of woman so new and
so stupendous will exercise a far-reaching effect on
family and home, on government and industry and
even on international relations, if for no other reason
than that in war women in Russia will play a more
decisive part than in any other land. Here, however,
I am chiefly concerned with the possible effect of the
new system of equality on the personal life of the
woman, on the kind of human being it is in time destined to make of her, is making of her already. One
thing stands out preeminently — under the Russian system she cannot endure as a mere Female Character, or
as a " mere object of sensuality " as the audaciously
realistic Tolstoy once expressed himself. She cannot
continue to be a mere ornament or a mere object of
adoration with her whole life wrapped up in man and
possible ways of rendering herself alluring. Of course,
women are women, and men will always be somewhere
in the foreground of their rational and emotional life.
The Russian woman is no exception, Revolution or no
Revolution. She has not abandoned decorativeness, not
even the Communist woman. Again and again I have
come on groups of young women, revolutionaries at
that, who railed at the government for failure to import in sufficient quantities foreign cosmetics which are
deemed immensely superior to the native output. Still
there is a reaction, a profound one, against the woman

making personal attractiveness the chief passion of her life. What scorn is levelled against her! As though she were perpetrating the vilest offence against society and herself.

Besides, under a system where she ceases to be dependent on men economically, where her energies find an outlet in the governing and productive processes of life on a plane of equality with men, where she is not only encouraged but in large measure compelled to work in factory or office, she is bound to cultivate a fund of fresh interests, a host of new diversions, to displace in great share her old absorption in her mere feminine self. She never can forget that she is a woman, but she is also being everlastingly and dramatically reminded that she is, in addition, a citizen, a worker, with obligations to her group and duties to the state, which she cannot afford to ignore or evade.

In the new society in Russia the woman has been achieving a physical freedom which she never had enjoyed. She suffers from the repression of the dictatorship, but everybody does that, including revolutionaries, even men in command of the dictatorship. Yet outside of this political control she is a free agent. In all my wanderings in Russia I have never heard a girl or woman say, " I wish I were a man so I could do as I like and go where I please." Women do stir about as they wish with as much liberty and unconcern as men.

Nor can there be any doubt that in the new society in Russia the woman, even with an irrepressible domestic disposition, is living a more rational life than in the old days, if only because of the opportunities not afforded her hitherto for the unfolding of her personal-

ity and intelligence. For good or for ill the slogan of
Kinder, Kürche, Küche — children, church, kitchen —
has ceased to be the guiding, if not grinding passion in
her life. Obstacles to her cultural and economic advance have been removed. She is penetrating with growing zeal countless fields of effort beyond the hearth.

And of course the new standards of sex are insuring
her an emotional freedom that man had regarded as
peculiarly his own. The launching of the single standard of morality, even if not yet universally observed, is
ridding her of fears and irritations that were often the
bane and the blight of her life. She can unfold herself
emotionally with hardly any more reserve and restriction than a man.

The question naturally arises if the Russian woman,
under the burden of her new privileges and responsi-
bilities, is not growing too independent, too aggressive,
too ambitious, too intelligent and thereby debasing and
perhaps killing romance? But as already indicated in a
previous chapter a knowledge of Russian history and
Russian literature disposes of the suspicion the question
implies. Beginning with Pushkin's Tatyana and ending
with Seifulina's Virineya, the ideal woman of the Russian novelist is usually singularly independent, singularly ambitious, and yet remains singularly romantic,
loves and is loved with no less and perhaps with greater
ardour than the so-called feminine type in western lands.
Need I repeat here further the experience of the Russian woman in the revolutionary movement, where
romances most sublime have flowered?

But is the Russian woman really a happier person
because of her new equalities? By all the canons of logic

and all the theories and prophecies of the world's feminists, whether Elly Ney or Charlotte Perkins Gilman or Margaret Sanger she should be. But is she? Panteleimon Romanov, one of Russia's living novelists, in his novel " The New Table of Commandments," attempts perhaps unconsciously to answer this epochal question. The heroine, a woman of culture and refinement, emancipated from old conventions, on realizing that her lover, a peasant by origin, but well-read, sensible and above all considerate of her feelings, is yet too full of ardour for the new life and new purpose to merge himself completely in his amour, says to him, " And do you know what I have often been thinking on those sleepless nights when you lay beside me and I feared to move lest I disturb you? I was thinking that if there was a Creator and if my life was ended and I had to come before Him, I'd come without a soul. He would have asked me, ' Why are you without a soul? ' and I should have answered with pride and joy, ' I have given all of it, O Lord, to that man there. I have nothing left for myself.' "

To which the new man with the new passions and new purposes makes reply:

" I too would have come before Him without a soul, and if He had asked me what I had done with it, I'd have pointed to the earth below and said, ' It has remained there, a tiny bit of it going into the life of every human being. . . . There on earth, Creator, it will be much safer than in Thy hands. . . .' "

The implication is clear — it is so much easier for a man to divest himself of his innermost self or rather to express it through a social purpose than it is for a woman. He can project himself spiritually into this purpose with greater ease and abandon than can a woman. I shall not presume to say that the author is right nor that he is wrong. Russian women by the thousands have shown that for a cause they could sacrifice self with as much abandon as men. But this cause — the Revolution — was a dream, alluring, overpowering. Now that the realization of the dream has commenced will the women in Russia begin to suspect that, despite equalities and opportunities, the new society is demanding too stern, perhaps too impossible a sacrifice, from them? I am merely posturing the question. Of this though there can be no doubt — because of the multitude of new rights and privileges that it has conferred on Russian women, the new society may eventually bring to them a great rapture, but it will not be without the cost of a great agony.

Part III

QUESTS

CHAPTER XVIII

ENGLAND

YOU do not any more than cross the Russian frontier than you plunge into a wave of war excitement which in itself makes Russia on first sight so much of a puzzle and a problem in this troubled world of ours. Flamboyant posters calling on the citizenry to be ready to repel outside foes peer at you from walls, fences, windows at every turn. At railroad stations, club-houses, parks, reading rooms you see impressive war exhibitions with all manner of guns, parts of aeroplanes, diagrams, statistical data, posters, gas masks, and wax figures showing soldiers in varied forms of physical disability, especially from gas attacks.

At bookstores shelves and windows carry big displays of war literature on every conceivable phase of war, and the public, particularly the youth, buys it and reads it eagerly. More, Russia is learning to shoot as no other land in the world. Everywhere you go in city and village you see rifle ranges where during leisure hours and on holidays throngs of men and women engage in protracted target practice. What is most impressive, because so terribly dramatic, are those endless Russian parades passing always, whatever the occasion, under slogans of war to death against outside enemies. Even now as I am writing this chapter such a parade is sweeping by my hotel in Moscow — heaving masses of youths, boys and girls, with bands, banners, rifles, floats, pouring into the inevitable Red Square in demonstration of a spirit of challenge that would be majestic if it were not so fierce.

What is it all for? Certainly not for mere sport. Russia is openly and earnestly preparing for war. She is convinced that sooner or later, and perhaps not in the distant future, she will be embroiled in a combat in which England directly and indirectly will play the leading part. She sees England mobilizing forces against her all over the world, and she dreads a war at this stage of her development more than any other calamity man or nature or both could visit on her, and for a very valid reason: a fresh conflict would halt the process of her recuperation and would subject her to a further and terrific blood-letting operation. She is determined not to be caught unawares.

It is easy to assume, as so many writers have been doing, that the Russian rulers are artificially inflating war excitement and distrust of England for the purpose of distracting the Russian masses from their own immediate distress. To view the movement with such pusillanimity is in my judgment to miss tragically the sweeping import of Russia's feeling toward England. One might be justified in so light-hearted an approach of the Russo-British conflict, if it were only revolutionaries who were seeing British war-clouds descending on Russia. But this is not the case, most emphatically not.

I had occasion once to be on a boat on the Volga that was packed with excursionists, who were mostly university men — jurists, physicians, teachers, administrators. They were no agitators, Bolsheviks, most certainly no war-lords. They were the old type of Russian intellectuals, in more than one sense the best friends England had had in Russia in the pre-war period. They had ever esteemed England highly for her democracy, her spirit of tolerance, above all for the hospitality she had extended to Russian men of intellect like Kropotkin, Herzen, Stepniak, Chaikovsky, even Lenine and a host of others, who had fled from their native land because of anti-Czarist efforts. Some of these men, had they had their way in the moulding of Russia's destiny on the abdication of the last Czar, would have gladly inaugurated in Russia a constitutional monarchy modelled on the English pattern. Yet these men in one voice spoke of England with disappointment and with rancour. Nationalists and patriots, these men agreed with the Bolsheviks that since the October Revolution England has been bent on a policy of breaking up Russia into a host of independent nationalities, so as once and for all to be rid of a united formidable Russia. Widespread among all groups of Russians, but particularly among the intelligentsia, is this feeling about England.

England of course has her grievances against Russia, many, varied and damning, as I shall point out presently. While Russia regards England as the fiercest enemy she ever has faced, England has reason enough to consider Russia as the most dangerous foe she ever has encountered. Russia since the Revolution has wrecked many a British dream. Here, however, in laying down the Russian side of the conflict I would emphasize that its roots are of no recent origin. England and Russia are ancient foes. For over a century these two vast and mighty empires have been swinging fists at each other, at times within very close striking distance. England has ever been actuated by a wish to keep all outsiders and especially Russia away from India and from all doors leading there, as well as to conquer new markets for her goods and for her capital, while Czarist Russia had been governed by an insatiate lust to add more and more territory, including if possible India, to her domains and to push out into warm waters. In the pursuit of these respective purposes England and Russia always found each other in the way — England not so much Russia, as Russia England — all over Asia. Hence in the Near East, in the Far East, in Central Asia, Russia and England had always been clashing. For the most part England had the whip-hand over Russia in so-called neutral territories in Asia, in Afghanistan, Tibet, Persia, Turkey, China. But now and then Russia would make serious encroachments on England's supremacy, as in Tibet and in Persia during the British war with the Boers. Both nations however through diplomatic skill managed to avoid an open break, and in 1907, when Russia was exhausted from the Japanese war and from her violent revolution, they actually concluded a military alliance directed, of course, against Germany. Yet that did not remove the source of their fundamental antagonism. At heart they remained foes, could not help remaining, for a strong British Empire was always a menace to old Russia, and a strong Russia was even more of a menace to the British Empire — everywhere in Asia.

When the Russian Revolution broke out England followed a policy which, whatever her real aims and motives, could not but encourage the Russians in the

belief that she was at last seeking her opportunity to
break the back of her ancient rival and forever rid
herself of the so-called Russian menace. Russia had
burst into a civil war and the Allies, as is known, had
intervened to help crush the Bolsheviks. England,
France and Japan were the most active supporters of
intervention — England more than the others. The
chief scene of intervention was European Russia, and
there France and England pursued aims that seemed
diametrically opposed to each other. Even the Paris
Temps was constrained to remark, " While France
is seeking to reunite Russia, England is striving to divide her." France of course had hoped that a reunited
Russia would again become her ally in a possible war
against Germany, England, however, had most to gain
from the dismemberment of Russia.

Politically these gains for England would have been
beyond the dream of any English statesman, would
indeed have brought to England the greatest triumph
of her history. They would have registered for her a
double victory — would have brushed out of the way
her sternest rival in Asia and given her a free hand
in all contested territory, and would have opened vast
new spheres of influence on the very territories of her
fallen enemy. No longer would England have to fear
an invasion of India, at least by Russia. No longer
would she meet with any appreciable outside interference in the pursuit of her policies in Afghanistan, Persia, Turkey, and this in itself would have strengthened
her authority in China, and more, much more. Since
a dismembered Russia would present the spectacle of
many new nationalities with little experience in gov-

ernment and in international affairs constantly brandishing swords at each other, they would have offered
the opportunity for strong influence by an outside
nation, and this nation would have been chiefly England, if only because of her richer diplomatic experience, her finances, her fleet, her merchant marine and
her proximity to many of these lands. England would
have enjoyed an ampler opportunity than any other
nation to become the dominating diplomatic influence
over most of the Russian territory, even as she later
did become that in the Baltic states. Indeed, if
Russia had been dismembered England would have
exercised supreme political power over practically the
whole of the Asiatic mainland, and that in itself together with her acquisition of new spheres of influence
in various parts of European Russia might have given
her the preponderance of power in Europe. In her
political influence she would have become the mightiest
empire the world had ever known.

Only slightly less immense would have been her
gains economically. She would have new and vast markets opened to her merchandise and to her capital.
She would surely have gotten control of the Caucasus
if only because of the new pathway it would offer to
Persia and India, and with the Caucasus in her hands
she would be mistress of some of the most immense oil
fields in the world.

At one time during the Russian civil war it did seem
as though Russia would break up. Siberia, the Caucasus, the Crimea, the Volga Basin, the north country,
the Ukraine, the central provinces were in arms against
each other. Meanwhile England had become dominant

in the Baltic, in the Caspian, in the Black and in the White Seas. She had virtually control of the Southern Caucasus, of the Archangel country in the north, she had pushed her way into Turkestan, and her influence was powerful in the Crimea and in Siberia. Fate seemed to have put all the trumps into British hands.

British diplomats and journalists disavow that the purpose of British intervention in Russia was to achieve the dismemberment of the Russian Empire. But Russians in and outside of Russia — some of the emigrés even more violently than do the Bolsheviks — contest this disavowal. One thing is emphatically evident, the policy England pursued in Russia — the spheres of influence she had established, the support she had offered separatist movements, the strategic position in which she had sought to intrench herself, particularly in the waters in and around Russia, could not but arouse in the Russians the suspicion that she was exploiting the fight on Bolshevism as a smoke-screen behind which to bring to fruition far more grandiose plans — the most grandiose any British statesman ever had cherished.

In the new Russian political literature, in the new histories the Russians are writing, they treat British intervention during the civil war under the heading of "the period of dismemberment," that is the period of British efforts to slash Russia to pieces. An entire young generation is being nourished on this notion. It has become to the Russians of nearly all groups and classes not only an inviolate conviction but a haunting obsession. England has become *the* enemy, *the* plotter, ever seeking to thrust a poison-dipped bayonet

into the very heart of the Revolution and of the
Russian nation — and this notion has kindled a mighty
flame of hate against England from one end of the land
to the other. Imagine high-school boys and girls in a
Siberian village boasting with glee of the success they
have been having during rifle practice in hitting for
their bull's eye the caricatured monocle of Sir Austin
Chamberlain!

However, the Red Army crushed all opposition.
With the exception of Poland and the Baltic states
all forces hostile to it, whether of White Russian generals or of foreign powers, were either vanquished or
put to rout. The military conflict with England which
had cost the latter half a billion dollars and not a few
lives was at an end. England even hastened to make
peace with Russia and paved the way for the Genoa
conference which gave the Soviets a chance to appear
before the world for the first time since their advent
into power. But the feeling of hostility between the
two nations did not and could not abate. It continued
to boil. The Soviet government had two forces to defend — the Revolution and the Russian Nation, and
rightly or wrongly it saw in England the implacable
enemy of both.

Russia launched an offensive against England with
some extraordinary weapons of her own, which could
not but rouse England's apprehensions and ruffle her
temper even more. Russian journalism armed with
Marxian prophecy began to make merry sport of England as a world power. It pictured her as weighted
down with senility and sunk in a morass of contradictions out of which only revolution could rescue her,

and that by asphyxiating her body politic. It pointed to
America as the young and lusty giant of the capitalist
world, skipping joyously about the earth and snatch-
ing England's crown of leadership in finance, industry,
commerce. As one Russian journalist once said to me:
" England is like an old woman that heroically persists
in painting her cheecks to sustain the illusion of youth
and power." Very brutally but very truly does this
expression convey the contempt of Russian journalism
for England. Still, the theoretic scorn of Russian journalism neither did nor could in itself achieve damage
to England, though it may have roused to fury the men
who clustered round the Baldwin cabinet and other
proud British patriots.

More pregnant with possibility for harm and therefore more distasteful to British sensibilities was the
action of the Russian trade unions. The British trade
unions had formed an alliance with them and they had
striven mightily, though in the main clumsily, to veer
British labour into channels of revolutionary methods
of procedure. During the miners' strike in England
they had contributed five million dollars to the support
of the strikers. The alliance between the Russian and
British trade unions came to an abrupt crash. The
British broke it off. It cannot be said that it ever did
affect British labour perceptibly in its political outlook
or tactics. The attempt of the Russians to exploit it
for such a purpose irritated not only conservative
leaders and their hosts of followers but the men in the
Labour Party, and only sharpened the feeling of bitter-
ness for the Russians.

Provocative of deepest exasperation to England were

the endeavours of Russian Communists and the Comintern, which to the British mind is wholly Russian because working in interests of Russia, to stir revolt in other lands and especially among colonial and semi-colonial peoples. They struck their severest blow at England in China. Invited by the Chinese the Russian Communists brought to China their experience in mass organization, mass propaganda and military warfare. With their help the Nationalists became the mightiest military force in China, the most important and best organized political body, and again with their help or rather their strategy they directed their chief fire against England. The famous Hong-Kong strike which had paralyzed British trade for months and nearly drove this once most prosperous British city in the Far East into bankruptcy, the nation-wide boycotts of British goods, the constant and violent agitation against England, in all of these the Russian revolutionaries had a firm and sometimes a decisive part. At present the Chinese Nationalists have driven the Russians from their ranks and their land, but the harm they have helped achieve in loss of trade and even as much in fall of British prestige not only in China but everywhere in Asia, is beyond repair.

However, it is not Russian journalism or the Russian trade unions or the Comintern and Russian revolutionaries or any other unofficial Russian or pro-Russian body that hold within them the greatest power for damage to British interests. It is official Russia, the Soviet Government itself that holds within it this power. Because of some of its external and internal policies it has become more formidable a foe to British supremacy and even security in Asia than the Czarist Government with all its armies and all its rapacity could ever be. Consider the damage Soviet Russia has already inflicted on England in Asia through her open support of the Nationalist movements of subject peoples. Here is Afghanistan most vital to England because of the vast barrier it forms between India and Russia. Had it not been for the moral stimulus and encouragement it received from Russia, it might never have launched into a war of independence against England. The British nearly won the war, but the Afghans triumphed at the peace table. They got their independence from England and primarily because it would have been dangerous to withold it in the face of a Russia championing it.

Here is Persia another barrier between India and Russia. The coming of the Soviet Government resulted in the scrapping of the Russian and was followed by the abandonment of the British sphere of influence in this ancient land of Asia. For the present revolutionary Russia has caused no special injury to British interests in Persia. But what will happen if a real Nationalist movement develops in the country? Persia may now be pacific, somnolent, self-satisfied. But so was China. One never can tell when a psychic cyclone will sweep over Persia and heave into being a militant Nationalist party. Such a party will inevitably lean on Russia for support. Indeed, Russia may be the galvanizing force of a Nationalist movement in Persia, and as in China will through her influence direct its fighting fury chiefly against England. Potentially Soviet Russia is the greatest menace the British have to reckon with in Persia.

Here is China. The Soviet Government annulled the

old treaties, signed new ones on the basis of full equality with the Chinese and with no pretensions to extra-
territoriality. She likewise cancelled the indemnities
that had been awarded to old Russia as her share of the
damages in the Boxer rebellion. This gave the Chinese
a fresh moral weapon in their crusade for equality and
independence and again to the severest detriment of
England.

Here is Turkey. The Russians helped Kemal Pasha
with arms in the Turkish war against the Greeks,
which in effect was a war against England. The slaughter of the Greeks is too recent an event to warrant a detailed account here. When it was over and the Greeks
in panic and woe staggered back to their own lands,
Kemal Pasha tore up the treaties the Allies had imposed on his country, and dictated his own terms to
his enemies, stripping England of all the prerogatives
she had wrested for herself from the Ottoman nation.

On front after front in which the two ancient rivals
in Asia have met, the Russians have dealt violent blows
to England, her trade, her investments, her prestige,
her power. In Persia, Afghanistan, Turkey, China, they
have helped deprive her of advantages and fortifications from which the Czar with all his armies and all
his lust for conquest never could shake her. They have
pushed their offensive further into fresh fields of action.
They have signed treaties of non-aggression with
Afghanistan, Turkey, Persia, and have been instru-
mental in bringing these three nations together to sign
similar treaties with each other. On the surface this
may seem like a harmless piece of diplomacy having no
bearing on England's position in Asia. But it establishes

a bond of sympathy between Russia and these nations as well as between them with each other and, in guaranteeing them against possible attack from the Russian side, hardens their spirit of independence and makes capitulation or even concession to England more difficult.

Certainly the new program of industrialization on which Soviet Russia has embarked holds a further though more indirect menace to England, particularly as Russia's Asiatic possessions are included in this program. True, Russia is colossally inefficient. She has made preposterous blunders in her industrialization projects. Yet she is pursuing her plans with fervour and energy. She has already built scores of electrical plants all over her Asiatic frontiers. Go to the city of Novo-Sibirsk, the capital of Siberia, which I recently visited, and you will find rows of modern brick and granite buildings where only a few years ago log-hovels sprawled. Go to Sverdlovsk, the capital of the Urals, and you will find it roaring with constructive effort — new factories and machine-shops in process of erection, not only in the city but all over this vast and immensely rich country which is right on the edge of Asia. Most significant of all are the new series of railroads projected for Asiatic Russia. One of them destined to play a historic part not only in Russia but in Asia will soon be finished. It will connect the vast Siberian with the Central Asiatic provinces of Russia and bring Russia, as Trotzky once said, much closer to India.

The scheme to industrialize Russia is no immediate threat to England, politically or economically, and will not be until it has been substantially realized, which will not so soon occur. When it is achieved, and Russia has factories in Asia to produce goods for foreign consumption, she will offer England no little competition, if only because of her geographic proximity to the Asiatic markets. She will also most assuredly enhance the political peril to England. England had cherished fear of an invasion of India when Russia had no industries in Asia and few railroad lines. How much graver and more real must this fear be when Russia has built a network of industries, especially metallurgical, in her Asiatic lands, and is in possession of three railroads starting from different points and moving southward toward Afghanistan. This treble line of railroads Russia will have in 1930, when the new Siberian-Turkestan road is finished.

Viewed from every conceivable angle the conflict between England and Russia has since the Revolution gained in intensity if not in savagery. Old suspicions, old intrigues, have grown more rampant. Old animosities have assumed a new fire, a new venom. Fresh frictions have leaped up everywhere. Under Czarism there always were mitigating circumstances that permitted of continuous compromises. There was, at least, an outward show of respect of one nation for another. There is only gruffness and contempt now. There was, further, the blood relationship of the Russian and English royal families. There was the rise of Japan, and while England had made an alliance with Japan as a threat to Russia, she could tolerate an aggressive Japan no more than a grasping Russia, and she could always count on Russia to support her in curbing Japanese lust for expansion. There was the rise of

Germany with her intrusion into Asia, threatening to dispute supremacy there with both Russia and England. There was the burst of Nationalist sentiment in Asia of equal menace to both empires.

These conditions now no longer obtain. The Russian imperial family is gone. Russia prefers to deal with Japan in her own way. German aggression in Asia is blasted for a long time to come, if not forever. As for the Nationalist movements — they are a real joy to the Russians. They thrive on such movements. Support of them they have woven into the very fabric of their internal and external policies. They are to the Russians a triumph, a weapon, a promise. It is not a matter on which they will mediate or compromise. The future of the Russian people and of the Revolution is inextricably interwoven with the spread and the ultimate enthronement of nationalism all over Asia.

Gone then are the common grounds on which old Russia and England could come together and hold back a catastrophe. Now there is nothing but conflict all along the vast social and political frontiers on which they meet. Nor can it be otherwise as long as Russia dreams and strives for a reintegrated and industrialized nation and persists in upholding the Nationalist movements of the world, while England clings to the preservation of her empire, especially in Asia. . . .

England has replied to Russia's retaliation with vigour and severity. We could hardly expect her to act otherwise in the face of the blows which Russia has inflicted on her in Afghanistan, Persia, Turkey, China, and in view of the possibility for further harm all over Asia including India. She broke relations with the

Soviets. The raid on the Russian Trading Headquarters in London was an excuse and most emphatically not a cause of this rupture.

A Russian historian in writing of the clash between England and Russia likens the two countries to two locomotives starting toward each other from opposite directions and along the same track. Must there be a collision? Skilled diplomacy may avert it. But the fundamental conflict will persist. A modernized and unified Russia supporting Nationalist movements is incompatible with a British Empire — especially in Asia.

CHAPTER XIX

REVOLUTION

AT the time of the British election in 1924 when
the Conservative Party hurled the so-called
Zinovyev letter into the campaign and thereby blasted
all chances of the Labor Party being returned to power,
George Bernard Shaw, in his wrath, sent a caustic
dispatch to the Moscow Izvestia, the official organ of
the Soviets. In this message he counsels the Russian
leaders to " dissociate themselves from the Third International as speedily as possible and to tell Zinovyev,
head of that body at the time, plainly that he must
choose between serious statesmanship and cinemato-
graphic nonsense."

This utterance of Shaw proves that even the most
brilliant minds of the world have failed to comprehend
the spirit and the temper of Russian bolshevism or of
the men sponsoring it. There have been writers and
political leaders, Lloyd George one of them, who in the
early days of the Bolshevik Revolution had assured
themselves and the world, that experience with practical affairs and contact with outside nations would
dampen the Communist ardour for world revolt. Twelve
years may not be a sufficiently long period to test this
prophecy, but thus far it has failed utterly of fulfillment. Now there are writers in this country and in
England who would have us believe that the Russian
Communist under the hegemony of Stalin has been

slowly withdrawing into his own nationalistic shell and seems content enough to leave the cause of world revolt to its own fate. The expulsion of Trotzky from the Party and from Russia would seem to lend colour to this theory, for Trotzky is the burning flame of the so-called " permanent revolution " which he is so violently championing. Yet nothing so much amuses the Russian Communists as the constant reiteration of this theory in bourgeois journals.

I happened to be in Moscow on the day of the funeral of Voykoff, the murdered Soviet Ambassador in Warsaw. The huge Red Square was jammed with crowds of soldiers and workers — over one hundred thousand of them — who came with bands and banners, glistening bloodlike in a hot sun, to pay a last tribute to their fallen leader. From the top of the Lenine Mausoleum where lies embalmed the body of Lenine, leaders of the Soviet Government, the Communist Party and the Third International delivered speeches. The most impassioned orator was Bukharin, the short, thick-set man with a massive head crowned with an upstanding tuft of greyish hair, who since the death of Lenine has been the *teoretic,* theorizer, and spokesman of Communist thought and policy. As he warmed up to his climax he exclaimed: " We announce to all our enemies that never for a minute, never for a second, never for one millionth of a second will our Party retrench from those proposals which it has inscribed on its banner, and on its banner it has inscribed the mighty slogan, the great watchword — international social revolution — the watchword of militant communism, which will battle until it has organized free labour on earth." His last words were: "Long live the cause that is destined to conquer the world."

There is not a Communist living but will subscribe with his very blood to these sentiments, which sound as much like a challenge as an oath. In the face of such and numerous similar pronouncements by Communist leaders and in Communist literature, all talk of an impending shift of attitude in Communist ranks in Russia, or of an abandonment even in part of the idea or the program of world revolt, is unworthy of serious consideration. The men and women indulging in these pacifying assurances clearly enough do not appreciate just what world revolution and proletarian dictatorship mean to the Communist. They mean everything, emotionally and intellectually. They are to the Communist *the* forces and the only ones that can eventually usher in social justice, as he understands the phrase, and world peace. They are the means, and the only means, of bringing salvation to mankind. He, therefore, regards world revolution not as an instrument of warfare but of peace, the mightiest the world has ever forged — the only one that eventually will rid humanity of all barbarities, including war. World revolution is to him at once a great hope and a great inspiration, a great weapon and a great aim.

An age or more hence when hardly any of the men who had participated in the October Revolution are alive, when, if Russia has peace, a generation has come into power which knows not the smell of powder, when Russia with the development of her immense natural resources has grown comfortable, the Russian Communist may cool in his ardour for world revolution. The

Soviet Government may yet become the ascendant power in Russia and keep the Communist Party subdued or at least subordinated to its own immediate international purposes and obligations. Even now there is a visible cleavage in policy between the Soviet Government and the Communist Party. Not a Communist living, for example, in and outside of Russia but regards the Kellogg Peace Pact as another nefarious intrigue of the bourgeoisie to blind the eyes and dull the minds of the masses. In no country which has had to consider the problem of joining the American Pact did the Communist faction in Parliament support such a move. In Germany, in France, in Poland, everywhere the Communists denounced it as a piece of bourgeois brigandage. But Russia, despite the control of the Soviet Government by the Communist Party, hailed the Pact with greatest enthusiasm and actually invited herself to sign it. Is it not also significant that in the conflict which had broken out in Afghanistan between Amanullah and Mohammedan leaders, the Russians had openly taken the part of Amanullah? Imagine Communists actually supporting a king and helping him retain his power!

Soviet policies may push the Communist in Russia farther and farther into the background. The time may yet come when the Russian Communist will become the most conservative radical in the world, when Communists in other lands will anathematize him as violently as he now anathematizes the non-Communist socialist. All things are possible in time. But at present the Russian Communist has not the least notion of pocketing his revolutionary ardour. He is a veritable flame of revolutionary enthusiasm. World revolution is one of the big sustaining forces in his life. It is the very soul of his revolutionary passion. He roars with amusement when he is informed that he is really cooling off . . . nowhere is there a perceptible sign of a process of cooling.

His plans and methods for world revolution are as fundamental as they are far-reaching. He realizes, of course, that it takes two to make a bargain and that his mere wish, however intense, to launch a revolution in any given place is insufficient to achieve it. He has always been saying that two elements are required to make a revolution possible, a subjective and an objective, that is, there must be a party, legal or illegal, which is physically and psychologically equipped to launch the revolution and there must be a condition in life, or what Lenine called an *imminently revolutionary situation*, which provides the opportunity for such a move. He is opposed to all forms of terror in peace times. The assassination of an individual capitalist or political reactionary, however hostile to labour or to communism he deems futile, utterly incapable of advancing in any way the growth of the *imminently revolutionary situation*, or of winning support for the Communist movement. He will have no terrorism. He is death on militant anarchism. Likewise, he is opposed to a so-called *putsch*, a mere helter-skelter assault on capitalist fortifications. He will have no rebellion just for the sake of rebellion. He is a practical, calculating warrior, with an eye always on possible results. He favours revolutionary action only when the two elements I have mentioned, the subjective and the objective, exist in a measure to give reasonable assurance of success. Under no other circumstances, so at least he insists, and for no other purpose will he counsel or countenance an uprising.

Now, whatever other beliefs the Communist may cherish there is one that he has abandoned — the belief that there is a spot anywhere in the world which is at present ripe for a Communist uprising. He sadly but frankly admits that there is no *imminently revolutionary situation* anywhere in any land, hardly even in China. He is even willing to confess that he, with all his hate of capitalism, can do little at present to foster the development of such a situation. It is beyond his power to bring or conjure it into being. But he does not despair. He believes with all his soul that sooner or later such a condition will bob up somewhere on the horizon — for it is in the very nature of capitalism to give it birth — and that his big job is to be prepared to take advantage of it. He, therefore, regards it as his immediate all-absorbing task or duty to forge into being the subjective element of the Revolution, the human forces that are to leap into action at the opportune moment and fight it out with capitalism and the bourgeoisie to the deathly end.

That is why he talks so much and so passionately of preserving the Russian Revolution. I happened to arrive in Russia at the time when England had broken relations with the Soviets and as I travelled about the country I ran into monster demonstrations against England, in cities and villages. The slogan under which these were held was — " The Revolution is in danger " — not Russia, but the Revolution, a significant phrase. The Revolution is higher than Russia, higher than any nation, any movement. It certainly is that to the Communist at present. He regards the Russian Revolution as the light-house of proletarian sovereignty in the tempestuous sea of capitalist domination. He points to it as a guide and inspiration to the masses all over the world — a force that must waken their revolutionary zeal, fan their fighting spirit. He views it as the mightiest immediate weapon at his command with which to inflame the-mass of humanity to revolutionary ardour. The Revolution, he never ceases to assure the world, must be saved even if it has to be carried to the Ural Mountains and tucked away in the snow-banks there. He is determined to defend it against all encroachments, internal and external, without terror, if possible, but if necessary, with terror, constant and ruthless.

How can it be saved? First by keeping Russia at peace with the outside world. Soviet diplomacy must steer clear from situations that smell of war, and when unexpectedly caught in them, must wriggle out with safety if not with glory. That is one reason why Soviet foreign policy, despite the fighting tone of its diplomatic notes, has been so conciliatory. The Soviet Government has learned to swallow rebukes quite gracefully. When Chang-tso-Lin, the late Manchurian war-lord, had slapped it in the face twice, once by seizing the fleet of the Chinese Eastern Railway and again by making a violent raid on the Soviet Embassy at Peking, it contented itself with a vitriolic harangue. I am reasonably confident that had Chang-tso-Lin or his successors seized the Chinese Eastern Railway, in which the

Soviet Government has a half interest, the Russians would not send a single soldier on Chinese soil to fight.

Peace under all circumstances, that is the slogan of the Communist in Russia. Hence his effort to influence foreign labour to help him in this aim. There may have been proletarian love in the contribution of five million dollars which the Russian trade unions had sent to the striking British miners in 1926, but there was also well-calculated purposefulness. I was in Russia at the time the money was being gathered, and Communists frankly admitted that it was good insurance money — insurance against war. British miners, after such a show of generosity on the part of Russian labour, were supposed to have something to say to their government if it ever encouraged or undertook a war on Soviet Russia.

Simultaneously the masses, says the Communist, must be reached through all available sources. They must be enlightened, energized, made into crusaders. They must at all times be reminded of the sins and villainies of capitalism. Their hate of the bourgeoisie must be continually fanned. A strike in America, an execution of a labour leader in China, a harsh note of Mussolini to Jugo-Slavia — all is grist for the Communist mill, fuel with which to kindle the revolutionary spirit of the masses. The Communist is at all times on the alert for opportunities to attack the bourgeoisie at every vulnerable point, to discredit it in every aspect of its everyday life, personal, social, official — all with a view of snapping whatever bonds of understanding and goodwill may be existing between it and the proletarian.

How does he transmit his ideas to outside labour?
The impression is widely prevalent that the Soviet
Government, through its embassies and trade bodies in
foreign lands, is the chief disseminator of Communist
propaganda. The raids on the Russian Trading Headquarters in London and on the Soviet Embassy in
Peking have disclosed evidence involving officials in
such propaganda, though the Soviet Government vehemently denies that the evidence is genuine. In view
of the disclosures in Germany of rings of forgers
who had for years been supplying the press and diplomatic representatives with all manner of manufactured
documents incriminating Russian Communists and
Soviet officials in foreign lands, the denials of the
Soviet Government cannot be readily dismissed. Russians of prominence in the government and in the Party
never tire of assuring the world that they ruthlessly
discipline Soviet workers abroad for participation in
political activities in any land where they are stationed.
The task of the Soviet Government, they protest, is to
maintain peace with the outside world, and any political
indiscretion of its representatives holds within it, under present strained relations with outside nations, the
possibility of war. Besides, they insist, the cause of
world revolution can progress well enough without the
surreptitious aid that Soviet workers in foreign lands
may be able or wanting to offer.

Indeed it can. It has ample supporters everywhere,
who have no official standing in Russia. There is the
Comintern, or the Third International. There is the
Profintern, or the Trade Union International. There
are the Communist parties in foreign lands. There

are the numerous Communist schools in and outside of
Russia, the Communist Youth Movement, the Communist feminine societies. All of these in their contacts with workers and other potential revolutionaries
anywhere in the world are to seek to win them to the
Communist gospel.

And who are the masses? The Communist answers
the question definitely enough. They are not the industrial workers alone. These are the most militant and
most desperate revolutionaries — always in the vanguard of the revolutionary procession, the chief shock
troops of the Revolution. But they must have on their
side the military man, the soldier and the sailor, and
also the farmer. The Communist is most explicit on
this point. Without their active support, the industrial
worker may find himself in a bad way just when he is
about to clinch his revolutionary victories. He may
be hacked to pieces and the Revolution again bottled
up. Communists in outside nations will always seek to
win the soldier and the sailor to their cause even as
much as the proletarian.

There can be no doubt that in any war to come the
nations of the world will have to face, together with
new physical weapons — new gases, new aerial attacks,
new explosives — the new distinctively human weapon of revolutionary propaganda, no matter who the
combatants involved. This propaganda will be widespread and intense, if only because a war from the
Communist standpoint is supposed to be especially
conducive to the creation of an *imminently revolutionary situation.*

The Communist, however, does not stop with the

masses. His goal is more far-reaching. He realizes very keenly that no movement requires at all times such dependable leadership as a revolution. It was lack of brave leadership, he insists, that was in part responsible for the failure of the Communist Revolution in Germany in 1923. If Scheidemann, he avows, leader of the Social Democrats, had had the fighting spirit of Liebknecht, Germany might now have been Soviet. If Ramsay MacDonald, Arthur Henderson and the other chiefs of the British Labour movement had been true crusaders of the labour cause, England might likewise, by this time, have been on the road to Sovietism. There is nobody the Communist so furiously despises as the non-Communist labour leaders. He speaks of them with vitriolic contempt. To him they are super-traitors of the proletarian cause, the champion scoundrels of all mankind. To him anybody, but especially a socialist or a trade union leader who ventures the assertion that labour and capital can compromise and co-operate for their mutual benefit is either a scamp or a lick-spittle, or both. He deems the conflict between labour and capital as beyond reconciliation save through the sword.

So the Communist, while striving desperately at all times to keep the Russian Revolution from collapsing and to excite and energize the masses of the world, is spending no little effort to develop new revolutionary leadership which in time will supersede the MacDonalds, the Scheidemanns and other pacifically-minded chieftains. This work again is carried on not by the Soviets but by the Communist bodies especially in the schools they maintain. In Russia there are many

such schools and the students are chiefly Russians,
though the number of foreigners, especially Asiatics,
is constantly increasing. In Moscow, for example, in
the University of the Toiling Masses of the East, there
are Turks, Hindus, Mongols, Persians, Koreans, Chinese and other Asiatics.

The presence of Asiatic students in the Russian
schools is no mere accident. In more than one sense
present-day Asia is a land of promise to the Communist — is almost the gateway to world revolution. The
ferment of Nationalist sentiment in Asia and the strife
for self-determination are to him a most welcome event
— a promise of triumph. A Nationalist revolution is
after all a revolution, a step in the direction of a Communist revolution. It is a blow at the prestige, and
even more at the pocket-book of the big capitalist nations of the world, and anything which batters down
their prestige and hits their pocket-book weakens them,
invites their economic disorganization, pushes them
closer and closer to the condition of an *imminently
revolutionary situation*. Rob England, says the Communist, of her privilege of exploiting China, India,
Egypt, and her other colonial and semi-colonial possessions and she must crash to ruins and become over-
ripe for a revolutionary outbreak and therefore for
Sovietism!

The question inevitably arises as to what justification the Communist has for thinking that an *imminently revolutionary situation*, like a stick of wood
plunged into a stream, must eventually rise to the surface of life? Has he learned nothing from the events
of the years that have passed since the end of the

World war? Nation after nation at one time had seemed
to be boiling with *an imminently revolutionary situation,* and yet when attempts were made to take advantage of it, it melted away like snow in fire. Here were
Finland, Estonia, Latvia, parts of the old Russian
Empire, within a stone's throw almost from old Petro-
grad, the citadel of the Revolution, yet when revolution had shot upward in these lands with a tumult that
sounded almost like a roar of triumph, it was quenched
in streams of blood. Here was Hungary; the Revolution
had actually swung into power there, but was swung out
again and gored to death. Here was Germany, in 1923,
with her Ruhr invaded, her currency fallen, hunger
stalking in the cities, France brandishing a sword over
her head — rotten-ripe it would seem for the Revolution, — and yet no sooner had it burst into flame in
Saxony, in Hamburg, than it was fiendishly smothered. Here were Java and China — Revolution had
raised its head in both lands with a sweep of terror,
but came to grief swiftly enough. There is not a region
anywhere in the world outside of Russia where the
Revolution had lifted itself into view but it was instantly hacked to death. In the light of these events
it would seem that the so-called *imminently revolutionary situation* is much further removed from reality
than the Russian or any other Communist had imagined, or is even now willing to admit that it was or is.

The Communist has since evolved a complicated
theory to explain away to himself and others the failure
of the Revolution to materialize. The subjective element of the Revolution, he avows, had not yet attained
real strength. Socialist leaders and labour chieftains,

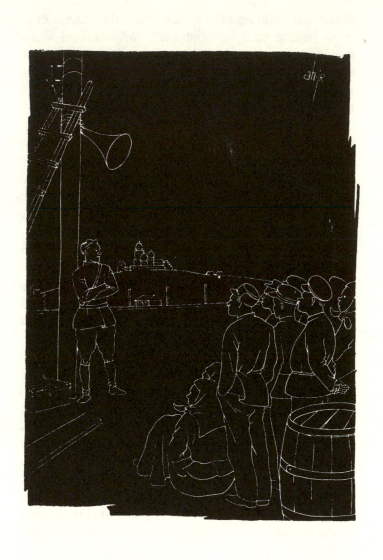

who should have been with and for the Revolution, had been opposing it too mightily. They will have to be re-educated or supplanted with men whose hearts are afire with revolt. He further admits that capitalism had managed to stabilize itself and thereby to push back indefinitely the much-sought-for *revolutionary situation*.* In other words there was not a mighty enough subjective element in the world to take advantage of the objective condition, and now the objective condition has been submerged — not destroyed but submerged. Sooner or later, he insists, it will leap up again. That is as inevitable as the rising and the setting of the sun. It is, he argues, written in all the laws of history, in all the laws of nature that this should be so. No capitalist trickery, no social patriot strategy can stave it off. If nothing else, a war, he protests, will body forth the *imminently revolutionary situation*. " If the bourgeoisie," exclaims Bukharin, " will unchain the furies of war — then in the end the proletarian will conquer the world." A war and its aftermath of wreckage, sorrow, desperation, in themselves symptoms of capitalist decay, will, he is certain, make the common man responsive to the revolutionary appeal.

But supposing there is no war? No matter, the Revolution, insists the Communist, must come anyway. If the whole world were to disarm and not a single drop of powder were to remain anywhere the Revolution would still make its advent. But under capitalism,

---

* The Stalin faction however, which is at present in control of the Communist party, is beginning more and more to view capitalist stabilization as being increasingly menaced by the conflicts arising from the search of capitalist nations for markets, for raw materials, for fields of investment.

argues the Communist, war must come. As long as each
nation is fighting its own battles for its own economic
well-being in outside markets the world over, and
particularly in more backward parts of the globe, there
are bound to be conflicts, jealousies, resentments which
in time of a crisis will and must precipitate armed encounters. " The monopolistic form of capitalism," reads
the resolution of the Sixth Congress of the Third International, " invariably is accompanied by *inescapa-
ble* imperialistic wars, which in their magnitude and
technical capacity for destruction, have no parallel
in the world's history." Wars, says the Communist, are
as natural to capitalist society, as storms to the ocean
or plagues to regions infested with swamps.

It is this theory of war as the breeder of revolution
that carries with it the mightiest challenge to the
capitalist or rather the Western World. The Communist is really serving notice on it — that, however stable,
protected and secure it may be now — in time of war
he will loosen on it all the furies at his command and
will seek once for all to settle the question of world
power or world rule with capitalism.

CHAPTER XX

WAR

IF the next war does not, somewhere or everywhere in the rear and at the front, burst into revolutionary conflagrations, it will not be because of failure of the Communist to hurl lighted torches of his own at places of strategic importance all over the fighting areas. Much, of course, will depend on the economic stability of the rear and the social solidity of the front of the nations involved in the fray. The more firm both, the more mighty will be the resistance to Communist manoeuverings. Despite its reputed prowess and Machiavellism the Third International, the directing head of the Communist fighting legion, is in time of peace and economic comfort nothing more, at best, than a bellicose general with grandiose schemes of conquest and a heart full of fire, but without an army, with hardly a fighting front. A war, more than any other social cataclysm, will put the revolutionary wrath, or fervour, or threat of the Communist to the most fierce test.

It may be, of course, that history will repeat itself and that the Communist, like the Socialist in 1914, will, when face to face with a real catastrophe, crash under the strain and find himself frozen out of revolutionary ardour. Who in 1914 would have imagined that the Socialist anti-war spirit would tumble like an edifice with the foundation washed away? Yet — there was no general strike. There were no refusals to take up arms. There was no compunction at one proletarian slaying another. With rare exceptions neither the French nor the German Socialists lifted their voices or their hands to paralyse the fighting dervishes their respective governments had hurled against one another. They swallowed their internationalism like a sugar-coated pill with hardly a twitch of the brow. Their blood proved thicker than water and more fiery than their socialist ardour.

The Communist outside of Russia may prove as derelict a revolutionary as the Socialist, but it would not be safe to count on it. Deriving his inspiration from the same " Communist Manifesto " and the same " Capital " of Marx, he is in his approach to his cause as different from the Socialist as are, to use a somewhat exaggerated example, the Christian from the Mohammedan. He has not the Socialist's sentimental aversion to bloodshed. He has no faith in the potency of pacifism — not the slightest. Not even the *bourzhui* had roused Lenine's wrath more robustly than had the pacifist, or brought down on himself a more furious castigation, and Lenine's followers share their leader's contempt for the pacifist. The Communist *is* a warrior. A conscientious objector is not admitted to membership in the Party. The Communist is a soldier in soul even more than in body, but under an international and not a national banner. Whatever his national origin, when mobilized by a capitalist government he must go to the front, so his teachers and Party tell him, and while there his mission is to kindle everywhere the flames of unrest, of rebellion, of mutiny. With all the energy and fervour at his command even at cost of life he is to push the fight from the furnace of a national into the crucible of class conflict. In any war to come, whatever the nations involved, the shadow of the Communist will hover over chancellories and general staff headquarters like a tormenting phantom. But whether the Communist will prove a Damoclean sword or a mere scarecrow, it would be futile to foretell.

Still, whatever the part he plays in a war between capitalist nations, there is no blinking the fact that in a war in which Russia is involved he will be a desperate force, if only because Russia, unless her present regime collapses, will march under the banner of communism and will be under the immediate and iron control of the Communist. Indeed, a war with Russia because of the presence of the Communist will be something new in the world. It will mean the ghastliest war known in history. It cannot be otherwise.

A war of nations at best is a brutal enough affair. A war of classes, a civil war, is even more so. A combination of the two, a war of nations and of classes fought simultaneously by the same peoples, bids fair to become the last word in human barbarism. Yet it is just this kind of a war Russia will have to fight if she ever faces a foreign foe, and it is just this kind of a war any nation will have to wage if it ever embarks on an armed conflict with Russia. A war with or against Russia must in the very nature of things be a double war, a war at the front and a war in the rear. The war in the rear, because disorganized and abortive as civil wars often are and involving as it must, indirectly at least, the civilian population of the given territory, including women and children, is sure to prove the more beastly of the two.

The Russians frankly and proudly protest that when they march to battle it will be not to fight a nation. Never, no matter who the enemy. It will be to liberate that nation from the yoke of the capitalist and the bourgeoisie. They will march to war under the slogans " death to the bourgeoisie " — " freedom and power to the proletarian," under the slogans not of a national but of a class war. They will appeal to enemy soldiers to align themselves with the Revolution against their own " exploiters and imperialists." This appeal may prove to be a voice in the wilderness. The response may elicit only heightened war fervour in the enemy ranks. But no matter. The Russians will continue their march forward or backward under the banner not of a national but of a class war, and that alone must make such a war more ghastly than any the world has known. It is easy enough to say that Russia is in no position at present to fight a first class war against a first class nation. I doubt if the Russians themselves will dispute this contention. But Russia is most certainly in a position to fight an atrocious war whoever the nations involved.

As already emphasized in the preceding pages the Russians are as convinced of the inevitability of war with a foreign foe, as they are of the ultimate success of their Revolution. To them the die is already cast, and they will have to spill blood, their own and that of others. They see in themselves not only a thorn but a spear in the side of the capitalist nations, piercing deeper and deeper into capitalist flesh, and they do not see how the capitalist world can remain indifferent to this thrust. Through their Revolution, they avow, they have crashed brutally into the so-called capitalist front. They have cut off one-sixth of the world's land from the normal processes of economic intercourse which are so necessary to the well-being of capitalism. They have fanned the resistance of colonial peoples to imperialist exploitation. They have fired the discontent, however invisibly, of the workers of the world. Their very existence with a Soviet government and a ruling Communist Party is both a symbol and a stimulus to further rebellion. Therefore, they are convinced that the capitalists of the world must make another attempt to smite them down, and that soon. For time, they insist, is on their side, altogether so. The longer the capitalists postpone the day of reckoning with them, the harder, they protest, they will be to conquer. They will grow more powerful and not only physically. If the capitalist world should delay the attack too long, they will be unconquerable morally, however badly they might be smashed physically. In another fifteen or twenty years, when the present older generation dies off, it will be about as safe to hold a Russia conquered by arms, so they earnestly believe, as to tame the ocean or a storm with machine guns. The new Russian humanity will be trained in a way of life and thought so utterly alien and hostile to any other outside nation that it will be unmanageable, save by people like themselves or in sympathy with their social faith and their mode of social behavior, which capitalist conquerors never will be. " Keep a bee-hive in your living room," said a Russian editor to me once, " and you may gather some honey, but you may also find yourself stung to distraction if not to death." That is precisely the way Russian revolutionaries feel about the possibility of any bourgeois nation ruling Russian territory inhabited by a humanity reared, as it will have been fifteen or twenty years hence, exclusively in Soviet ideas. The bourgeois nations, the Russians reason further, cannot help realizing the danger of a postponement of hostilities. They must in sheer self-interest hurry their reckoning with Russia, or rather the Russian Revolution, or else bow to its inevitable blows.

The Russians may be taking their menace to capitalist nations too seriously. They have been living in an atmosphere of tumult, rumor, panic, threat. They have been sundered from the outside world and their fears and premonitions loom to them more awesome perhaps than to others. They may be seeing too much red, too much fire, too much dynamite. But the fact is that they do see themselves surrounded by armed legions ready at some unforeseen moment to leap at them.

This is one reason they are eager to exploit every circumstance to keep down military tension in their part of the world. Epochal is the significance of Russia's support of the Kellogg Pact. She was among the first nations in the world to sign it, and she even used it as a basis to band together a group of her immediate neighbors including Poland and Rumania, her stanch foes, in a protocol of her own. Of course her diplomats dismiss with cutting irony the notion

that the Kellogg Pact is a panacea for peace. But it
invites an atmosphere and a psychology of peace and
may hold in leash longer than would otherwise have
been possible the dogs of war, and that in itself is to
Russia in her present state of internal distress a welcome boon. Every day of peace is victory. Every new
brick she lays, every bolt she fastens, every shovelful
of dirt she digs up, every move of her hand to make
Russia a modern nation, economically self-sufficient,
she regards as an achievement and a triumph. No nation ever needed peace more desperately than Russia.
The Kellogg Plan was to her a gleam of light, even if
transitory, in an ocean of uncertainty and gloom. If the
world would accept her proposal for complete disarmament, made by Litvinov in Geneva, she would have no
reason in the world to conjure up some irremovable obstacle to prevent its realization, as diplomats and publicists have so often said she would. To be relieved of
the fear of war during this period of reconstruction
would be an immense gain for the Russia of the Soviet
Union. To strip the bourgeoisie of the world of weapons
with which to hold down colonial peoples and to suppress uprisings of proletarians, would be even more
of a boon to the Russia of the Communist. Russia would
have every reason to welcome disarmament because, in
her own Marxian phraseology, she would have " nothing to lose and a world to gain."

Since Russia is convinced that she cannot escape a
war, whom does she regard as her possible enemies? In
America the opinion is widespread that Russia is more
likely to clash with Japan than with any other nation.
Yet despite the frequent diplomatic tilts between the

Nipponese and the Muscovites over Manchuria and over rights in far-eastern waters, despite Japan's obvious designs on the Chinese Eastern Railway in northern Manchuria, of which Russia is a half owner, and on Russia's maritime provinces in the Far East, for the present Russia does not single out Japan as a possible antagonist in the battle-field. Even if Japan were to make an outright seizure of the Chinese Eastern and venture a step or two farther in her aggression and annex portions of Russian territories in the Far East, Russia will not meet the challenge with armies. Not at present. Russia may secretly incite local uprisings of her nationals in territory occupied by Japan. She may seek to promote guerilla warfare on her enemy, and she is a past master in the game of such warfare, as the Japanese have had occasion to learn during their occupation of Siberia in 1922. Russia may go further and repeat Trotzky's tactics against the Germans after Brest-Litovsk, break the peace and refuse to fight, save with propaganda calculated to stir rebellion in the enemy's rear, but she will not hurl armies against Japan, no matter what the provocation. The Russian leaders know that they are no match for Japan, especially in territory so far removed from their base of supplies. The Russian leaders realize only too keenly that they have not the remotest chance of winning a war against Japan and they know further, at least they speak of it frankly enough, that if they were to centre their fighting energies on Japan they would expose themselves to attack in the European territories and invite another but more energetic effort to overthrow them.

Fifteen or twenty years hence, when Siberia and the

Far East have had some industrial energy blown into them, and their population has swelled perceptibly, Russia may sing a different tune, may accept a challenge to war. But at present, however painful it may be to her to see herself thrust back from the Pacific Ocean, in the event of course that Japan decides on such a manoeuvre, and her vast Siberian and Asiatic possessions shut off from an outlet to the open sea, she will not embark on a war with Japan, if only because she will not want to divide her fighting energies, all of which she needs to guard the frontiers nearer Moscow. In fact the Russian leaders hold a clash with Japan so remote a possibility that in speaking of war they hardly ever mention her as a possible antagonist, save in the event that a coalition is formed in which Japan joins.

When one surveys the horizon for possible foes of Russia the eye inevitably falls on England, certainly the Russian eye does, for it is with England, as already explained, that Russia clashes most violently and over a multitude of issues in which both national and revolutionary aims coalesce. But if only because of her geographic position England alone will never venture a war on Russia. Her navy can easily shut off Russia from the seas, but cannot even bottle her up, not to say conquer or even seriously cripple her. If England ever engages in combat with Russia it will be others besides the English or the British who will bear the brunt of the fighting on land, and whoever else these other nations may be, Poland must be one of them.

Indeed, whoever may be seeking to strike at Russia

by land must do it through Poland and Rumania, but
chiefly through Poland and the Poles. Poland is the
most strategic gateway to Russia and is psychologically
and physically best equipped to co-operate in a campaign against her big Slavic neighbour. The Russians,
when they speak of an invasion of their territories, take
it for granted that Poland will be somewhere in the
front of the invading procession.

The ancient feud between these two nations has not
abated through separation, has if anything gained in
intensity. They are constantly picking quarrels with
each other, officially and unofficially. There are not
very many issues of the *Pravda* of Moscow that do not
print scathing cartoons of Poland in the garb of a gen-
darme of the capitalist nations of the world, or editorials bristling with savage resentment at something or
other that some Polish official of prominence has said
or done. The Polish leaders do not neglect to remind
their public and the world at large that Russia *is* the
enemy they must always be prepared to meet in battle.
The constant wrangling of these two nations over
Lithuania, over hegemony in the Baltic, over trade
agreements, over Communist conspiracies against the
Polish Republic and counter-revolutionary plots against
the Soviet regime, carries in it enough explosive substance to precipitate a clash at any moment deemed
opportune by either party. Now that they have both
signed the Protocol to the Kellogg Peace Pact we may
expect an abatement but not a cessation of their ancient
enmity.

It may be that Poland will fight Russia alone with
what help in military leadership, finance, and supplies it

may procure from other powers unfriendly to Russia. It may be that it will battle against Russia with the aid of Rumania, her closest ally, or with several other little nations who may be wanting to settle old scores with Russia. Most likely Poland will be only part of a coalition headed by England or by England and France. The Russians are convinced that England, unless headed by a radical Labour Government, will inevitably be involved in any war against her. But whoever or whatever the nations that find themselves embroiled in combat with Russia, Poland cannot escape participation, hardly any more than can our own South when the United States faces a foreign foe in the battle-field.

Yet whether Poland fights Russia alone or with the help of others a war between these two nations, even more than between Russia and any other foreign power, will rouse the mightiest of passions on both sides, for the Poles hate the Russians only a little more than the Russians hate them, and the Russians hate the Poles as they do no other people in the world. Hostile as they are to England, they bear no animosity toward the English. But in the case of Poland, there is personal animosity on both sides. To Poland a war with Russia would mean the defence of her national integrity, a struggle against communism, against atheism. It may mean an opportunity to bring under Polish domination the lands that had once been part of the Polish Kingdom, principally White Russia and the Ukraine. Once before in 1920 Poland, through Pilsudki, had made an effort to wrest some or all of these territories from Russia, an effort that nearly ruined the long sought for and dearly purchased independence of the Polish nation.

To Russia a war with Poland would, to use Bolshevist parlance, be a war against landlords, capitalists, imperialists. There would be more or less of the passion of a holy war on both sides — there would be that in any war with Russia — fought with all the desperation and all the madness that such passion engenders. And it would be of course a double war, a war at the front and a war in the rear, as any war with Russia must be.

As soon as Polish armies occupied a village or a town, Polish rulers would scrap the Soviet government and bring back a bourgeois regime. The Polish secret service would comb the country for Communist sympathizers. In war nations do not take chances, especially with Bolshevik sympathizers who would be certain to have their hearts with the cause not of Poland but of the home country and of the Revolution. As a matter of protecting themselves against Bolshevik backfire Polish military leaders will seek to root out Bolshevik adherents. As a matter of keeping the Bolshevik taint from seeping into their military ranks or into the civilian population back of the lines, Polish authorities will seek to hunt down the civilians in conquered territory carrying this taint or suspected of carrying it. The secret service will be busy and so will the firing squad.

The Russians will be no more merciful with political foes. In territory they conquer they will immediately scrap the existing government, set up a revolutionary tribunal, nationalize property, enthrone Sovietism. Opponents of the new regime will be tracked down and dealt with summarily. There will be executions, for there will be civil war.

In other words, no sooner has either of the armies conquered a certain territory than the ground is laid for a new warfare; in the case of Poland against Communist hegemony and Communist followers and sympathizers, in the case of Russia against a capitalist hegemony and against foes of Sovietism. There is class or civil war in the territory of either conqueror.

And what will be the fate of war prisoners that either side captures? It is well enough to say international law protects them against molestation when they refrain from resistance. The Russians with their missionary zeal will be glad enough to spare proletarians or peasants, and others whom they may hope to convert to their gospel. If they discover in their midst convinced *fascisti* or others committed to the overthrow of Sovietism, will they seek to bolshevize them too? Certainly Poland or any other nation at war with Russia will have no occasion to bring missionary effort of their own into play — not with Communists or others in close sympathy with the Communist and communism. It would be the most futile of tasks. A Communist saturated with Communist principle and passion is as open to the persuasion of an opposing social creed as an old-fashioned Calvinist is to the teachings of Buddha.

Most horrible, in my judgment, must be the war on youth, and possibly also on women. I mean the war in the rear. Now whatever one may think of the Russian Communists they have been successful in rousing the support of the younger generation, especially in the city. In every manner possible they have catered to the spirit of adventure in youth. They have fostered athletic games, picnics, dramatic performances, revolutionary festivals. They have sought to stir youth to a new feeling of self-importance, to a new passion, a new hope. They have placed youth in the position of weightiest responsibility. They have imbued youth with a zest for conflict, aye, for conquest on the revolutionary front.

A somewhat similar condition abounds on the Polish side. The patriotic organizations and the church have, during the past years, stirred a mighty sentiment of patriotism in youth. The Polish youth is on the whole perhaps the most patriotic element in the country, and with the exception of a small coterie of Communists and Russian sympathizers, it hates Russia as no other nation. Many of these youths will volunteer for service at the front or will stay at home to perform the tasks of civilians.

Consider then the position of this youth, both Polish and Russian, eager, impassioned, reckless of consequences, devoted to the respective cause their government is championing, the one bred only in the Bolshevik spirit, the other tempestuously anti-Bolshevik. Will miltary leaders and revolutionary tribunals spare them? They did not always do so in the war they fought in 1920, and at that time the youth of these lands especially in Poland had not yet been worked on by the propaganda of their respective political leadership. It had not the definitely fixed political and social orientation, the enthusiasm, the desperation and the fighting spirit it has now, and it was not so stirringly conscious of its own powers and its own importance. In war rulers see only their aims ahead and anything and anybody in the way must be dug up and buried like weeds before a plow.

It is not merely youth that will be involved. There are women on the Russian side who are fanatically devoted to Bolshevism, and women on the Polish side who are just as frantically opposed to Bolshevism. There are peasants in Poland lusting for land and ready to slay those holding it or keeping them from seizing it; and there are peasants in Russia hating Bolshevism and ready to slay anyone defending it. Indeed, one shudders to think of the brutalities that must accompany a war between Russia and any nation, and especially a war between Russia and Poland.

Russia needs peace desperately. Poland needs it no less. When one considers the multitude of internal and external difficulties that beset either of these nations, one wonders how they ever can muster sufficient audacity to launch into an armed conflict. But then — in 1920 Poland was in far more desperate straits than now. She was a boiling cauldron of chaos and enthusiasm. It was still a question whether internal wrangling would not wreck the very independence for which it had so long and so valiantly been fighting and hoping. Yet that did not halt Pilsudki from hurling his fighting legions against his nation's ancient enemy, only to be driven back in agony and humiliation to the very gates of Warsaw.

Despite the Kellogg Pact both nations have signed no one can tell when and what untoward circumstance may hurl them against one another and loosen on their nationals, if not on all Europe, the bloodiest holocaust of the ages. And the war that Russia will fight against Poland will be more or less the kind of war she will be fighting against any other nation. It will be a double war, at the front and in the rear. So that in time of war as well as peace Russia is a new force on earth — indeed a world that never was.

CHAPTER XXI

AMERICA

I HAD strayed once on a hot Sunday afternoon into a village on the Volga and ran into the most extraordinary procession I had ever witnessed even in Russia, a land of bizarre processions. It was a wedding, celebrated in Soviet style, that is outside of the church. Bride and groom in ornate costumes, their arms twined round one another, were sitting in a small cart which was drawn not by the far-famed Russian *troika*, but by a tractor, a Fordson, which whined and chugged and sputtered merrily as though responding to the mood of the occasion. Cart and tractor were hung with lithographs of Karl Marx, Lenine, Kalinin and other Bolshevik heros, and were draped with red bunting and banners, embroidered in white and orange with spectacular slogans of the Revolution. Leaders of the local and of surrounding Soviets, including an elderly muzhik with a flowing beard, had perched themselves on improvised seats of the tractor and on all sides followed men, women, youths, in festive garb and singing lustily to the accompaniment of accordions and tambourines.

Up and down and around the village the procession swirled, gay, boisterous, triumphant, like an army returning from victory. Finally it halted in the public square. The engine was silenced, and so were the accordions and the tambourines. The shouts of the crowd dropped to a whisper as gentle-toned as the rustle in a forest. A youthful official with shaven head, gleaming eyes, and a red badge pinned to the bosom of his blouse leaped on the tractor, and in a voice vibrant with fervor he assured the audience that they were participating in no ordinary event. To think that in a village as deaf and slothful as theirs, where some folk still shared their abodes with pigs and chickens, mere muzhiks could be united in wedlock, not by a dark-minded Orthodox priest intoning incomprehensible verses to a non-existing God, but amidst revolutionary chants and in revolutionary fashion with bride and groom riding in a cart drawn by a tractor — a Fordson, brought all the way from America! An occasion of triumph it was for everybody in the village. The very Fordson, he ex-claimed, was a symbol of a new day and a new joy — of the machine against the church, of science against superstition, of man putting himself in tune with na-ture! Other speakers followed each in his own fashion reiterating the sentiments of the first orator and point-ing to the mud-crusted grey Fordson as evidence of the supreme triumph of the Revolution in the village.

The tractor was then set in motion again. The ac-cordions crashed into a fresh tune, the tambourines banged away once more, the crowd burst into song and marched on, this time to the home of the bride. I joined in the celebration, and when my American origin became known I was accepted not only as a guest but as a hero of the village. Peasant after peasant insisted on shaking hands and drinking to my health and to the health of Khord (which is the way peasants pronounce Ford's name) who had given Russia the Fordson, to

the health of all America. Questions followed. Who was
this man Khord? Where and how did he live? Was it
true that he was richer than the former Russian Czar?
Would I tell him that Russian muzhiks wanted him to
come and build a factory in Russia so folks could buy
tractors and even automobiles cheap? People were rich
in America, were they not? Every peasant there had a
Fordson of his own and an automobile? If only Russia
could be like America!

More goblets of vodka, more gulpings of *samogon*,
more toasts to that man Khord and to all America,
very many more!

Now on previous occasions I had come on incidents
which emphasized glowingly the admiration which Russians of all shades of political opinion cherish for
America. There was that desolate Tatar village where
an aged radiant-eyed Mullah on learning that I was
from America insisted that I be his guest for several
days, and where peasant after peasant amidst cere-
monious curtseying presented me gifts of honey in expression of gratitude to America for the food she had
sent to their village in the days of the famine. There
was that dreamy-eyed Ukrainian school-master who
had languished for a decade in a Siberian jail and had
once stood in the shadow of a firing squad and who,
as we lay on the grass in his orchard with a starry
heaven and a brilliant moon gazing down on us, chatted
on endlessly and with an ever-rising surge of passion
of the greatness and happiness that would come to Russia when she had machines and factories and railroads
like America.

There was that group of peasant girls at the fair in

Poltava who, evenings when their work of selling home-made pottery was over, would gather round an open fire in front of their straw tents to cook their food and to bombard me with questions as to life in America, of boys and girls, schools and books, homes and clothes, love and marriage. There was that Cossack schoolman in the Kuban who was so overjoyed at meeting a man from America in his own *stanitsa* that he almost gathered me in his arms, rushed me off to his home, called a group of neighbours together and insisted that I tell them all I knew of the cultivation of cotton in America and of building silos. There was that gathering of pro-letarians in Stalingrad who drank goblet after goblet of vodka to the triumph of the American Revolution, and who were yet wishing with all their hearts that the new tractor factory they were building would prove at least as successful as the Ford plant in America. There was that conductor in Moscow who blazed with wrath when I hopped on a trolley while it was in motion, and threatened to turn me over to a militiaman if I did not pay a fine, but who on sight of my American passport mellowed into gentleness and begged me never again to violate the law of the city by jumping on or off a car while it was in motion. There was that seventeen year old factory girl, Tanya, the daughter of a proletarian in a northern town who wished me to look up John Dos Passos somewhere in America and tell him that his novel " Manhattan Transfer " was the most entrancing book she had ever read, and who assured me that it was her dream someday to visit the land of " Manhattan Transfer," and with her own eyes see all the wonders that it possessed.

Indeed, what American who has ever wandered into a Russian village did not find himself surrounded by crowds of muzhiks who were only too eager to lavish on him hospitality and adulation? Yet never before in all my journeyings in Russia had I been so aware of the sincerity and even the pathos of this widespread adoration of America as at this wedding in a Volga village with a Ford tractor as the real celebrity of the event. True enough was the remark of an American post-graduate student in Russia that there is something almost pathological in Russia's worship of America and things American. It certainly is an extraordinary phenomenon.

On first reflection this seems almost like an amusing anomaly. No nations in the world appear to be so far apart in their approach to life as do America and Russia. Contrasts between them peer, almost shriek, at the visitor at every step. Individualism versus collectivism; exaltation versus degradation of private property; middle class versus proletarian sovereignty; official recognition versus official denial of religion; official respect versus official indifference to the family. Burrowing further one encounters the clash over the issue of world revolution, which the ruling Party in Russia is upholding. If this Revolution ever does bud forth the final battle for supremacy will be fought by America against a Union of Soviets in which Russia may hold a dominant position. World revolution may of course prove as much of a chimera as the prophecy of that Apostle of Doom on Long Island who some time ago had sallied forth with a group of his followers to meet the end of the world. In an appraisal of the relations between the two countries, however, it is well to note the clash involved.

Still, obvious and basic as are the contrasts and conflicts, the very word America has attained a magic quality in the Russian language. It is a symbol of something youthful and invincible, above all indispensable to the salvation of the proletarian revolution, of Russian humanity, of all humanity. Several years ago a certain Ossinsky, a Russian official of note, had, on his return home after a sojourn of several months in America, delivered a number of lectures in which he sought to tarnish the virtues with which Russians had endowed America; aside from involving himself in a rough tilt with an astute American journalist he succeeded only in making himself doubted and distrusted. The Russian mass, bolshevik and non bolshevik, will not drag America from the pedestal on which they have hoisted her.

Many are the reasons for Russia's fervour for America. Because of their geographic separation Russia and America, unlike Russia and England, have not been treading on each other's toes. The name of America has never appeared with discredit in Russian social and political literature. During the days of the recent famine America fed millions of Russians all over the country. Immigrants from Russia have been constantly providing succour to relatives and friends in their homeland. Never has this succour been so precious as now, with chaos and uncertainty facing large masses of the Russian population. Hundreds of thousands of Russians are reposing faith in salvation from ruin in the possibility of obtaining through the aid of American relatives a knitting, sewing or some other kind of machine with which to earn their own living with their own hands and in their own homes. Russia's need of credits, the most desperate need of the moment, with which to bring to fruition an immense industrialization project is another force making her look with longing to America. Fear of war, which haunts her like a gruesome spectre, further draws her sympathetically to America. If only to protect her investments in Europe, America, the Russians hope, will frustrate the realization of what they regard as a sinister conspiracy to drag them into war.

Nor have the Russians been unmindful of the service which America has rendered to the cause of Russian territorial integrity. Despite an absence of political relations with the Soviet government America has held to a policy of the preservation of Russian territorial unity. She has acknowledged the independence of Poland and the Baltic states, but so has Russia herself. Had it not been for America Russia might now have been cut off from an open road to the Pacific and her precious maritime provinces in the Far East might have been annexed by Japan. The records speak only too plainly. Hughes never had penned a more decisive note during his incumbency in office as Secretary of State than he had to the Japanese Government on May 31, 1921.

" In view," he wrote, " of its conviction, that the course followed by the Government of Japan brings into question the very definite understanding concluded at the time troops were sent to Siberia, the Government of the United States must in candour explain its position and say to the Japanese Government that the Government of the United States can neither now nor here-after recognize as valid any claims or titles arising out of the present occupation and control, and that it cannot acquiesce in any action by the Government of Japan which might impair existing treaty rights or the political or territorial integrity of Russia." These words sound almost like an ultimatum. No doubt it was to American advantage to keep Japan from intrenching herself on the mainland of Asia, but it was certainly to Russia's immense benefit to have Japan withdraw her troops from all Siberian territory.

These are all links in a chain of sentiment and consideration that draw Russia to America. But they are not the sole links nor, as far as the masses are concerned, the weightiest. There are others that flow out of a new consciousness and a new vision that has seized leaders and masses. A result of the Revolution they reveal now with a gush of pathos and now with a burst of humour an aspect of Russian humanity and a failing in Soviet administration that would require the genius of a Gogal adequately to portray. I had better be concrete.

Once just before departing from Moscow for London I wished to leave a forwarding address in the Post Office of the Prombank where I had been receiving my mail. I had been directed to see a certain clerk, he passed me on to another, and this one to a third, and that one to a fourth, and when I finally reached the sixth clerk I was informed that no forwarding address could be left in the Prombank Post Office! Once again while in Verkhne-Udinsk, Siberia, I went to the Soviet Shipping Office to find out on what date I could sail for the town of Seleginsk. It was the same story, one clerk palming me off to another, until my patience was so taxed that I turned to the manager with a burst of exasperation and demanded that he put me in touch with someone in the Shipping Office who knew something about sailings. With extreme courtesy and with profuse apologies, he directed me to a clerk on a floor above his office. This clerk was away to his lunch. I waited for him, and when he returned he wrote out for me a list of sailings to Seleginsk. When I asked him what the fare was he told me that only the ticket agent could supply me with that information. He looked at his watch and assured me that if I hurried in a cab to the wharf I should find the ticket agent still on duty. I dashed into the street, jumped into a cab and asked the driver to make haste. On my arrival at the wharf I found the ticket office closed. It had been closed for several hours, so waiting peasants had told me and none of them knew when it would be open!

My classic experience with Russian incompetence and irresponsibility came my way on my first trip to Kharkov, the capital of the Ukraine and a growing metropolis in Russia. I had arrived in the city late in the evening after a protracted sojourn in Ukrainian villages. The banks had already closed for the day and I found myself with a little more than a rouble in cash in my possession — not enough to pay for a drive up-town to one of the leading hotels and to buy food. As there was a small government hotel near the station, I went there. The clerk registered me in the books, assigned to me a room and on learning that I was not a member of a trade union, informed me that it would cost me two and a half roubles instead of forty kopecks to have my passport registered. I made no complaint. I was weary and saw myself happily settled for the night in a clean bed for the first time in weeks. I had already lifted my suitcase to go to my room, when the clerk demanded payment in advance!

I explained to him my predicament as to ready Russian cash. His brow furrowed and with a profusion of regrets he informed me that he would have to refuse me occupancy of the room. I offered him an American travellers' check. He waived it aside. He had no authority to accept foreign checks or foreign currency. Would he wait until morning when I could go to the bank and draw money against my letter of credit or cash a travellers' check? No, he could not do that — it was against the rules, and pointing to a long sheet of hand-written paper pasted on a pillar in the hall he said, " read it." I did and found that he was acting in full accord with written instructions. Would he hold my suitcase, or typewriter or overcoat or all of these as security until morning? No, he was not allowed to hold a guest's baggage and again he pointed to the list of written instructions. What then was I to do — spend the night in the street? He shrugged his shoulders. He was sorry but he was helpless. I pulled out all my Moscow credentials to impress him with my importance, but of no avail. Never had I known an official more zealous to fulfill the letter of the law than was this clerk. I would have promised him a gratuity, but that is always a dangerous affair in Russia — the laws against bribery are the most severe in the world. I ap-

pealed to his sense of sportsmanship. He remained un-
impressed. In sheer desperation I resorted to terror —
I would frighten him into a compromise. I pictured to
him the dire consequence which he might have to face if
I disclosed the incident in the foreign press — a regularly accredited American journalist being compelled to
spend the night in the streets, because a clerk in a government hotel would not allow him to occupy a room
unless he had made payment in advance! A look of
concern crept into his eyes and after some reflection he
volunteered to rouse the manager out of bed and present my case to him.

After a protracted absence he returned beaming with
joy. Yes, the manager would make a concession to an
American journalist. I gave him my passport and in doing so remarked casually that in the morning when I
went to the bank I should need it back to identify myself. A cloud swept over his face. No, he could not do
that — an inspector might drop in and discover a violation of the ordinance and then there would be trouble.
" But," I protested, " without the passport the bank
will honour neither my letter of credit nor my travellers'
check? " Again he shrugged his shoulders. He was
visibly distressed. Once more he pointed to the list of
written instructions. Once more he reminded me that if
he was discharged for violation of rules he, as a non-
Party man, would have to idle about and starve. He did
not know what he could do. At last he hurried to the
manager, wakened him once more, held another conference and finally returned with the news that an exception would be' made in my case, provided I would
promise to pay up early in the morning as soon as the

banks opened and before an inspector might stumble into a discovery of a violation of rules.

Anyone who travels extensively in Russia is destined to encounter similar or even more distressing experiences resulting from stupid ordinances and even more from tragic incompetence and a lack of a sense of responsibility on part of clerks and officials. The inability to perform a task properly is an ancient Russian malady, but never has it loomed so devastating as now during this period of revolutionary upheavals when every misstep and every miscalculation spells misfortune and sometimes tragedy. The Russians are not bad mathematicians. The columns of figures that appear daily in the press testify to a love for mathematical calculations. Yet somehow they find it difficult or painful to master the axiom that the shortest distance between two points is a straight line and not a circle. Not a day passes but the newspapers all over the country print tales of laxity and incompetence which would be amusing were they not revelatory of a condition too tragic to be viewed with levity.

That is one reason the Russians look with such envy to America. The very word America in Russian parlance implies competence, responsibility, punctuality, accuracy, diligence. To work like an American means to work well with zest, tenacity, economy of energy and materials. America has replaced Germany as the symbol of exemplary service. Every apprentice in every shop and factory knows that to work like an American means to work with earnestness, with devotion, with an eye to results. Let a Russian meet an appointment on time — alas how rarely it happens! — and he will be greeted with the laudation that he is a real American. Is there any country in the world which has translated so many American business manuals as has Russia? Is there a high-school or university student, a foreman or director of a factory who has not read and re-read and ruminated over these manuals on American methods of work, American system of service, American habit of punctuality? America is to Russia the great god Brown of achievement.

Even more impressed are the Russians with what they call American *technika* — meaning the American machine. Looking out on a modern world after a long night of feudalism, Russian masses thrill to the machine as perhaps no people in the world. In one of the most successful plays of the post-revolutionary period, " Rails Hum," several scenes are laid in a railroad shop. Engines shriek and whine, hammers thump and thunder, fires roar and crackle, and men in boots, in overalls, faces daubed with soot and grease, skip earnestly about, shouting orders, manipulating levers, handling switches, merging themselves with the machine as though it were a comrade in arms and the biggest plaything in the world. Readers of these pages who have seen the Russian motion picture " Potemkin," will recall the zest and the joy with which its creator continuously flashed on the screen the engines and guns and belts and pieces of mechanism of the naval boat. It seemed as if the director wished to infuse a soul into the very smoke and steam that the stacks belched forth.

To the Russians, not only to the Bolsheviks, the machine is the most extraordinary achievement of man.

It is a power not of enslavement but of liberation and will redeem man from need and toil if only it be placed under proper social control. The machine will make man not a robot but a master of himself and of the world about him. No mystic energy that man need bother about lies beyond it. No riddle that he need worry over lies wrapped in its inner mechanism. A play like Eugene O'Neill's " Dynamo," is inconceivable in present day Russia. The very problem it postures would, to the revolutionary at least, seem absurd if not reprehensible. The machine to him is no source of evil but a fount of everlasting good. It is in the words of O'Neill's Reuben " the hymn of Eternal Generation, the song of Eternal Life." All of Reuben's fret and fuss over the " Big thing," the mystery, the meaning, the morality of the Dynamo, Electricity — of the Machine, would only amuse the Russian revolutionary. He sees in it its own finality, its own fulfillment. Without it, life to him is an eternal damnation, an endless night of darkness and horror. Tolstoy and Gandhi and all the prophets of economic primitivism and naturalism are to him only deluded and futile prattlers.

It is a sight ever to be remembered to watch a crowd of proletarians scrutinize a newly received piece of mechanism from a foreign land, or a crowd of muzhiks gather about the first tractor that has arrived in their village. They thrill with ecstasy to the sight and sound of wheels, belts, pistons, rods. No wonder that the machine plays so heroic a part in Russian motion pictures, in the graphic arts, and in dramatic pieces. The Russians have endowed it with a triumphant personality, not like the Someone in Grey in Andreyev's " Life of

Man " who is a reminder of the terror of life and the futility of death, but like some fairy god-mother always ready to brush away all evil and all torment.

With such fervour for the machine it is only natural that they should look with longing to America. America to them is the symbol of the triumph of the machine. A Ford Factory, a Brooklyn Bridge, a Woolworth Building, a Mississippi Dam, a Hudson River Tunnel; automobiles, cameras, typewriters, engines, mowing machines, boots, coats, in fabulous quantities — these are all fruits of the American machine, of American *technika*. America may be reactionary, capitalistic, imperialistic. She may be executing a Sacco and a Vanzetti, but she can produce as no nation in the world. She is mistress of the machine. She has much, therefore, very much to teach Russia — more than any other nation, and Russia, insists the revolutionary, shall and must learn from America, if she is to realize her social and economic destiny!

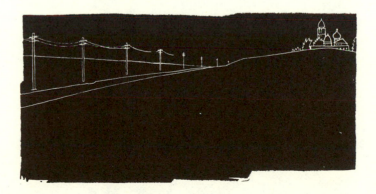